NEW HAVEN'S COLUMBUS DAY PARADE AND MONUMENT

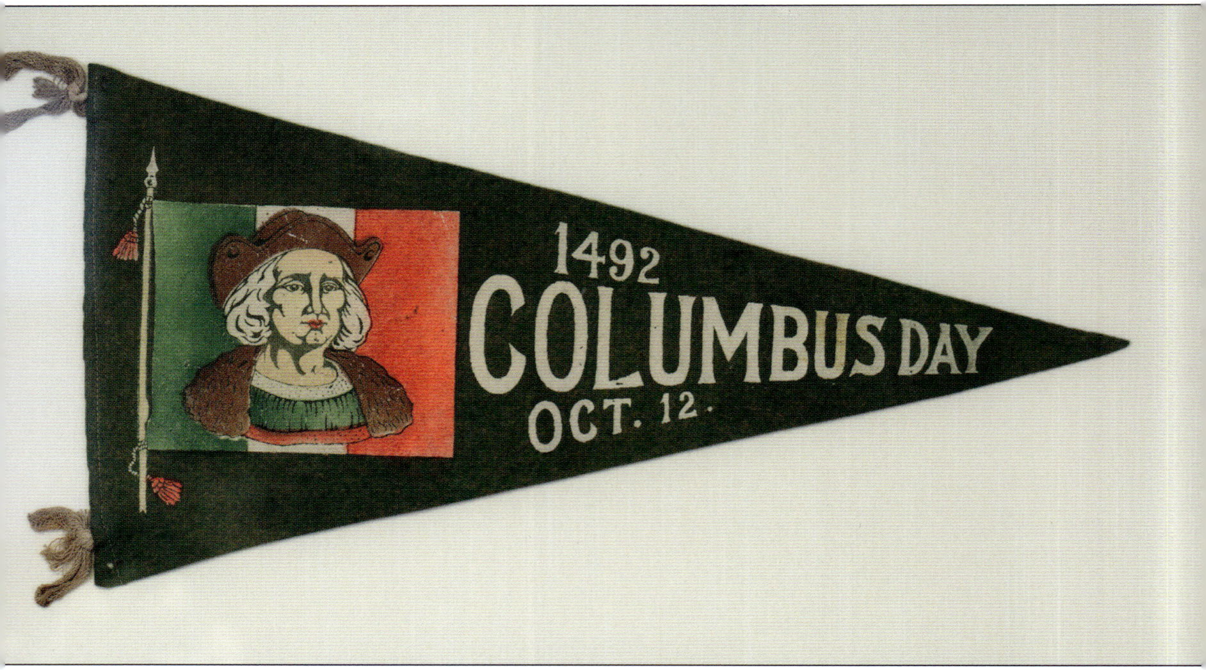

"Columbus Day, October 12, 1492" Pennant. This pennant was created for the 400th anniversary of Columbus's first landing in what is now the Bahamas, an event celebrated in New Haven and in many cities across the United States in 1892. Pennants such as these, stenciled with words and images on long tapering triangles of felt, were tied to dowels and used in parades, such as New Haven's first Columbus Day Parade. This Columbus Day pennant was donated to the Santa Maria Maddalena Society by Stephen Melillo, the proprietor of American Memories, a company located on Wooster Street in New Haven. Melillo is a member of the society, and donated the pennant for display in the clubhouse. He opens his storefront on busy weekend afternoons and evenings, when people come to stand in line for pizza at Sally's and Pepe's. Melillo has been collecting pennants and memorabilia since he was a boy; the Columbus pennant is a rarity. (Photograph by William Sacco, Santa Maria Maddalena Society.)

Front Cover: Michael Celentano, of New Haven, peers around his sail (Photograph by Melanie Stengel, *New Haven Register*; see page 57)

Upper Back Cover: The Dante Club in a 1960s parade (Alphonse Lauro; see page 43)

Lower Back Cover: (left) Woodward School students in the 1993 parade (Photograph by Jeanette Glicksman, *New Haven Register*; see page 56); **(center)** the restored Columbus Monument being unveiled in Wooster Square in 2004 (Photograph by John Cummings, Knights of Columbus; see page 64); **(right)** Lancraft Fife and Drum Corps, who formed in 1888 in North Haven, Connecticut, perform at the wreath-laying ceremony at the Columbus Monument on October 8, 2016 (Author's collection).

NEW HAVEN'S COLUMBUS DAY PARADE AND MONUMENT

Laura A. Macaluso

ARCADIA
PUBLISHING

ISBN 978-1-4671-2687-8

Published by Arcadia Publishing
Charleston, South Carolina

Printed in the United States of America

Library of Congress Control Number: 2017933488

For all general information, please contact Arcadia Publishing:
Telephone 843-853-2070
Fax 843-853-0044
E-mail sales@arcadiapublishing.com
For customer service and orders:
Toll-Free 1-888-313-2665

Visit us on the Internet at www.arcadiapublishing.com

Ancora Imparo.
Michelangelo Buonarroti (1475–1564)

Contents

FOREWORD

At the unveiling of the New Haven Columbus Monument in 1892, on the 400th anniversary of Columbus's historic voyage, Mayor Joseph Sargent said: "May this statue serve to eliminate any differences between Italians and Americans. May this statue maintain peace and prosperity for future generations." With those words ringing in our ears, this book honors our common heritage, one that continues to be a part of our daily lives, and helps ensure that no Italian American in the Greater New Haven community forgets where we came from. Our roots remain a part of us forever.

For over a hundred years, Italian Americans have come to the Columbus Monument in Wooster Square to pay respects to Signore Columbo, to reflect on our values, and to commemorate our old and new homes. From the day that Christopher Columbus first set foot in the New World, to this very moment more than 500 years later, we are and remain one people—united by heritage, tradition, and the eternal bonds of family and community.

Just as America changed us, we changed America. Let us celebrate that change by sharing it with family and friends, and remembering our proud history as Italian Americans. For me, growing up in Wooster Square, in New Haven, the spirit of Italy was never stronger. I learned about the world and formed my values wherever people gathered to share their lives and help one another—in our local parish, the mother church, St. Michael's, my grandmother's pastry store, Canestri's, and around our kitchen table.

This book is a testament to how dearly we hold and cherish our Italian heritage and how large a part it plays in our daily lives. It speaks to the reach of our Italian community—an extended family that continues to prosper and thrive. But Columbus is not just for the Italians—his legacy belongs to all immigrants. As Italians worked to become part of American society, they used Columbus to help them connect to American history. It was not always easy, but they did it, just as every immigrant who comes to our shores becomes a part of the American tapestry.

—The Honorable Rosa DeLauro, Congresswoman, Third District

ACKNOWLEDGMENTS

Acknowledgements begin with the current members of the 2016–2017 Columbus Day Committee of Greater New Haven for their desire to see 125 years of history documented and shared with the publication of this book. They are Theresa Argento, Rita Barbieri-George, Paul Criscuolo, Peter DeBrino, Peter Desio, Richard DiPalma, Charlotte Gambardella, Arthur Giulietti, Laura Florio Luzzi, Joanne Mallinson, Louis Onofrio, Richard Ramadei, Magdalen Sparaco, and William Zampa.

Further, the Honorable Rosa DeLauro, congresswoman for the Third District, is thanked for graciously writing the foreword during an unusual political year. I am also grateful to Jennifer Lamb, district director for Rep. DeLauro, who coordinated this effort.

The following people provided access and guidance regarding resources: Richard Biondi, Alison Boetelho, Frances Calzetta, Mary Christ, Peter Desio, Angel Diggs, Charlotte and Peter Gambardella, Frank Grazioso, Robert S. Greenberg, Alphonse Lauro, Anne Ostendarp, Laura Parisi, Anthony Riccio, Frances Skelton, and Vivian-Lea Solek.

Many thanks go to Bill Sacco, as always, for his photography. Finally, Liz Gurley, title manager at Arcadia, deserves *mille grazie* for making this book happen—it was a close call, but, with her expert guidance, we got there.

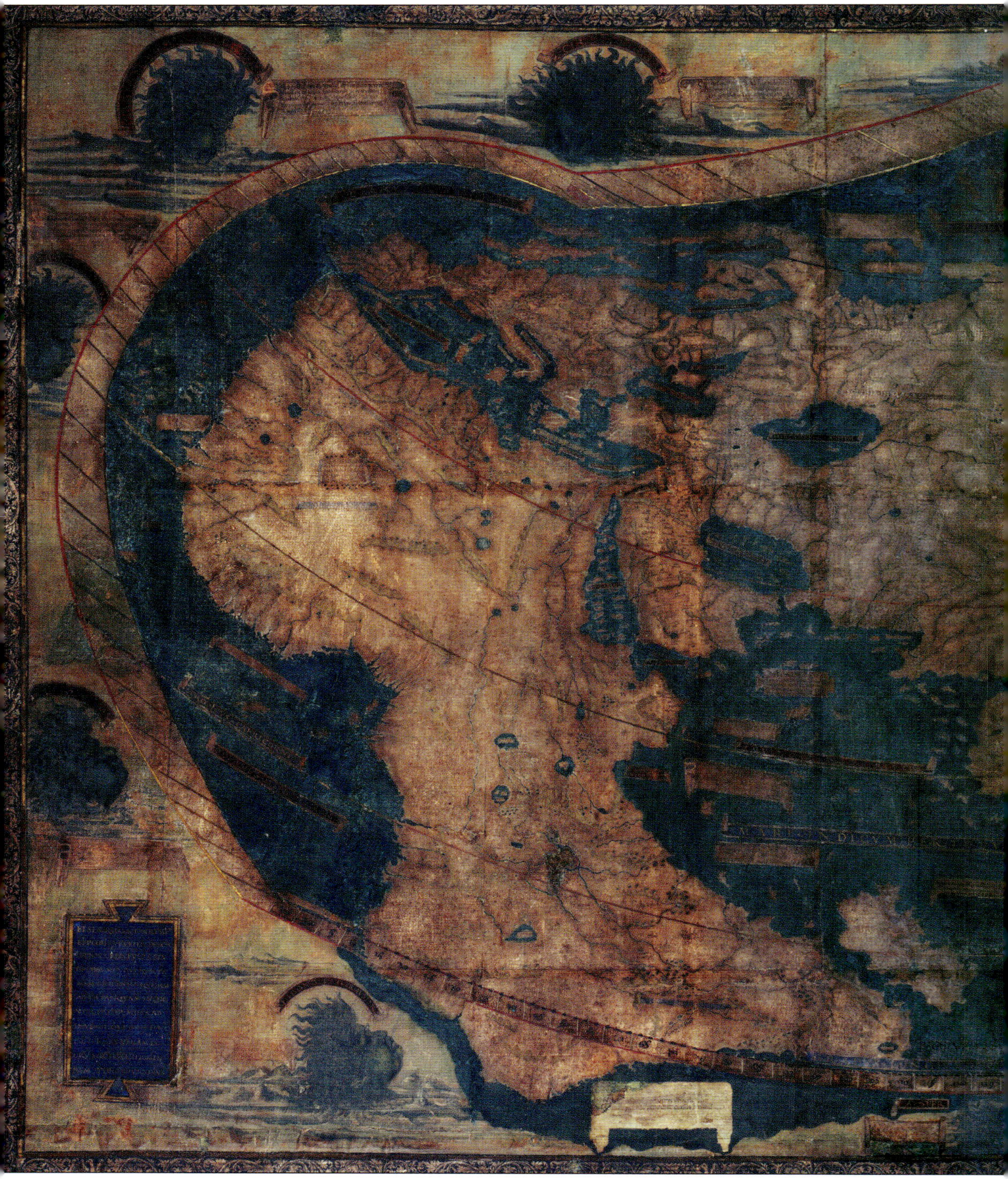

Map of the World of Christopher Columbus, c. 1489. German cartographer Heinrich Hammer drew and colored this map while working in Florence, Italy. According to the Beinecke Library, which received the map as an anonymous donation in 1962, the Martellus Map (Latin version of Hammer's name) is the "best contemporary cartographic representation of Columbus' conception of the world at the time of his first voyage." Although the map is hard to read today due to 500

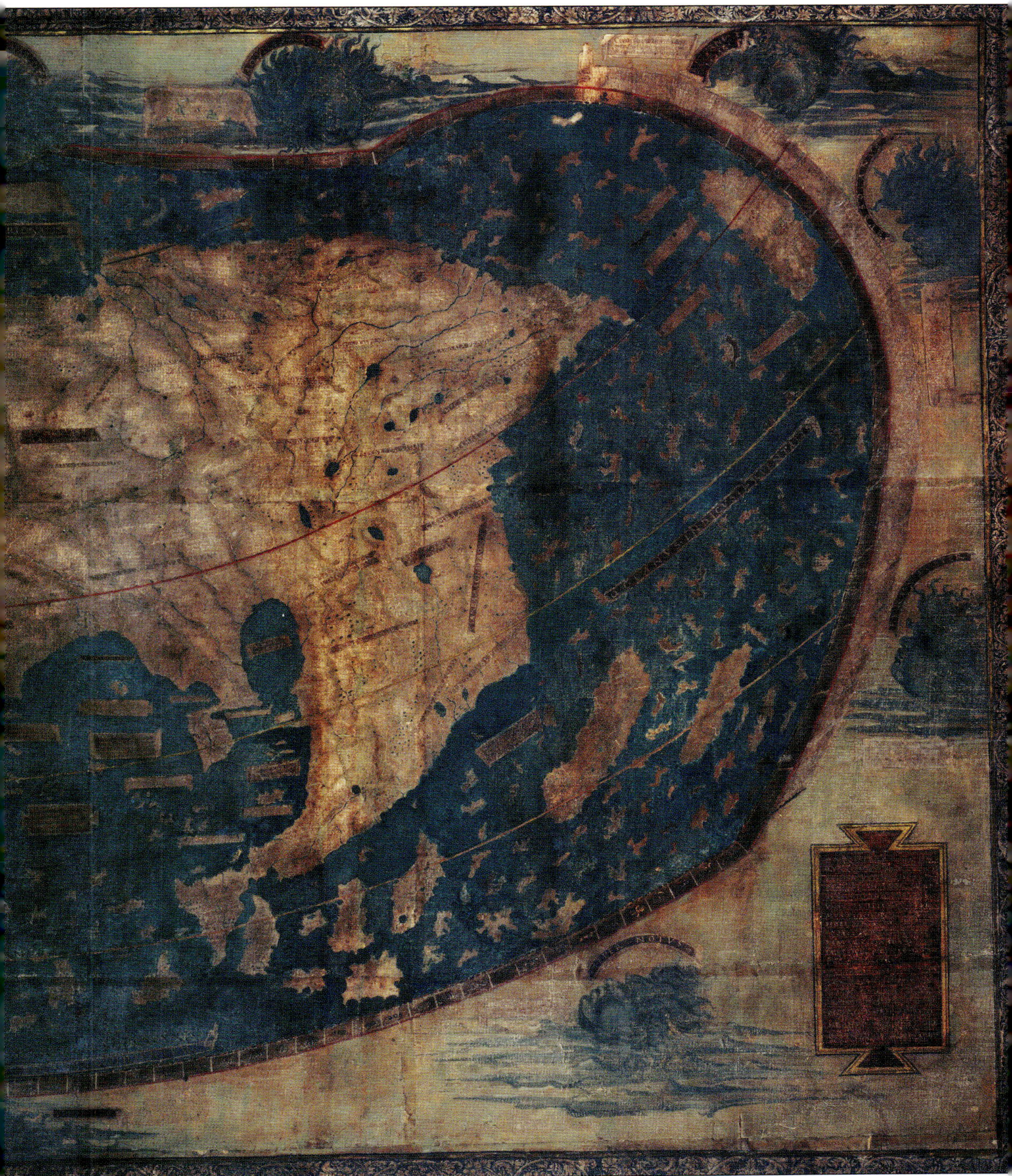

years of fading and wear, a multispectral imaging of it was done in 2014–2015, bringing to light details that are difficult to read with the naked eye. The map shows the spread of continents across the earth—from the west to the east. Documents from the Columbus voyage demonstrate that it was this map Columbus used to plan his voyage. (Beinecke Rare Book & Manuscript Library, Yale University.)

Introduction

This book marks the 125th anniversary of the installation of the Columbus Monument and 64 continuous years (more or less) of the Columbus Day Parade. It is a good idea to remember this anniversary, because today, Columbus is being challenged across the United States, with many American cities replacing Columbus Day with Indigenous Peoples' Day, a trend that began in the late 20th century but which has picked up steam in the first two decades of the 21st century. This book demonstrates why Columbus remains important to the city of New Haven and New Haven County and how one immigrant group—southern Italians—used the figure of Columbus to establish connections and contributions to its homeland more than 100 years ago.

The creation of the Columbus Monument in 1892—the first monument of many to Columbus in the state of Connecticut—was, in fact, a way for the Italians of the Elm City to mark their presence in what was a heavily Yankee Protestant place. Even the Irish, who emigrated to New Haven earlier and also withstood years of derision and marginalization from the Yankee patrician class, did not erect a public monument as early as the Italian community. The Columbus Monument is the first work of public art erected by an ethnic group in New Haven and the Columbus Day Parade is its descendant, a community-spirited event played out every year in both New Haven and the surrounding towns of Branford, East Haven, Hamden, North Haven, and West Haven, where many children and grandchildren of the original immigrants resettled after redevelopment in the 1950s and 1960s and the decline of the city due to poverty and the loss of industrial jobs.

Italians were the largest ethnic minority in New Haven by the turn of the 20th century, and their place in city history is remembered in the Columbus Monument and Columbus Day Parade and also in the city's food culture, some of it located in the Wooster Square neighborhood, whose heart is the monument and park, sometimes referred to as "Columbus Park." But the book also notes how Columbus became an important figure not only for the Italian and Italian American communities but also for all of the city's Roman Catholics. For example, when the Knights of Columbus formed in New Haven in 1882, eventually becoming the largest fraternal lay Catholic organization in the world, they chose Columbus for the name of their new organization. The Knights of Columbus were, in fact, the first to hold a Columbus Day Parade in New Haven, in 1892—the year the monument was installed by the Italian community and the United States of America was awash in celebrations for the 400th anniversary.

John Noble Wilford wrote that "every generation creates the Columbus it needs," and, true to form, the figure of Columbus continues to be revived in different forms in New Haven. For example, one of the city's most recent Percent for Art projects at Columbus Family Academy highlights the story of "discovery" through artwork placed throughout the interior and exterior of the school (see chapter 4). Although Columbus himself is de-emphasized in this presentation, he is there, whether you draw his face and figure or not. In New Haven, his name lives on in a school, a road, a monument, a park, and a parade, for starters. Thus this book offers a chance to remember many of the people who contributed to the Columbus story in New Haven—those individuals and organizations that volunteer tirelessly for years, if not decades, to maintain the Columbus presence in the Elm City. In 2017, this is not an easy position to be in, considering the severity of the backlash against Columbus and the holiday formally (and federally) dedicated to him 80 years ago, in 1937. Even the City of New Haven bowed to this pressure in 2014, renaming Columbus Day "Indigenous Peoples' Day"—if only for that year. Other cities, such as Seattle and Minneapolis, have changed over to this permanently. I recently had the good fortune of having a conversation with a young man of the Catawba Nation (in South Carolina). I told him about this book, and it was clear that Columbus is a hated figure in his native community—and with good reason: the legacy of Columbus and Christian culture came at an immeasurable price for Native Americans, a price they are still paying, more than 500 years after his arrival in the western hemisphere. I argue, though, that it is equally important to recognize how Italian communities like New Haven used the figure of Columbus to establish a formal presence in the city, especially important for a group of people disparaged and marginalized from power structures—not unlike the story of so many other immigrant groups, arriving one after the other and finding deep hostility before uneasy acceptance.

This young man suggested that from their perspective, what would be better would be community conversations about each other, so that Italian Americans could understand the Native American viewpoint and vice versa. Some of that kind of cross-cultural work happened in New Haven in the 1990s, demonstrated by a photograph in chapter 4. But more needs to be done so that Connecticut—the state with the largest Italian American population in relation to size in the country—understands why Columbus was needed at the turn of the 20th century, and ways in which the 21st century can re-create the Columbus it needs. Considering the current national and international conversation about immigrants, emigrants, and refugees, the subject is a timely one. The book will serve as a historical document, helping the city to remember its past, while continuing traditions into the future.

The story of the Italians in New Haven is well-known by now. The first histories of the Italians in New Haven and Connecticut were written in the 1920s and 1930s, when Italian Americans themselves began documenting their own history as a way to celebrate the achievements of those who preceded them. Often, these histories were shaped around the biographies of the men who became civic leaders, either through their successful businesses (such as Paul Russo and Sylvester Z. Poli) or through their positions in education, religion, or medicine (such as Dr. William Verdi). It would be another 50 years before an Italian American held the highest seat of political power in the Elm City—that of mayor—but the journey from new immigrant to mayoral office for Italians was relatively short: the first Italians documented in New Haven arrived in the 1880s. By the 1920s, the number had grown from a trickle of individuals to an influx of immigrant families called in one history "honest, laborious workers" employed in the city's many factories, but especially the "Sindaco Sargent" or Sargent Company, which targeted southern Italians from the *mezzogiorno* to come to New Haven to work in its brick buildings on Water Street. William Celentano, born of working-class Italians, became the city's first Italian American mayor in 1945. And, in terms of writing history, only recently, thanks to the work of Richard Biondi and Anthony Riccio, have the contributions of Italian American women and other "everyday" folks been documented and published.

As noted, the Italians in New Haven were preceded by the Irish, who, in the 1840s and 1850s, came to New England and places like New Haven due to the famine. Seventy-six percent of New Haven's immigrants in 1880 were Irish, many of whom settled around the Wooster Square area. But in the 1890s, the Irish hold on the city was challenged by a new group of immigrants: the Italians, who themselves fled poor, farming communities in the southern areas of the peninsula and who saw the United States with its growing industrial labor needs as a solution to their poverty. Italians arrived in New Haven, moving into places such as the Hill and Wooster Square neighborhoods, and took on the mantle of Columbus at just the right moment: as seen in chapter 1, the United States already had a long relationship with the Italian explorer, because the Columbus story contributed to the greater national narrative of the discovery of a new land, and then of the trials and tribulations of the earliest immigrants who endured (hence the Connecticut state motto, *Qui Transtulit Sustinet* [He who transplanted still sustains]).

In this special corner of the world, Wooster Square, an identity was formed combining the Old World and the New. Of the many firsts for an ethnic group in the city and state, Italians in New Haven purchased the Congregational-turned-Baptist church facing the square, transforming it into St. Michael's Roman Catholic Church (1899), began the first Italian society in the state, La Fratellanza (1884), and erected the first public monument (1892). The Columbus Day Parade and the Columbus Monument are contemporary reminders of this history. Similar to New Haven's St. Patrick's Day Parade, the Columbus Day Parade has had its starts and stops; although no historical photographs seem to survive from before the 1950s, we know the parade did occur, likely between the turn of the 20th century up until the 1930s—a parade ribbon with the date 1928 supports this statement. The parade was not held during the 1930s and World War II era, years of the Great Depression and the enlistment of hundreds of soldiers from New Haven—including many Italian Americans. After the war, during the 1950s and 1960s, as discussed in chapter 3, the parade had its first revival, thanks in large part to the large role of politics in New Haven life and the election of the city's first Italian mayor. But by the end of the 20th century, American society was changing yet again. The Columbus Day Committee, once a sponsored program of city hall, became its own not-for-profit organization, and plans were made to celebrate the 500th anniversary of Columbus in America in 1992. At the same time, Native Americans and others began actively protesting Columbus Day events across the country—including in New Haven. By the turn of the 21st century, few people were watching the parade in the Elm City and thus the committee decided to bring the parade to the surrounding towns with large Italian American populations. And so, New Haven's Columbus Day Parade now visits towns in New Haven County, including Branford, East Haven, Hamden, North Haven, and West Haven, alternating each year to share the connection of Columbus with the local Italian American diaspora. Although the parade has changed over time, the intent is the always same: ethnic pride and patriotism.

One

Columbus Craze

The United States of America was crazy for Columbus in the 19th century. Although George Washington was the beloved father of the country, Christopher Columbus was second only to him among historical figures—and far above most of the Founding Fathers who are remembered today. One of those of the Revolutionary generation, Thomas Jefferson, kept a portrait of Columbus in his home, Monticello, calling him and Amerigo Vespucci "early American worthies."

The first American writers, such as Washington Irving, wrote about Columbus as early as 1828, and numerous prints of the navigator and the story of his journeys across the Atlantic—which became known as the "Discovery of the Americas"—were bought and sold, decorating American homes, put into scrapbooks, and hung in school classrooms. As the century drew to a close, architects and artists began planning for the largest exposition in American history (at the time): the World's Columbian Exposition, which would celebrate the 400th anniversary of the first Columbus journey to the Americas, giving the United States international exposure.

World's fairs were extravagant spectacles of sight (and site): buildings, lakes, and even whole cities were designed and built in short amounts of time to holds thousands of visitors coming to see the latest in industry, science, and the visual arts. These world's fairs were a product of the Victorian era, and driven by the Industrial Revolution. Not surprisingly, the first world's fair was the Crystal Palace Exhibition in London in 1851. The World's Columbian Exposition, held in Chicago on the shores of Lake Michigan in 1893, showed the world that the United States was a competing world power.

Although famous architects and urban planners such as McKim, Mead & White and Frederick Law Olmsted came together in 1891 to move the project forward, the exposition did not come together until a year after the 400th Columbian anniversary. But it was no matter. Americans flocked to the so-called White City in droves, visiting from across the country and collecting souvenirs of Columbus in the form of prints, medals, ribbons, plates, and clocks (great examples of which can be seen in the Columbus Gallery at the Knights of Columbus Museum). With the figure of Columbia at the heart of the World's Columbian Exposition, the first American world's fair was a massive success and the pinnacle of national interest in Columbus.

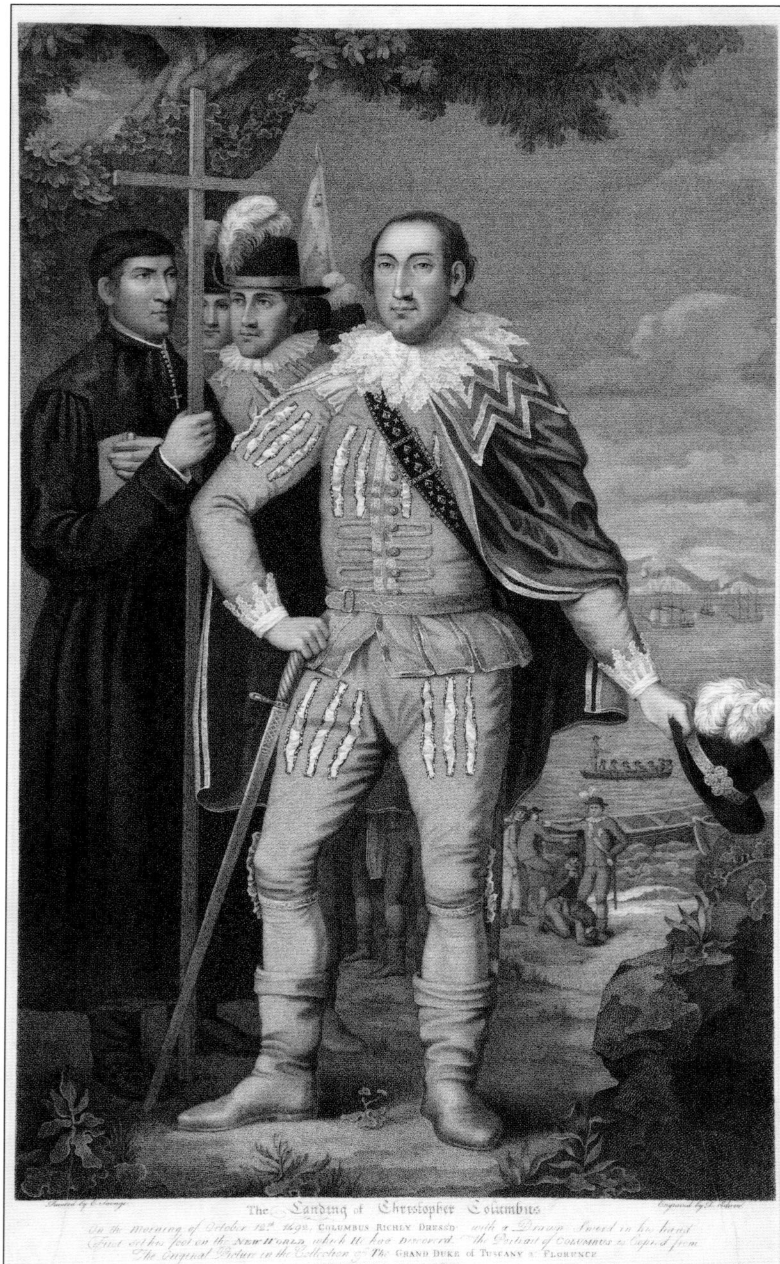

THE LANDING OF CHRISTOPHER COLUMBUS, DAVID EDWIN, 1800. As early as the founding of the country in 1776, long before Italian immigrants arrived in large numbers, Americans were celebrating Christopher Columbus as one of the key historical figures of the new country. This print and the caption below it demonstrate how early the image of Columbus as "discoverer of the New World" was imprinted into the American imagination and myth. Part of the caption reads, "On the Morning of October 12, 1492, Columbus richly dressed, with a drawn sword in his hand, first set foot on the New World, which he has discovered." The role of Christianity was prominent from the start, as was de-emphasizing all of the sailors (seen in the background) who helped him get there. (Yale University Art Gallery.)

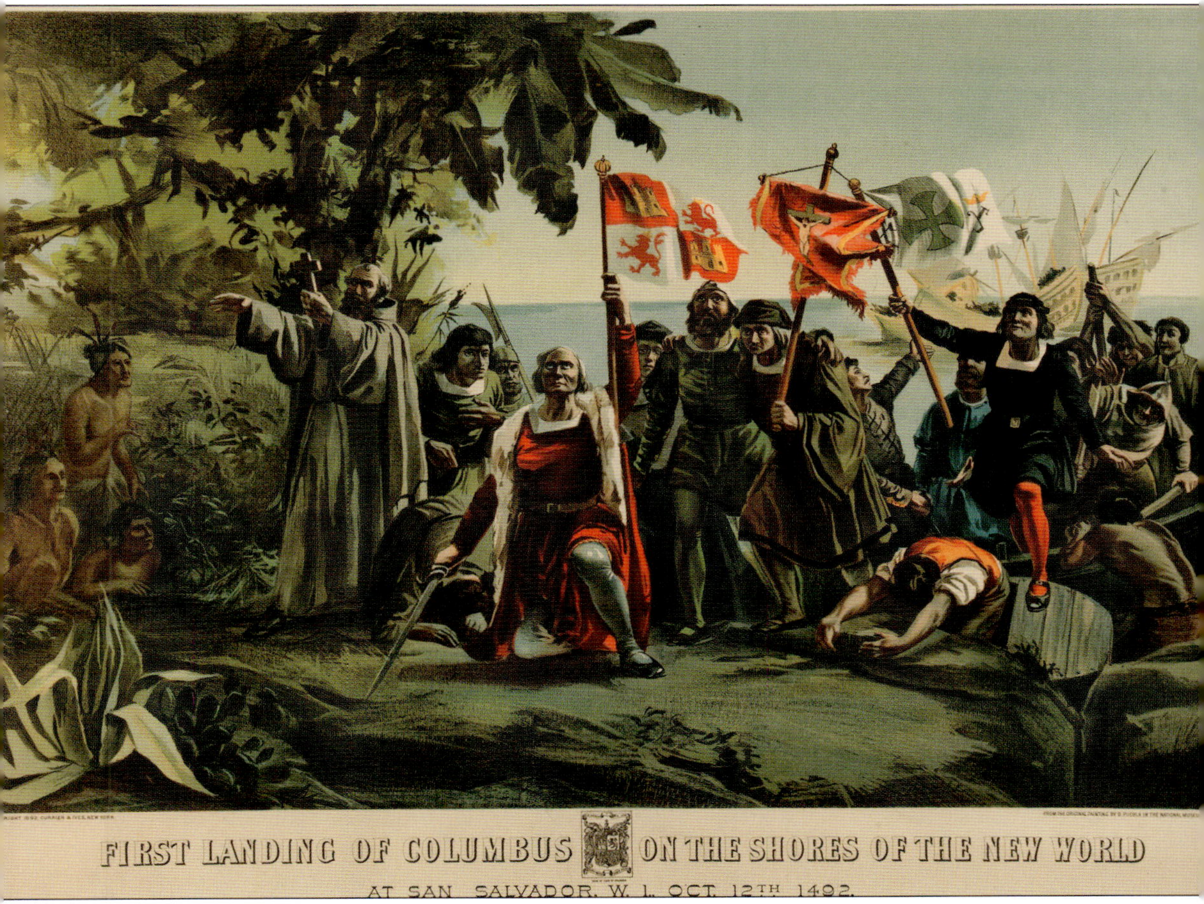

FIRST LANDING OF COLUMBUS..., CURRIER & IVES, 1892. Likely available for purchase at the World's Columbian Exposition, this iconic image of Columbus, translated into low-cost color prints by the New York firm Currier & Ives, would have been displayed in American homes across the nation. (Yale University Art Gallery.)

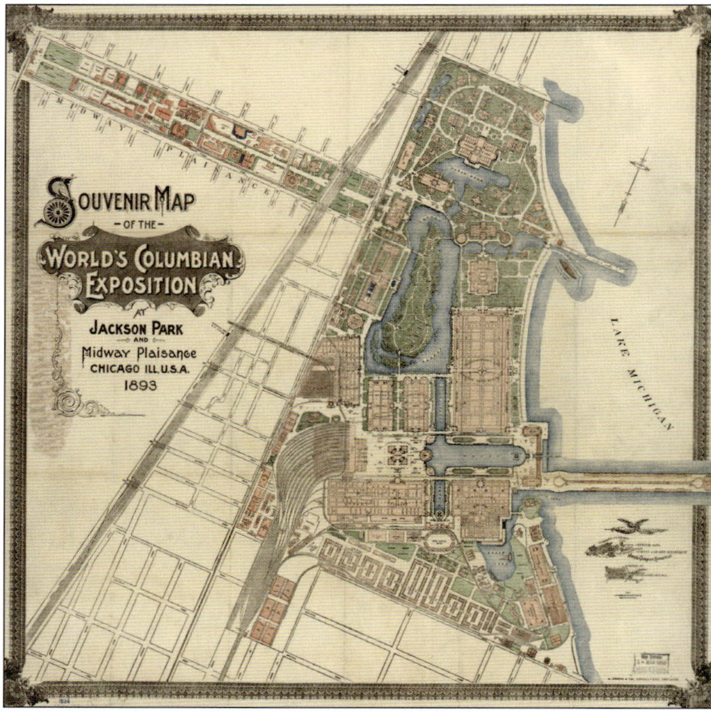

Souvenir Map, World's Columbian Exposition, Hermann Heinz, 1893. The World's Columbian Exposition, laid out on the grounds of Midway Park in Chicago, on the banks of Lake Michigan, was the culmination of a year of planning, in which architect and artists built a "White City" out of plaster and wood. They were a year behind schedule. (Library of Congress.)

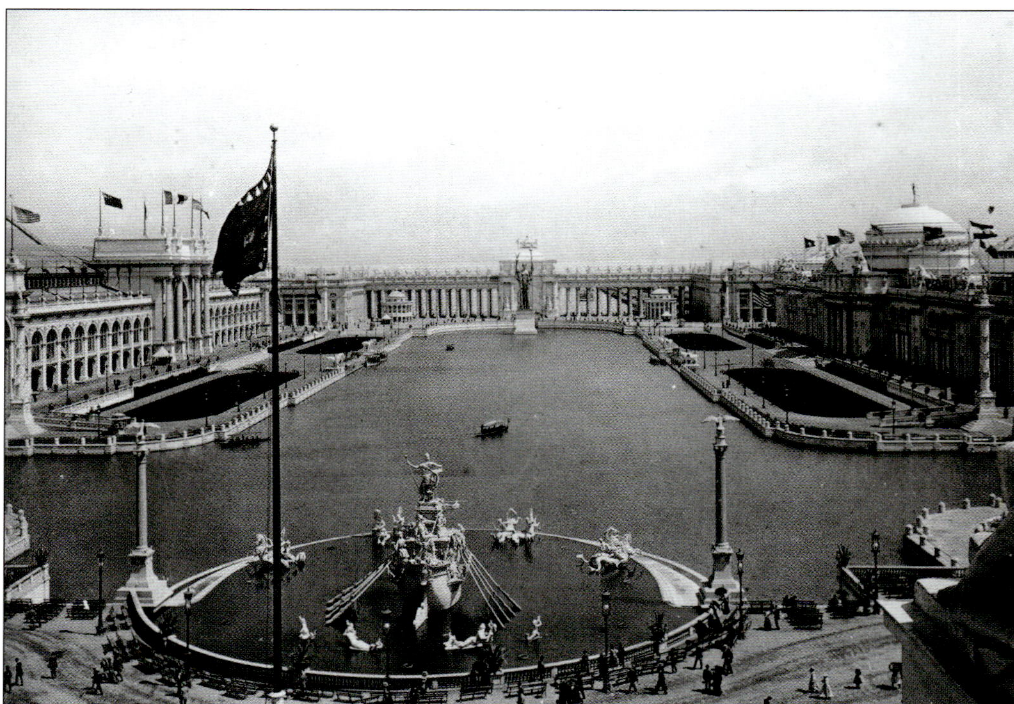

Court of Honor, World's Columbian Exposition, 1893. The Basin and the Court of Honor are seen in a view looking east from the Grand Plaza. In the foreground, two electric fountains flank the Columbian Fountain. All of these buildings were created with wood and plaster and built in the Neoclassical style. (Library of Congress.)

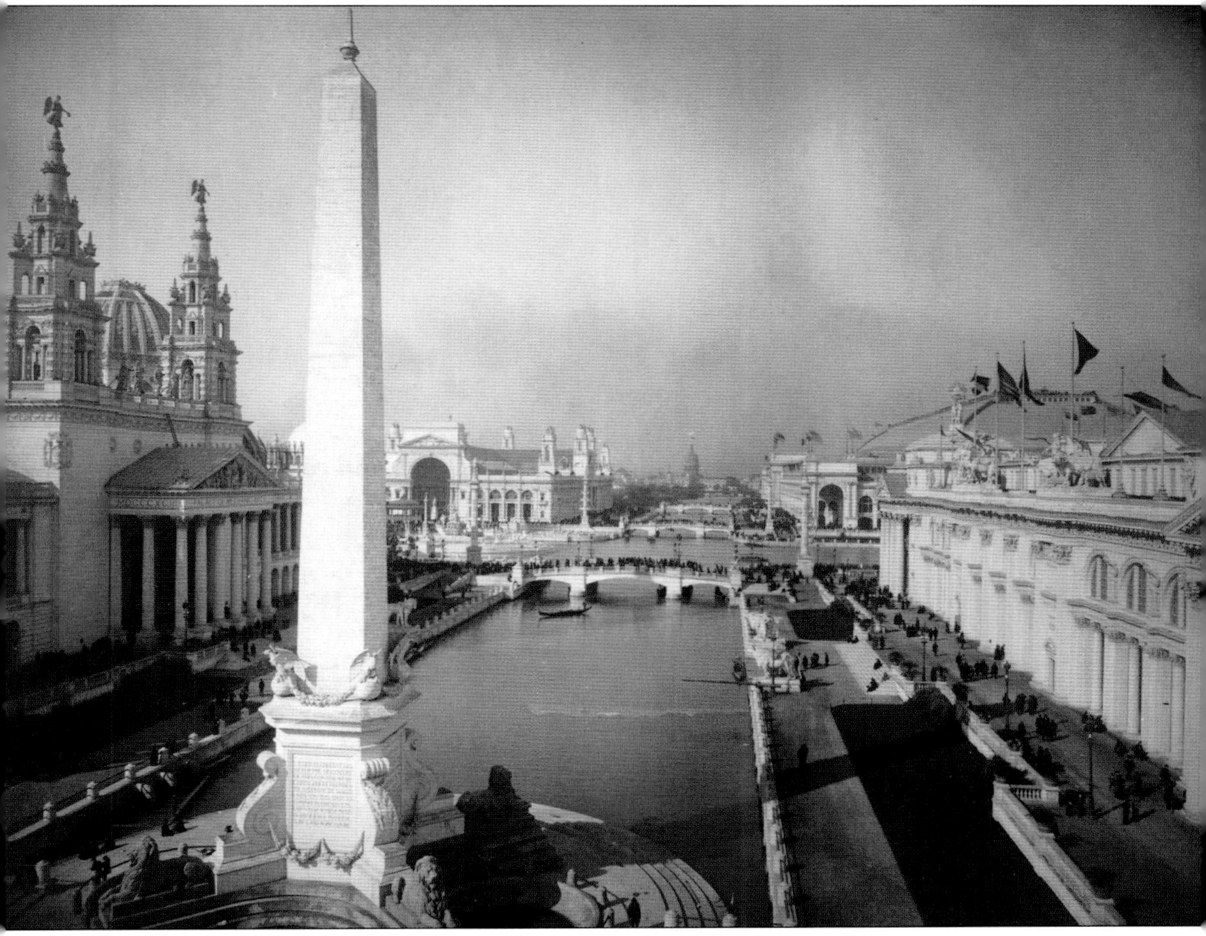

BIRD'S-EYE VIEW, FRANCES BENJAMIN JOHNSON, 1893. The Neoclassical architecture was complemented by an obelisk—another favored form for American public commemoration. The Washington Monument sits on the National Mall in Washington, DC, which is a similar layout and form to the Midway of the World's Columbian Exposition. (Library of Congress.)

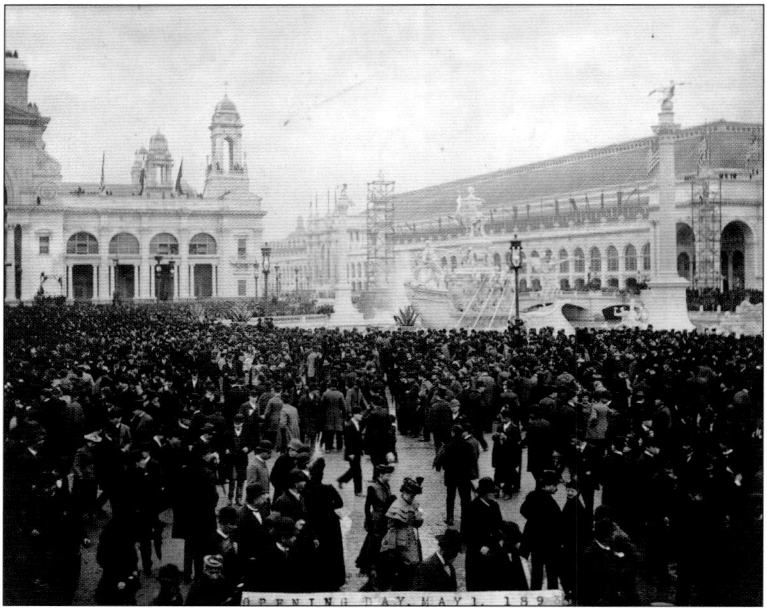

OPENING DAY, WORLD'S COLUMBIAN EXPOSITION, MAY 1, 1893. Crowds came from far and wide, including from abroad, to visit the "White City"—a city built within the city of Chicago to celebrate the 400th anniversary of Columbus in the New World. The exposition was open for six months. (Photograph by C.D. Arnold, Library of Congress.)

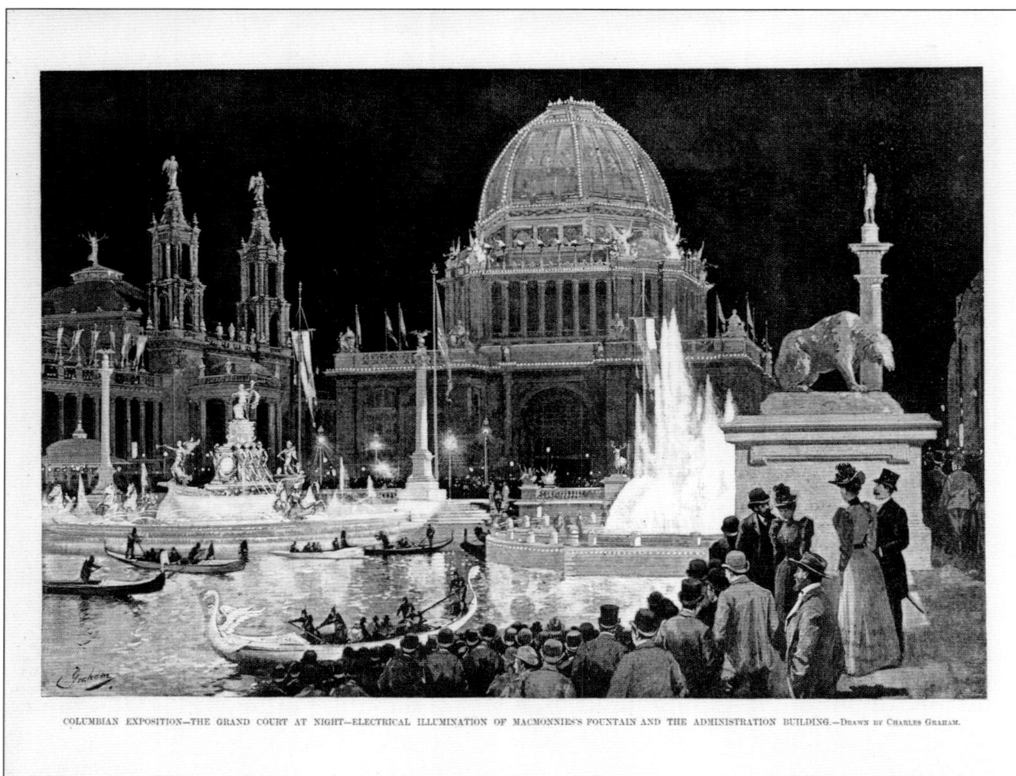

GRAND COURT AT NIGHT, ELECTRIFIED, CHARLES GRAHAM. The Grand Court centerpiece was the Administration Building and basin filled with sculpture, most importantly Frederick MacMonnies's Columbian Fountain, a huge barge with the figure of Columbia—which represented the New World, and more specifically, the United States. Gondolas and twinkling electrical lights created a romantic scene. (Library of Congress.)

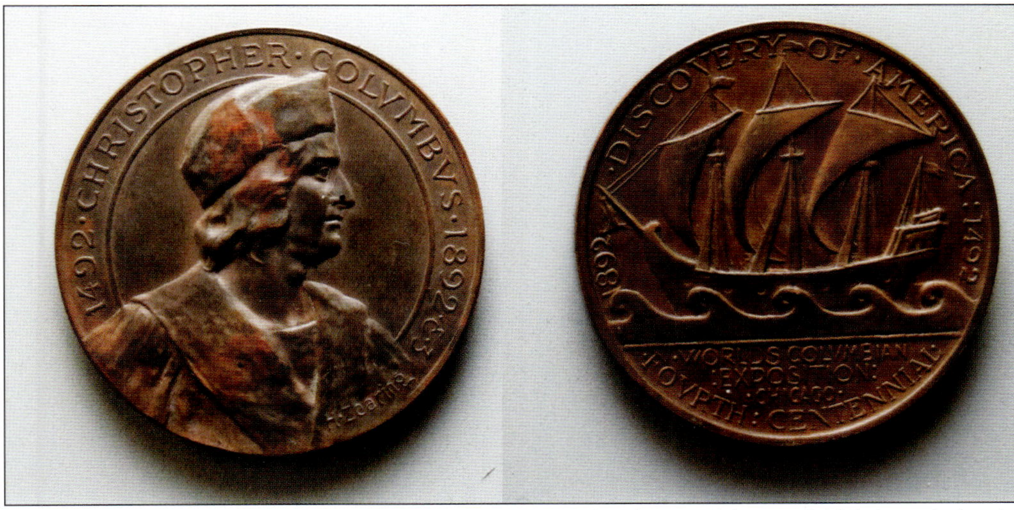

Bronze Souvenir Medal, Henry H. Zearing, 1893. The design of this medal likely includes the same image used by many artists, including Alfons Pelzer, the artist of the Columbus Monument in Wooster Square in New Haven. The images, both obverse and reverse, are plainly presented, with a look back to the Mediterranean in the stylized ocean waves, much like a fresco from ancient Greece. (Yale University Art Gallery.)

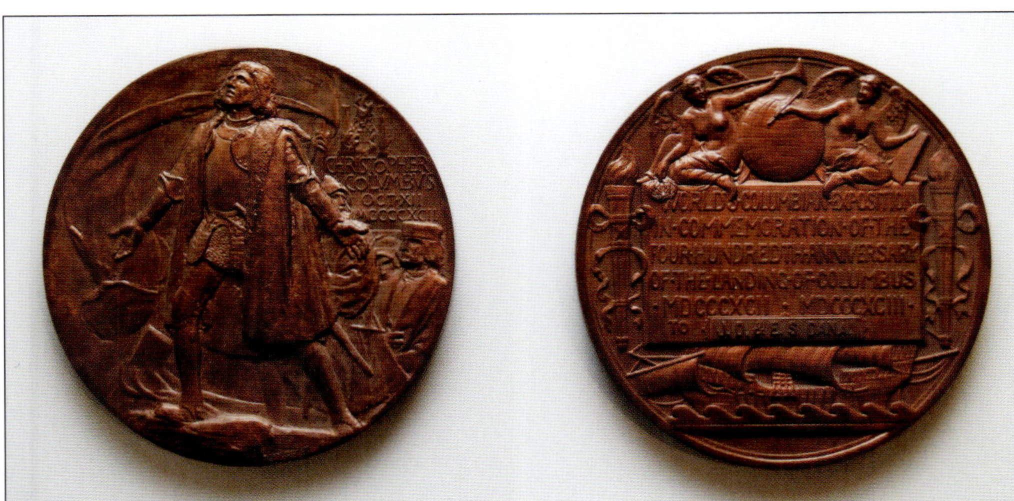

Bronze Medal, Augustus Saint-Gaudens and Charles E. Barber, 1893. Saint-Gaudens was the premier American sculptor of the Gilded Age. This medal was cast at the Scovill Manufacturing Company, in Waterbury, which specialized in bronzes and metalwork. The pose of Columbus with outstretched arms (supplication to God) is seen often, including in the huge bronze figure at the Knights of Columbus Museum. (Yale University Art Gallery.)

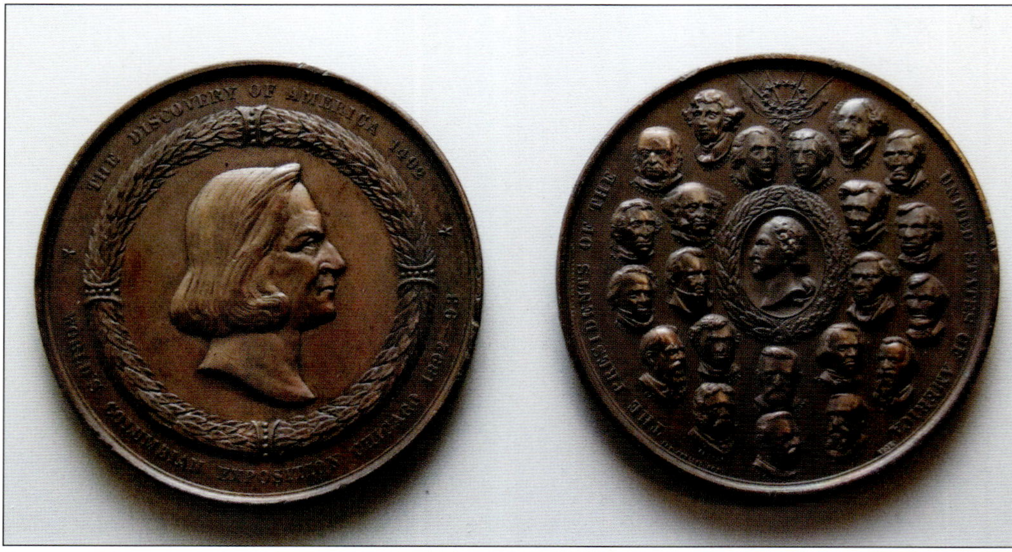

Bronze Medal, Columbus and Washington with American Presidents, 1893. Although the artist of this medal is unknown, both the profile of Columbus and that of Washington sit inside a laurel wreath frame, a symbol of victory from the classical world, indicating the artist was familiar with the history of art and its symbols throughout the western world. (Yale University Art Gallery.)

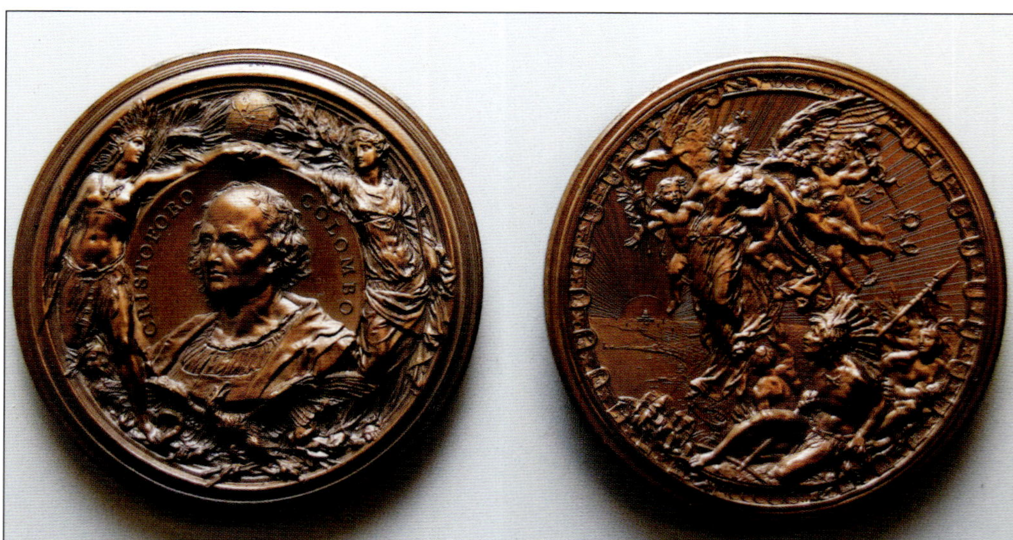

Bronze Medal, Angelo Cappuccio and Ludivico Pogliaghi, 1893. One of the more ornate souvenir medals of the exposition, the design here shows that Cappuccio and Pogliaghi were European-trained. On the obverse, the portrait of Columbus is shown with female personifications of the Old World (woman at right) holding hands with the New World (Native American woman). (Yale University Art Gallery.)

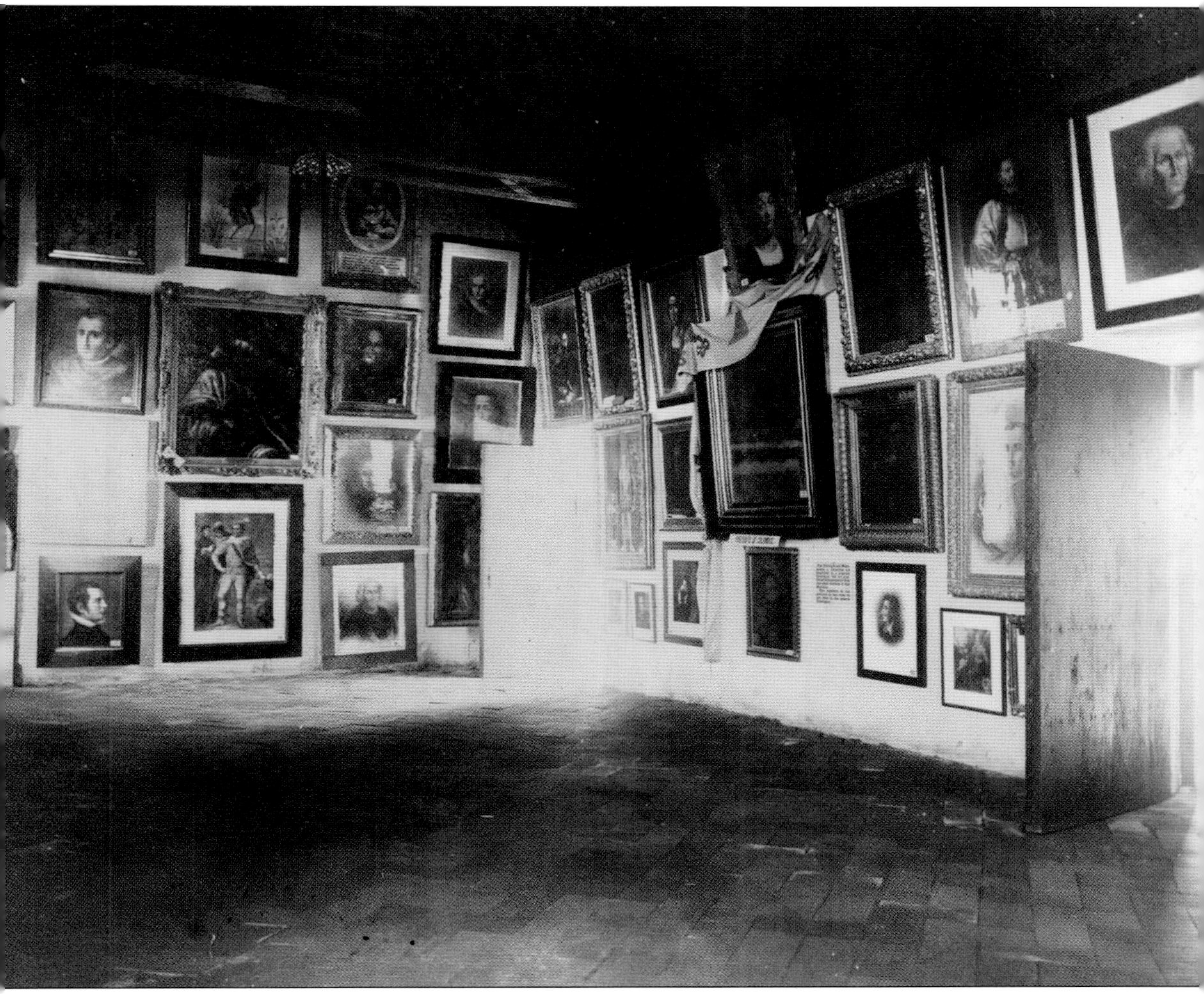

Columbus Room at the World's Columbian Exposition. Columbus appeared in many forms and in many places at the World's Columbian Exposition, including in this room, filled from floor to ceiling with images of the navigator. (Photograph by the Souvenir Photograph Co., Library of Congress.)

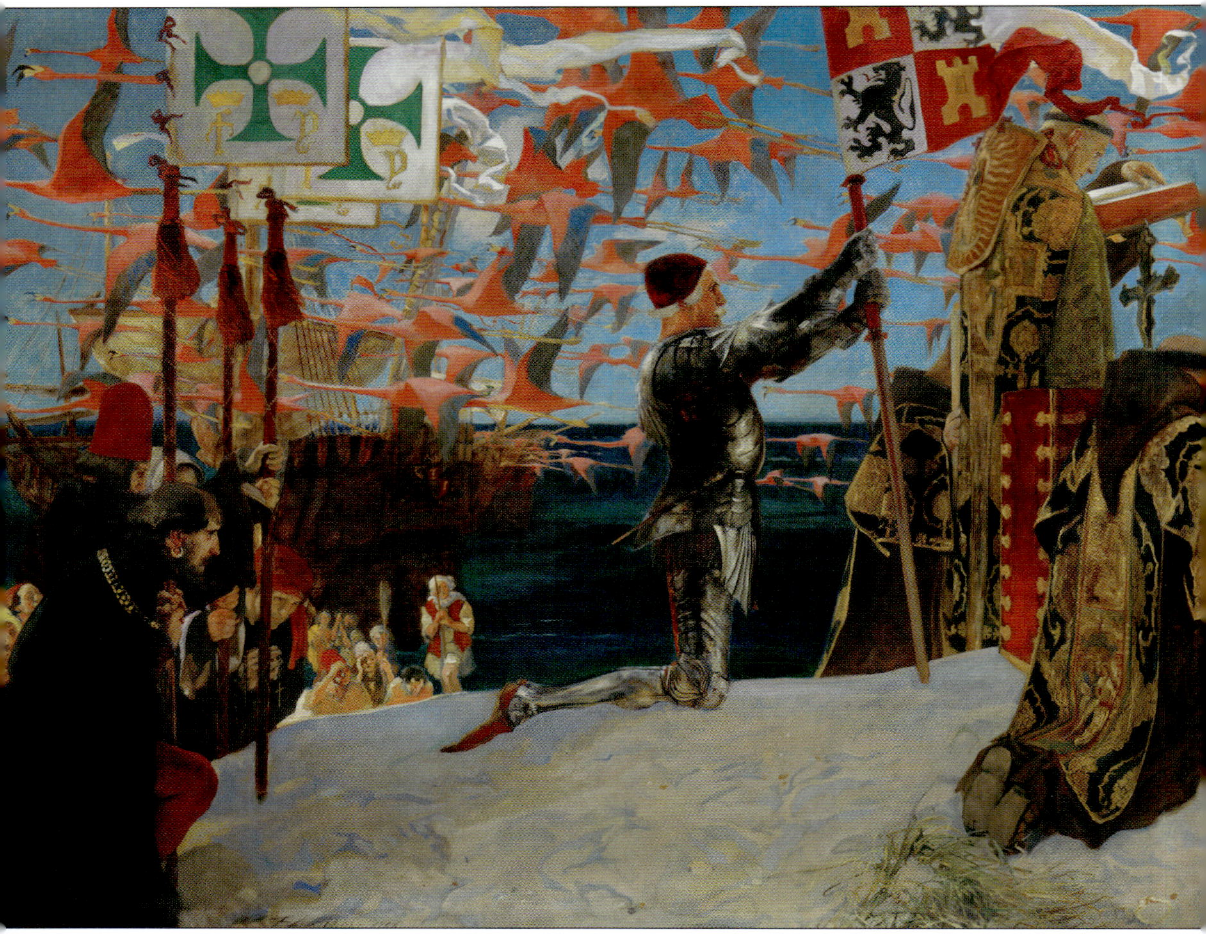

Columbus in the New World, Edwin Austin Abbey, 1906. Abbey was a muralist and illustrator, and created many works of art from Shakespearean and Victorian-era stories. The Yale University Art Gallery has many studies of this painting in its collection, including one for the pink flamingoes, which are shown filling the air with their flight. The pageantry of Abbey's paintings is similar to the pageants and parades Americans favored in the late 19th and early 20th centuries. (Yale University Art Gallery.)

Two

The Columbus Monument in Wooster Square

The fact that the Wooster Square Historic District was the city of New Haven's first local historic district (1970) and was subsequently listed in the National Register of Historic Places (1971) demonstrates the value of the neighborhood to the identity of New Haven, a city of 19 unique neighborhoods spread around the original Nine Square Plan of 1638/1639. Although known today for its status at the epicenter of "apizza" (New Haven–style pizza), the Wooster Square neighborhood changed shape many times over the course of its almost 200-year-old life: its architecture was built up, razed, and built up again, and generations of Americans settled there, placing a toehold in the industrializing city and later dealing with the effects of deindustrialization. First named for David Wooster, a New Haven resident and Revolutionary War general who died in the Battle of Ridgefield, the green square is bounded by an elegant iron fence designed by Mayor Philip Galpin around 1860. Various styles of 19th- and 20th-century architecture and the planting of Japanese cherry trees provide the square with a refined sense of self today. But in 19th-century New Haven, as waves of immigrants transformed the city from its Yankee roots, Wooster Square became *the* neighborhood—first, for the Irish, and then, at the end of the 19th century (coinciding with the 400th celebration of Columbus in the New World), into a place still identified today as having strong Italian American roots, even though most Italians moved out of the city to the suburbs in the second half of the 20th century.

One of the reasons Wooster Square retains its Italian American flavor is due to the work of the Columbus Day Committee of Greater New Haven, which organizes a wreath-laying ceremony at St. Michael's Church the weekend of Columbus Day. Priests bless wreaths from all of the local Italian societies, organizations, and other friends, such as the Knights of Columbus, which are then paraded across the square and hung around the iron fence that encloses the Columbus Monument. To get from Wooster Square to Wooster Street (where the apizza restaurants reside), a person can take DePalma Court, which passes by Paul Russo Memorial Park. Few people realize the little area of grass is named for the man who organized Italians' efforts into the city and state's first successful public art project for them: the installation of the Columbus Monument in Wooster Square in 1892.

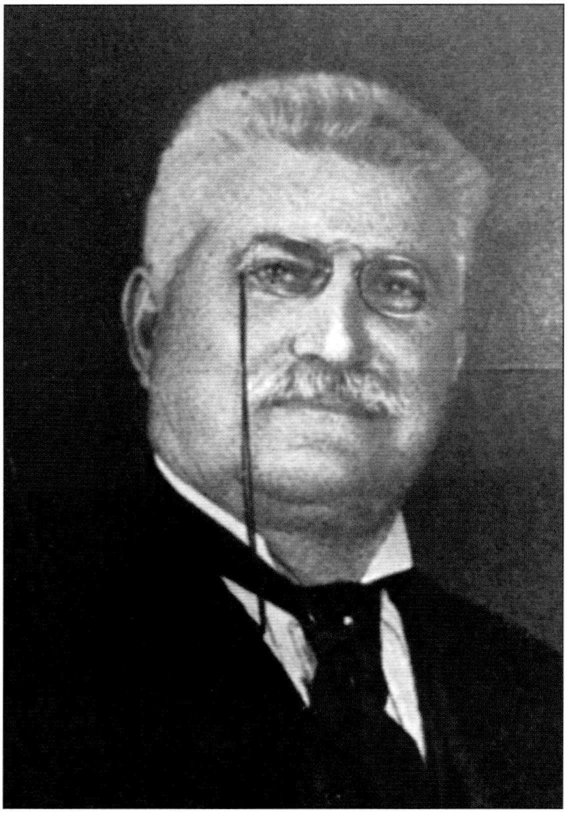

PAOLO RUSSO. Paolo "Paul" Russo, born in 1859 in Viggiano in the province of Basilicato, Italy, came to New Haven via New York City with his parents, quickly establishing himself as a hardworking, entrepreneurial, and intelligent advocate for the Italian community. He became a business owner and was utilized as a court translator, eventually becoming the first Italian to graduate from Yale Law School (in 1893)—at the very same time he helped the Italians of the city and state to mark their presence in the Elm City by installing the Columbus Monument in Wooster Square. This advertisement for Russo's insurance company, providing "Assicurazioni per Case ed Automobili" (insurance for homes and cars) appeared in the newspaper *La Parola Cattolica* in 1936. Russo was loved by the Italian community of New Haven and Connecticut, earning the nickname "Papa Affetuoso" (affectionate father). (Both, Italian-American Historical Society of Connecticut.)

ST. PAUL'S CHURCH
41 Alling St., Allingtown
Rev. Michael P. Barry, Pastor.
Masses at 7:30, 8:30, 9:30 and 11:30 a. m.

ST. PETER'S CHURCH
174 Kimberly Ave.
Rev. Wm. P. Kennedy, Pastor.
Masses at 7, 8:15, 9:30 and 10:45 a. m.

ST. ROSE'S CHURCH
119 Blatchley Ave.
Rev. John J. Fitzgerald, Pastor.
Masses at 7, 8:30, 9:45 and 11:00 a. m.

ST. STANISLAUS' CHURCH
790 State Street
Masses at 7, 8:30, 9 and 11 a. m.

ST. JOSEPH'S CHURCH
117 Edwards St.
Masses at 7, 8, 9:15 and 10:45 a. m.

ST. JOHN'S CHURCH
Davenport Ave. cor. South St.
Rev. Francis Murray, Pastor.
Masses at 7, 8, 9 and 10:30 a. m.

ST. MARY'S CHURCH
7 Hillhouse Ave.
Rev. E. A. Baxter, Pastor.
Masses at 6, 7, 8, 9, 10 and 11 a. m.

West Haven—
ST. LAWRENCE CHURCH
Rev. Jeremiah Curtin, Pastor
Rev. J. H. Grady, Rev. A. M. Finnance, Assistants.
Sundays Masses at 7:15, 8:15, 9:15, 10:15, 11:15. Children's Mass in basement at 8:15.

ST. PAUL'S CHURCH
41 Alling Street
Rev. Michael P. Barry, pastor;
Rev. J. M. Coughlin, assistant.
Sunday Masses at 7:30, 8:30, 9:30 and 11:30 a. m.

ST. JOHN THE BAPTIST'S CHURCH
786 Dixwell Ave.
Rev. W. L. Kiernan, Pastor.
Masses at 7, 9:30 and 10:30 a. m.

East Haven — Foxon Park
OUR LADY OF POMPEI. CHURCH
Rev. T. Lawrason Riggs, Administrator, New Haven.
Mass 8:25 a. m. Sundays.

ST. VINCENT DE PAUL'S CHURCH
Rev. Dr. Joseph J. Joyce.
Sundays Masses at 7:00, 8:30, 10:00 and 11:00 a. m.

Hamden—
ST. RITA'S CHURCH
Park Ave.
Rev. Francis E. May.
Sunday morning masses at 7:50 and 9:20.

New Haven—
SACRED HEART'S CHURCH
Cor. Columbus Ave. & Liberty St.
Rev. William Redding, Pastor.
Masses at 6, 7, 8:15, 9:30 and 10:45 a. m.

ST. AIDEN'S CHURCH
124 Fountain Street
Rev. Fr. E. Wilson, Pastor.
Masses at 7:30, 9:00, 10:15 and 11:30 a. m.

ST. BONIFACE'S CHURCH
636 State Street
Rev. Jorn A. Heller, Pastor.
Masses at 8:15 and 10:45 a. m.

ST. BRENDAN'S CHURCH
Cor. Whalley & Ellsworth Aves.
Rev. John McLaughlin, Pastor.
Masses at 7, 8, 9 and 10.45 a. m.

ST. CASIMIR'S CHURCH
Greene Street
Rev. V. P. Karkauskas, Pastor.
Masses at 8:15. 9:15, 10:30, and 11:55 a. m.

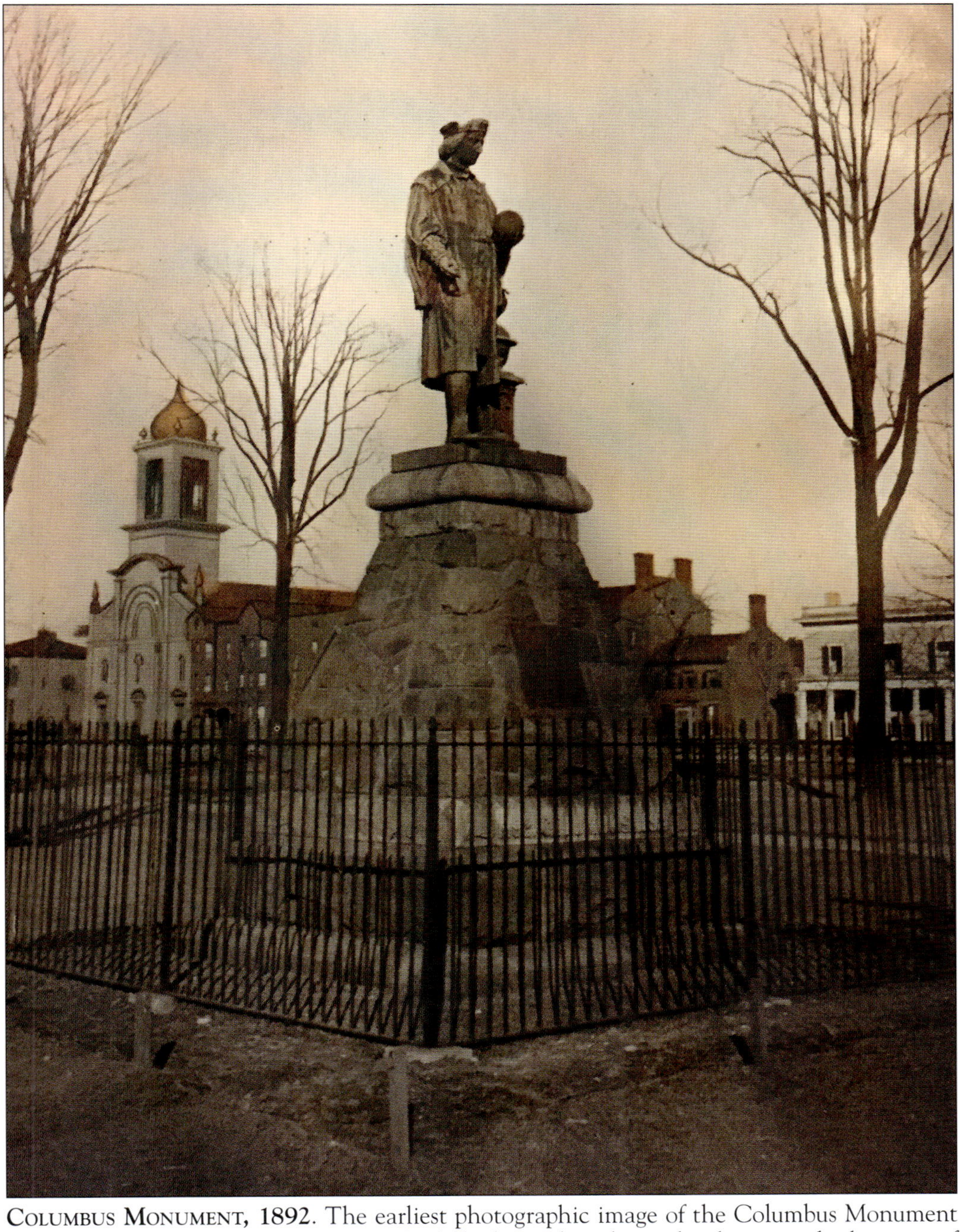

Columbus Monument, 1892. The earliest photographic image of the Columbus Monument (which has a hand-tinted application of color), shows the relationship between the location of the monument—which originally had a view out of the park, down the street to Long Island Sound—and St. Michael's Roman Catholic Church behind it, with its bell tower and onion dome, later Romanized with a Latin cross. The photograph also shows that the original Columbus Monument, upon installation in 1892 by and for the Italian Americans of the city and Connecticut, is a different version than the bronze monument reinstalled in its place in 1955. This first monument was made out of copper, with an interior armature of steel, much like the Statue of Liberty, which was a few years older, installed in New York Harbor in 1886. (Author's collection.)

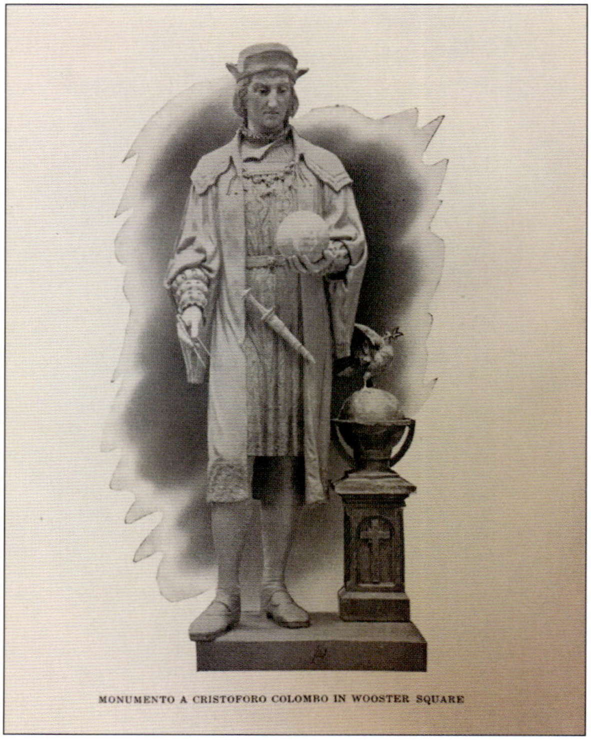

MONUMENTO A CRISTOFORO COLUMBO IN WOOSTER SQUARE. This graphic print of the Columbus Monument in Wooster Square shows details that were not brought forward in the bronze replacement statue. Alfons Pelzer is responsible for this design, and the W.H. Mullins Company of Salem, Ohio, offered these statues for sale, likely at a fraction of the cost of casting a bronze. (Author's collection.)

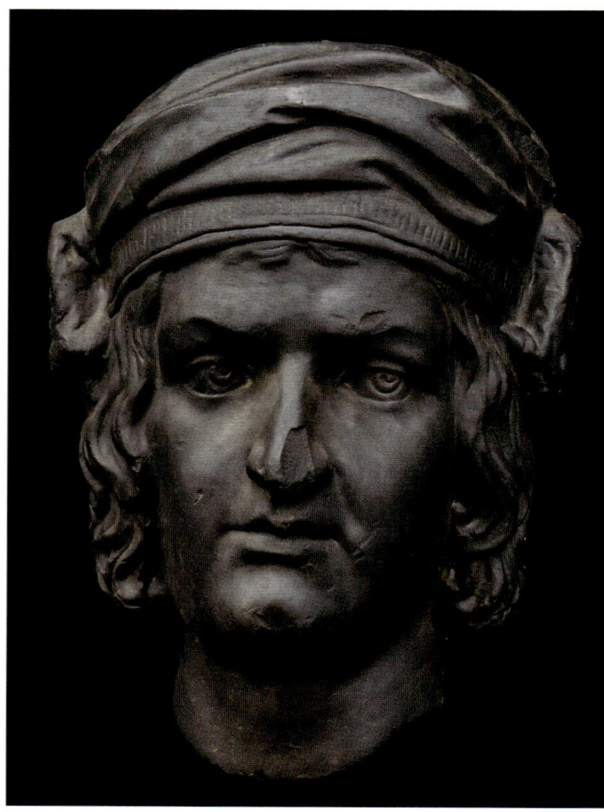

PLASTER HEAD OF COLUMBUS. Although it is not known what this plaster mask of Columbus was intended for (or copied from), it shows a traditional version of the navigator, in the Renaissance style. Plaster copies were often made during the bronze casting process. (Italian-American Historical Society of Connecticut.)

Columbus Monument, Phillipsburg, New Jersey, 1892. This copper monument, from the same Alfons Pelzer design as New Haven's, was installed and dedicated in October 1892 at the (former) St. Philip and St. James School (now a parish center called Mercy Hall). Unlike the Italian Americans of New Haven and Connecticut, who raised funds for their purchase of the copper Columbus through picnics and various group outings, the church group in Philipsburg raised its funds through the creation of a silver medal, copies of which sold for $1 each. The original Columbus Monument in New Jersey lasted longer than New Haven's, although it has gone through numerous conservation treatments and repairs, including a 1991 effort at the Cavalier Renaissance Foundry in Bridgeport, Connecticut. Similar to New Haven's bronze version, this Columbus Monument does not include the globe and dove, which appear in the original design. (Both, author's collection.)

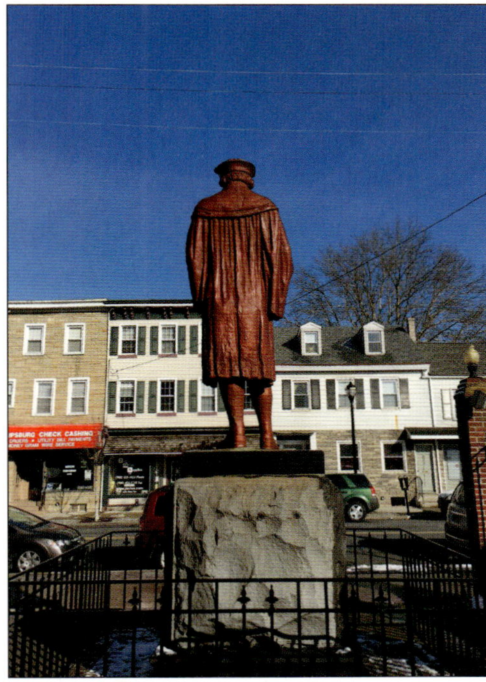

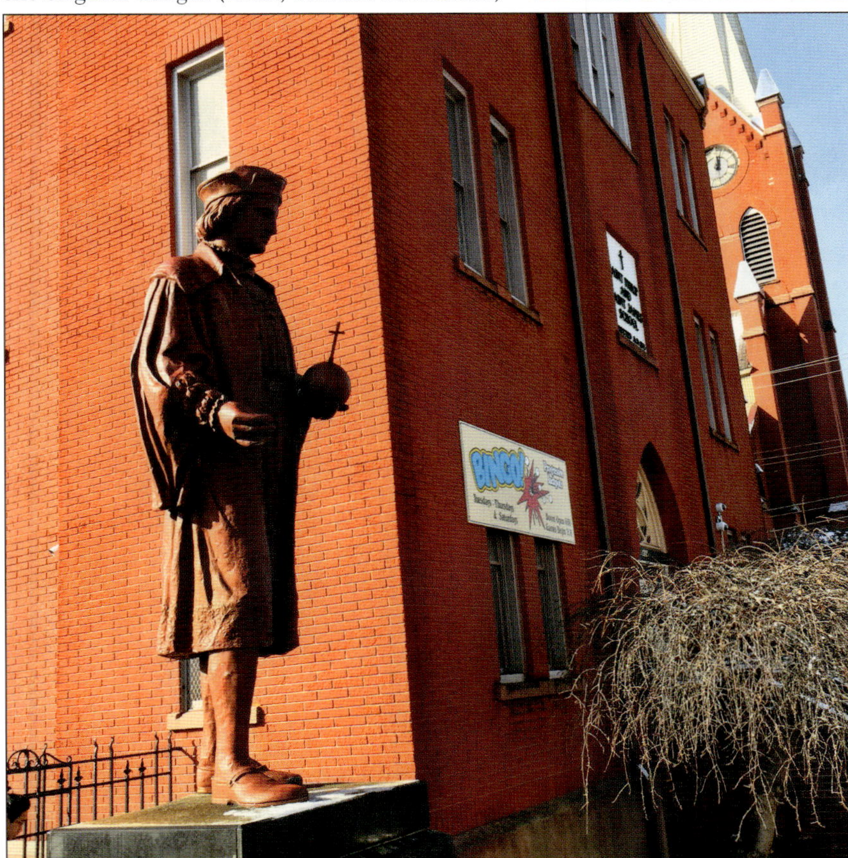

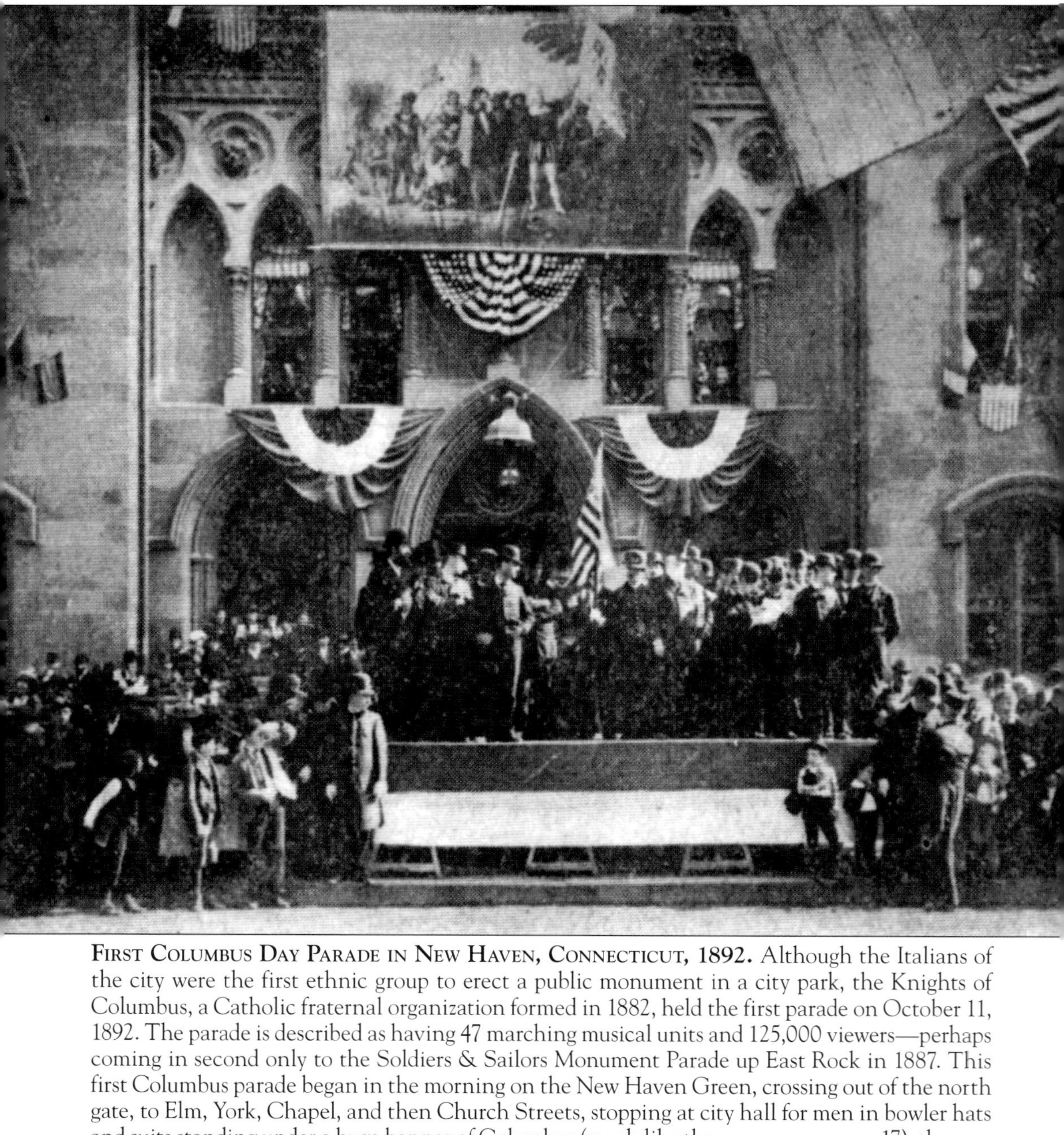

FIRST COLUMBUS DAY PARADE IN NEW HAVEN, CONNECTICUT, 1892. Although the Italians of the city were the first ethnic group to erect a public monument in a city park, the Knights of Columbus, a Catholic fraternal organization formed in 1882, held the first parade on October 11, 1892. The parade is described as having 47 marching musical units and 125,000 viewers—perhaps coming in second only to the Soldiers & Sailors Monument Parade up East Rock in 1887. This first Columbus parade began in the morning on the New Haven Green, crossing out of the north gate, to Elm, York, Chapel, and then Church Streets, stopping at city hall for men in bowler hats and suits standing under a huge banner of Columbus (much like the one seen on page 17), then on to Elm Street, to Grand Avenue, to Franklin and Chapel Streets, and to Wooster Square, then to Olive Street, where the line halted for 15 minutes to reform, then restarted from Chapel to Howe Streets, to Howard Avenue, to Congress Avenue, to Church and Temple Street, passing again through the green for a final review. (Local History Room of the New Haven Public Library.)

Columbus Day Parade Badges and Pin, October 11, 1892. Wearing ribbons, badges, and buttons to parades was a common feature of American culture in the 19th and early 20th centuries. These were created for use by members of the Knights of Columbus, who organized the first large Columbus Day Parade for the city of New Haven in 1892. The organization of mostly Irish American men took the name "Knights of Columbus" in 1882, and many founding members fought in the American Civil War in the name of preserving the Union and under their Catholic faith, thus ready to defend religious freedom and civil liberties. Although the Knights of Columbus discussed erecting a monument to Columbus for the 400th anniversary, the Italian Americans with Paul Russo's guidance got there first. (Right, Knights of Columbus Museum; below, Santa Maria, Council No. 8 badge, Robert S. Greenberg, Made in New Haven.)

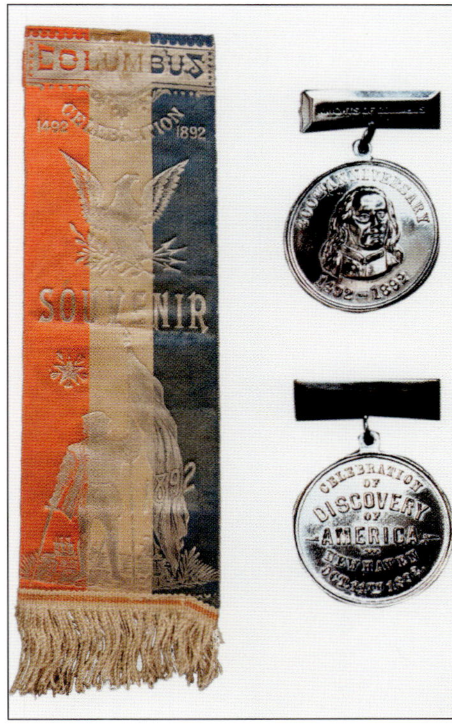

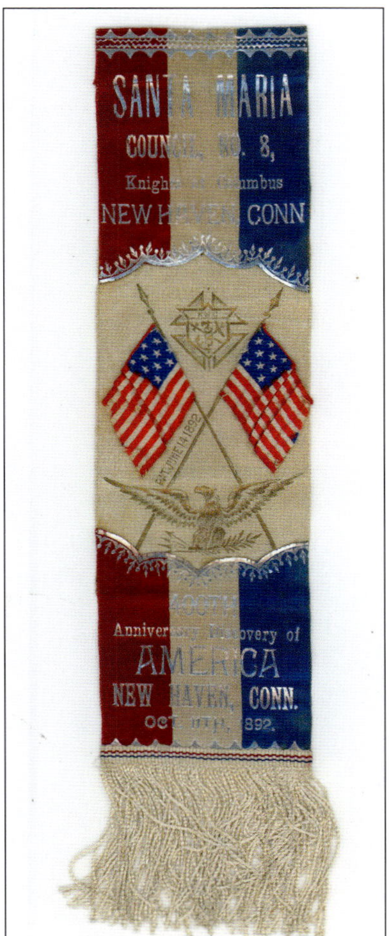

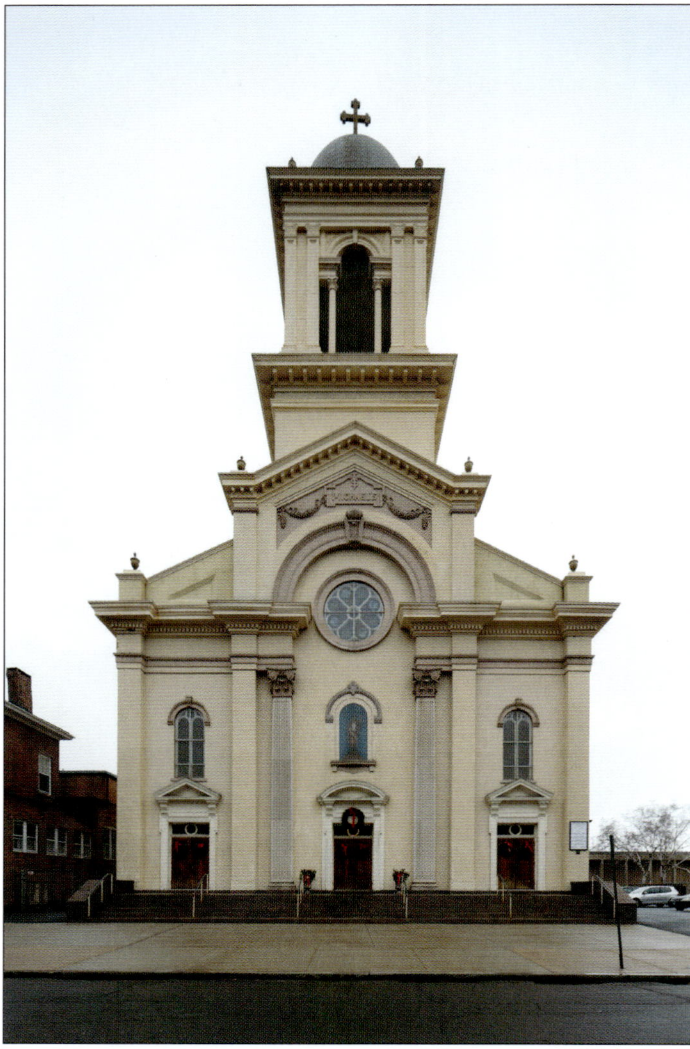

Facade, St. Michael's Roman Catholic Church. St. Michael's is the oldest Italian church in the state of Connecticut and the site of the annual wreath-blessing ceremony for Columbus Day. St. Michael's has been the mother church for the New Haven Italian community since 1899. Italian immigrants arrived at the end of the 19th century, pushing into the Wooster Square neighborhood and working in the city's many factories. (Photograph by William Sacco.)

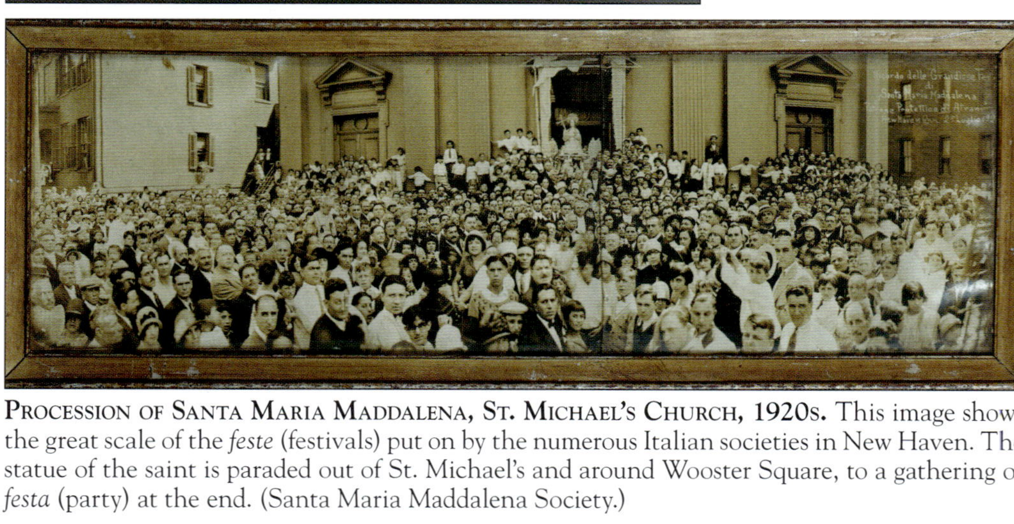

Procession of Santa Maria Maddalena, St. Michael's Church, 1920s. This image shows the great scale of the *feste* (festivals) put on by the numerous Italian societies in New Haven. The statue of the saint is paraded out of St. Michael's and around Wooster Square, to a gathering or *festa* (party) at the end. (Santa Maria Maddalena Society.)

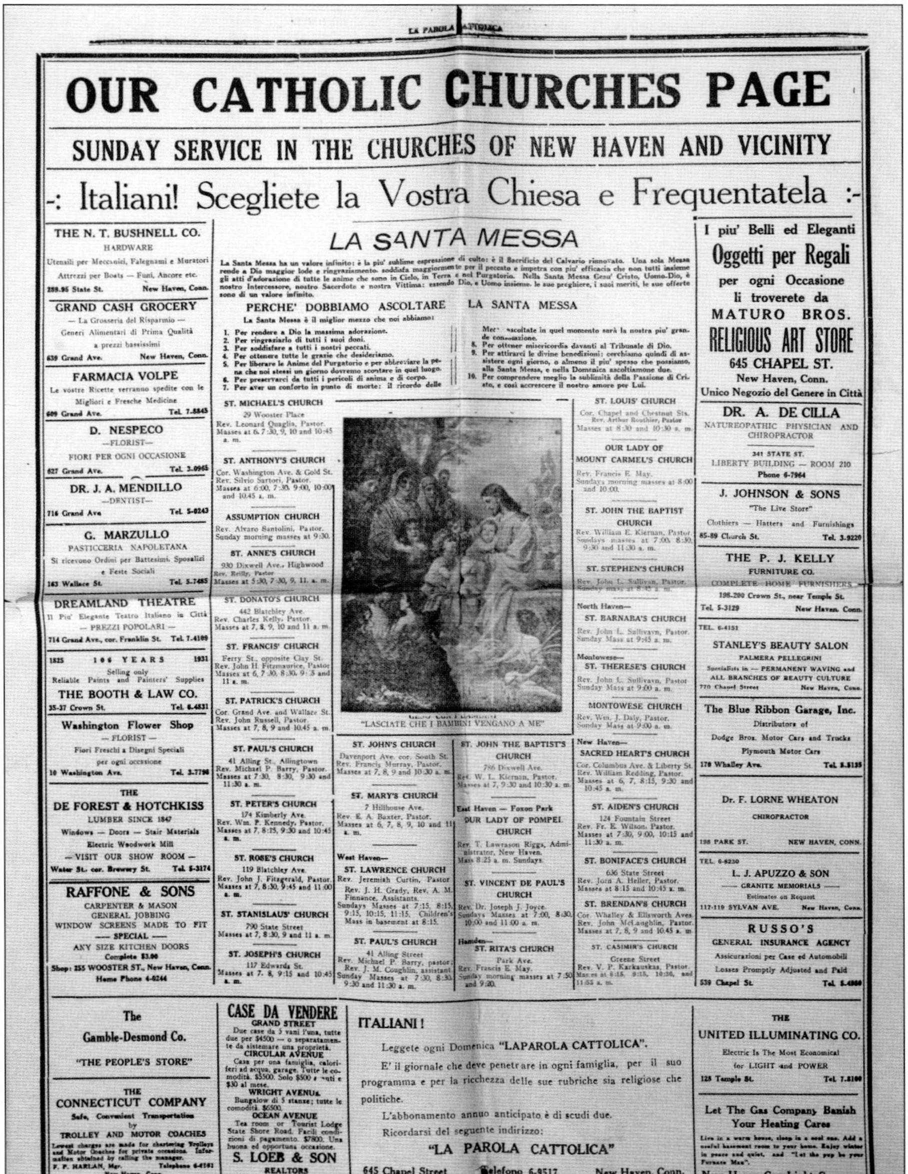

OUR CATHOLIC CHURCHES PAGE

SUNDAY SERVICE IN THE CHURCHES OF NEW HAVEN AND VICINITY

-: Italiani! Scegliete la Vostra Chiesa e Frequentatela :-

THE N. T. BUSHNELL CO.
HARDWARE
Utensili per Meccanici, Falegnami e Muratori
Attrezzi per Boats — Funi, Ancore etc.
288.95 State St. New Haven, Conn.

GRAND CASH GROCERY
— La Grosseria del Risparmio —
Generi Alimentari di Prima Qualità
a prezzi bassissimi
639 Grand Ave. New Haven, Conn.

FARMACIA VOLPE
Le vostre Ricette verranno spedite con le
Migliori e Fresche Medicine
609 Grand Ave. Tel. [illegible]

D. NESPECO
—FLORIST—
FIORI PER OGNI OCCASIONE
627 Grand Ave. Tel. 3.0965

DR. J. A. MENDILLO
—DENTIST—
716 Grand Ave Tel. 5-0243

G. MARZULLO
PASTICCERIA NAPOLETANA
Si ricevono Ordini per Battesimi, Sposalizi
e Feste Sociali
163 Wallace St. Tel. 5.7485

DREAMLAND THEATRE
Il Piu' Elegante Teatro Italiano in Città
— PREZZI POPOLARI —
714 Grand Ave., cor. Franklin St. Tel. 7.4109

1825 106 YEARS 1931
Selling only
Reliable Paints and Painters' Supplies
THE BOOTH & LAW CO.
35-37 Crown St. Tel. 6.4831

Washington Flower Shop
— FLORIST —
Fiori Freschi a Disegni Speciali
per ogni occasione
10 Washington Ave. Tel. 3.7798

THE
DE FOREST & HOTCHKISS
LUMBER SINCE 1847
Windows — Doors — Stair Materials
Electric Woodwork Mill
— VISIT OUR SHOW ROOM —
Water St., cor. Brewery St. Tel. 5-3174

RAFFONE & SONS
CARPENTER & MASON
GENERAL JOBBING
WINDOW SCREENS MADE TO FIT
—— SPECIAL ——
ANY SIZE KITCHEN DOORS
Complete $3.00
Shop: 255 WOOSTER ST., New Haven, Conn.
Home Phone 4-0244

LA SANTA MESSA

La Santa Messa ha un valore infinito: è la piu' sublime espressione di culto: è il Sacrificio del Calvario rinnovato. Una sola Messa rende a Dio maggior lode e ringraziamento, soddisfa maggiormente per il peccato e impetra con piu' efficacia che non tutti insieme gli atti d'adorazione di tutte le anime che sono in Cielo, in Terra e nel Purgatorio. Nella Santa Messa Gesu' Cristo, Uomo-Dio, è nostro Intercessore, nostro Sacerdote e nostra Vittima: essendo Dio, e Uomo insieme, le sue preghiere, i suoi meriti, le sue offerte sono di un valore infinito.

PERCHE' DOBBIAMO ASCOLTARE LA SANTA MESSA

La Santa Messa è il miglior mezzo che noi abbiamo:

1. Per rendere a Dio la massima adorazione.
2. Per ringraziarlo di tutti i suoi doni.
3. Per soddisfare a tutti i nostri peccati.
4. Per ottenere tutte le grazie che desideriamo.
5. Per liberare le Anime del Purgatorio e per abbreviare la pena che noi stessi un giorno dovremo scontare in quel luogo.
6. Per preservarci da tutti i pericoli di anima e di corpo.
7. Per aver un conforto in punto di morte: il ricordo delle Me[illegible] ascoltate in quel momento sarà la nostra piu' grande con[illegible]azione.
8. Per ottener misericordia davanti al Tribunale di Dio.
9. Per attirarci le divine benedizioni: cerchiamo quindi di assistere ogni giorno, o almeno il piu' spesso che possiamo, alla Santa Messa, e nella Domenica ascoltiamone due.
10. Per comprendere meglio la sublimità della Passione di Cristo, e così accrescere il nostro amore per Lui.

ST. MICHAEL'S CHURCH
29 Wooster Place
Rev. Leonard Quaglia, Pastor.
Masses at 6, 7:30, 9, 10 and 10:45 a. m.

ST. ANTHONY'S CHURCH
Cor. Washington Ave. & Gold St.
Rev. Silvio Sartori, Pastor.
Masses at 6:00, 7:30, 9:00, 10:00 and 10.45 a. m.

ASSUMPTION CHURCH
Rev. Alvaro Santolini, Pastor.
Sunday morning masses at 9:30.

ST. ANNE'S CHURCH
930 Dixwell Ave., Highwood
Rev. Reilly, Pastor
Masses at 5:30, 7:30, 9, 11. a. m.

ST. DONATO'S CHURCH
442 Blatchley Ave.
Rev. Charles Kelly, Pastor.
Masses at 7, 8, 9, 10 and 11 a. m.

ST. FRANCIS' CHURCH
Ferry St., opposite Clay St.
Rev. John H. Fitzmaurice, Pastor
Masses at 6, 7:30, 8:30, 9: 5 and 11 a. m.

ST. PATRICK'S CHURCH
Cor. Grand Ave. and Wallace St.
Rev. John Russell, Pastor.
Masses at 7, 8, 9 and 10.45 a. m.

ST. PAUL'S CHURCH
41 Alling St., Allingtown
Rev. Michael P. Barry, Pastor.
Masses at 7:30, 8:30, 9:30 and 11:30 a. m.

ST. PETER'S CHURCH
174 Kimberly Ave.
Rev. Wm. P. Kennedy, Pastor.
Masses at 7, 8:15, 9:30 and 10:45 a. m.

ST. ROSE'S CHURCH
119 Blatchley Ave.
Rev. John J. Fitzgerald, Pastor.
Masses at 7, 8:30, 9:45 and 11:00 a. m.

ST. STANISLAUS' CHURCH
790 State Street
Masses at 7, 8:30, 9 and 11 a. m.

ST. JOSEPH'S CHURCH
117 Edwards St.
Masses at 7, 8, 9:15 and 10:45 a. m.

[illegible]
"LASCIATE CHE I BAMBINI VENGANO A ME"

ST. JOHN'S CHURCH
Davenport Ave. cor. South St.
Rev. Francis Murray, Pastor.
Masses at 7, 8, 9 and 10:30 a. m.

ST. MARY'S CHURCH
7 Hillhouse Ave.
Rev. E. A. Baxter, Pastor.
Masses at 6, 7, 8, 9, 10 and 11 a. m.

West Haven—
ST. LAWRENCE CHURCH
Rev. Jeremiah Curtin, Pastor
Rev. J. H. Grady, Rev. A. M. Finnance, Assistants.
Sundays Masses at 7:15, 8:15, 9:15, 10:15, 11:15. Children's Mass in basement at 8:15.

ST. PAUL'S CHURCH
41 Alling Street
Rev. Michael P. Barry, pastor; Rev. J. M. Coughlin, assistant
Sunday Masses at 7:30, 8:30, 9:30 and 11:30 a. m.

ST. JOHN THE BAPTIST'S CHURCH
786 Dixwell Ave.
Rev. W. L. Kiernan, Pastor.
Masses at 7, 9:30 and 10:30 a. m.

East Haven — Foxon Park
OUR LADY OF POMPEI CHURCH
Rev. T. Lawrason Riggs, Administrator, New Haven.
Mass 8:25 a. m. Sundays.

ST. VINCENT DE PAUL'S CHURCH
Rev. Dr. Joseph J. Joyce.
Sundays Masses at 7:00, 8:30, 10:00 and 11:00 a. m.

Hamden—
ST. RITA'S CHURCH
Park Ave.
Rev. Francis E. May.
Sunday morning masses at 7:50 and 9:20.

ST. LOUIS' CHURCH
Cor. Chapel and Chestnut Sts.
Rev. Arthur Routhier, Pastor
Masses at 8:30 and 10:30 a. m.

OUR LADY OF MOUNT CARMEL'S CHURCH
Rev. Francis E. May.
Sundays morning masses at 8:00 and 10:00.

ST. JOHN THE BAPTIST CHURCH
Rev. William E. Kiernan, Pastor.
Sundays masses at 7:00, 8:30, 9:30 and 11:30 a. m.

ST. STEPHEN'S CHURCH
Rev. John L. Sullivan, Pastor.
Sunday mass at 8:45 a. m.

North Haven—
ST. BARNABA'S CHURCH
Rev. John L. Sullivavn, Pastor.
Sunday Mass at 9:45 a. m.

Montowese—
ST. THERESE'S CHURCH
Rev. John L. Sullivavn, Pastor
Sunday Mass at 9:00 a. m.

MONTOWESE CHURCH
Rev. Wm. J. Daly, Pastor.
Sunday Mass at 9:00 a. m.

New Haven—
SACRED HEART'S CHURCH
Cor. Columbus Ave. & Liberty St.
Rev. William Redding, Pastor.
Masses at 6, 7, 8:15, 9:30 and 10:45 a. m.

ST. AIDEN'S CHURCH
124 Fountain Street
Rev. Fr. E. Wilson, Pastor.
Masses at 7:30, 9:00, 10:15 and 11:30 a. m.

ST. BONIFACE'S CHURCH
636 State Street
Rev. Jorn A. Heller, Pastor.
Masses at 8:15 and 10:45 a. m.

ST. BRENDAN'S CHURCH
Cor. Whalley & Ellsworth Aves.
Rev. John McLaughlin, Pastor.
Masses at 7, 8, 9 and 10.45 a. m.

ST. CASIMIR'S CHURCH
Greene Street
Rev. V. P. Karkauskas, Pastor.
Masses at 8:15, 9:15, 10:30, and 11:55 a. m.

I piu' Belli ed Eleganti
Oggetti per Regali
per ogni Occasione
li troverete da
MATURO BROS.
RELIGIOUS ART STORE
645 CHAPEL ST.
New Haven, Conn.
Unico Negozio del Genere in Città

DR. A. DE CILLA
NATUREOPATHIC PHYSICIAN AND CHIROPRACTOR
341 STATE ST.
LIBERTY BUILDING — ROOM 210
Phone 6-7964

J. JOHNSON & SONS
"The Live Store"
Clothiers — Hatters and Furnishings
85-89 Church St. Tel. 3.9220

THE P. J. KELLY
FURNITURE CO.
COMPLETE HOME FURNISHERS
198-200 Crown St., near Temple St.
Tel. 5-3129 New Haven, Conn.

TEL. 6-4151
STANLEY'S BEAUTY SALON
PALMERA PELLEGRINI
Specialists in — PERMANENT WAVING and ALL BRANCHES OF BEAUTY CULTURE
770 Chapel Street New Haven, Conn.

The Blue Ribbon Garage, Inc.
Distributors of
Dodge Bros. Motor Cars and Trucks
Plymouth Motor Cars
170 Whalley Ave. Tel. 5.5135

Dr. F. LORNE WHEATON
CHIROPRACTOR
198 PARK ST. NEW HAVEN, CONN.

TEL. 6-8230
L. J. APUZZO & SON
—— GRANITE MEMORIALS ——
Estimates on Request
117-119 SYLVAN AVE. New Haven, Conn.

RUSSO'S
GENERAL INSURANCE AGENCY
Assicurazioni per Case ed Automobili
Losses Promptly Adjusted and Paid
539 Chapel St. Tel. [illegible]

The
Gamble-Desmond Co.
"THE PEOPLE'S STORE"

THE
CONNECTICUT COMPANY
Safe, Convenient Transportation
by
TROLLEY AND MOTOR COACHES
Lowest charges are made for chartering Trolleys and Motor Coaches for private occasions. Information obtained by calling the manager.
F. F. HARLAN, Mgr. Telephone 6-4161
New Haven, Conn.

CASE DA VENDERE
GRAND STREET
Due case da 5 vani l'una, tutte due per $4500 — o separatamente da sistemare una proprietà.
CIRCULAR AVENUE
Casa per una famiglia, caloriferi ad acqua, garage. Tutte le comodità. $5500. Solo $500 [illegible] e $30 al mese.
WRIGHT AVENUE
Bungalow di 5 stanze; tutte le comodità. $6500.
OCEAN AVENUE
Tea room or Tourist Lodge State Shore Road. Facili condizioni di pagamento. $7800. Una buona ed opportuna occasione.
S. LOEB & SON
REALTORS
151 Court St. New Haven, Ct.

ITALIANI!

Leggete ogni Domenica "LAPAROLA CATTOLICA".

E' il giornale che deve penetrare in ogni famiglia, per il suo programma e per la ricchezza delle sue rubriche sia religiose che politiche.

L'abbonamento annuo anticipato è di scudi due.

Ricordarsi del seguente indirizzo:

"LA PAROLA CATTOLICA"
645 Chapel Street Telefono 6-9517 New Haven, Conn.

THE
UNITED ILLUMINATING CO.
Electric Is The Most Economical for LIGHT and POWER
128 Temple St. Tel. 7.8100

Let The Gas Company Banish Your Heating Cares
Live in a warm house, sleep in a cool one. Add a useful basement room to your home. Enjoy winter in peace and quiet, and "Let the pup be your Furnace Man".
New Haven Gas Light Company

"OUR CATHOLIC SERVICES PAGE," FROM *LA PAROLA CATTOLICA*, MAY 23, 1936. This page, which encourages Italians of the Elm City with the words: "Italiani! Scegliete la Vostra Chiesa e Frequentatela!" ("Italians! Choose your church and attend frequently!"), lists the city's Roman Catholic churches, showing just how large the city's Catholic population had grown by the first half of the 20th century—which included Poles, Irish, and Italians (on this list, St. Michael's remains first). A mixture of English and Italian words demonstrates how two cultures begin to blend into one. For Italian Catholics, images of Mary, Jesus, and the saints was a tradition, seen here in the picture of Jesus with young children, with the caption, "Lasciate che i bambini vengono con me" ("Let the children come with me"). This newspaper, printed in New Haven on Chapel Street, was donated to the Italian-American Historical Society of Connecticut by Frank Grazioso. (Italian-American Historical Society of Connecticut.)

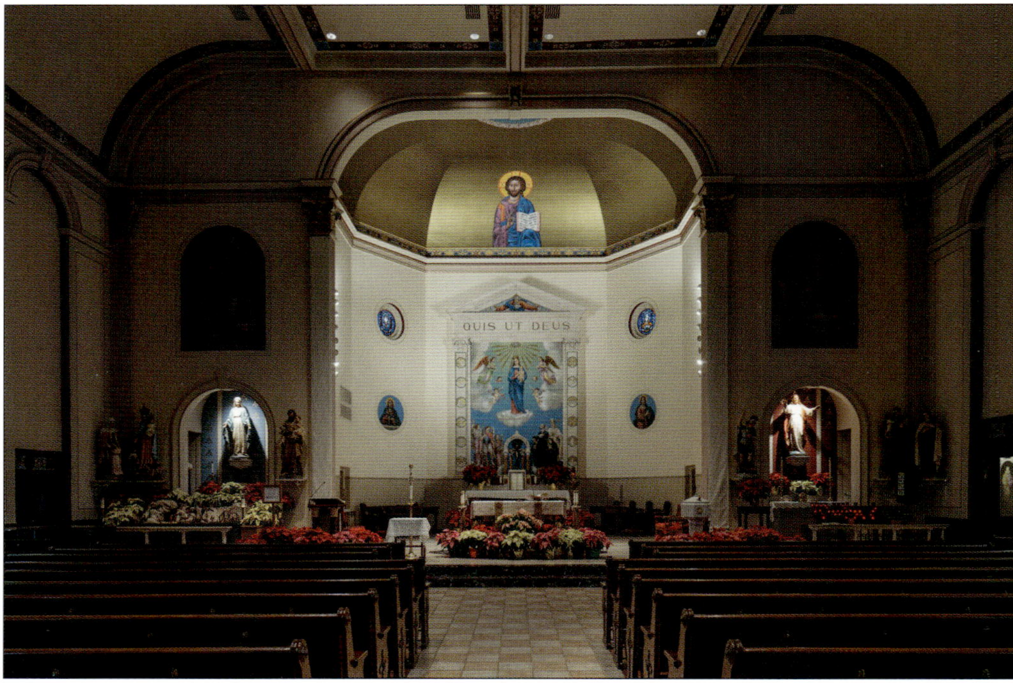

Interior, St. Michael's Roman Catholic Church Nave (above) and Chapel (below). According to architectural historian Elizabeth Mills Brown, very little is left of the original 1855 Congregational church, but the decorative elements—paintings, frescoes, statues, and stained glass—demonstrate the Catholic use of art to teach scripture and church history. The dozens of statues on display in the chapel (works of art) represent the patron saints of different Italian villages and towns of the immigrants who came to New Haven. Each of these separate villages and towns had its own saints and its own traditions, and when transplanted to New Haven, developed its own mutual aid societies. Still in existence, for example, are the Società di Sant'Andrea Apostolo (from Amalfi) and the Santa Maria Maddalena Society (from Atrani), each with its own statues and saint procession days. (Both photographs by William Sacco.)

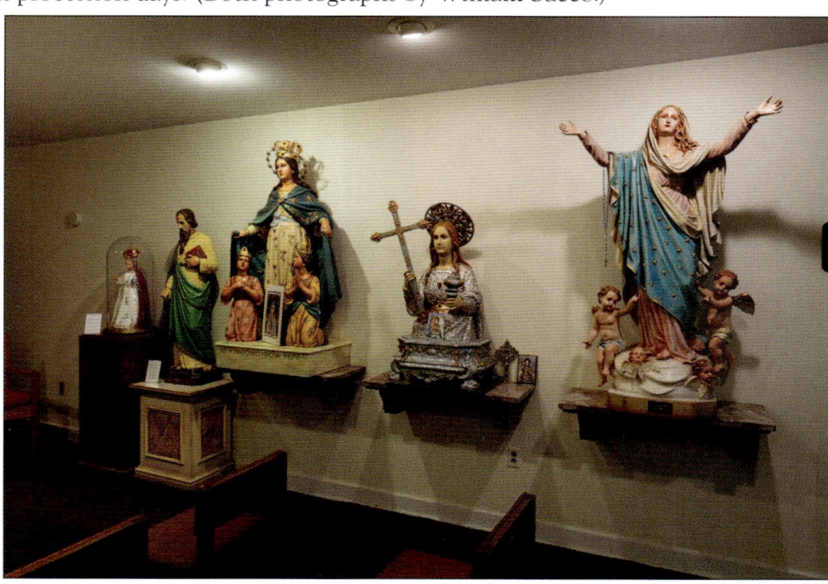

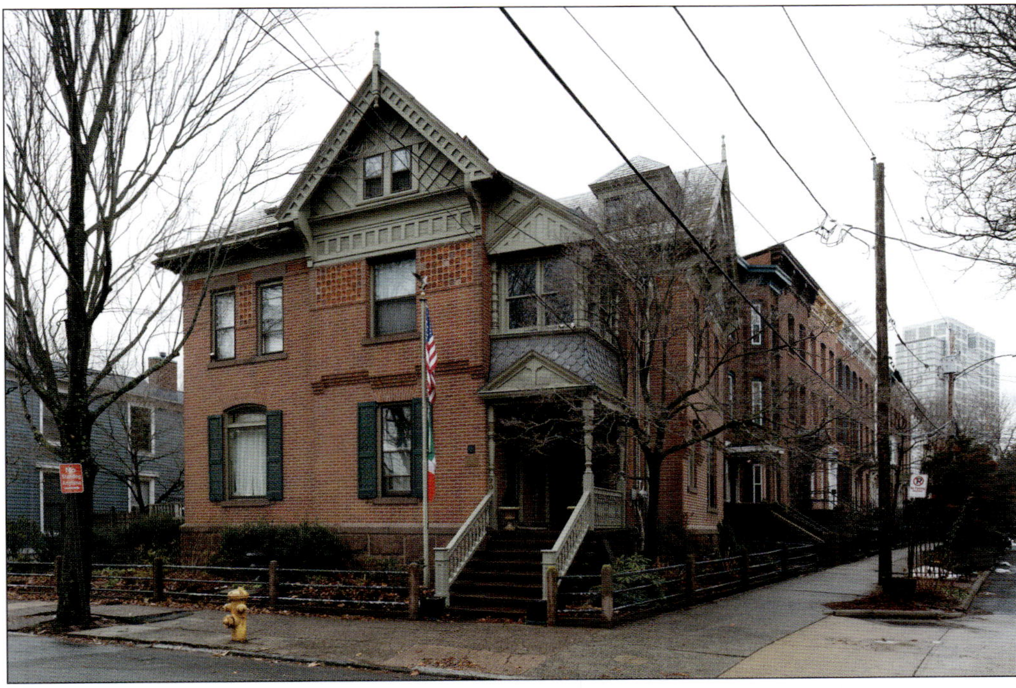

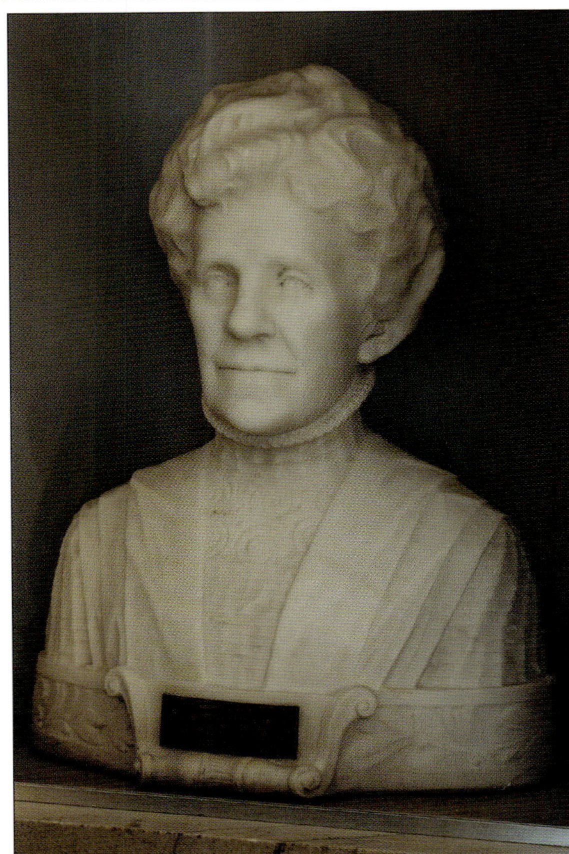

FORMER ITALIAN CONSULATE (ABOVE) AND BUST OF AUGUSTA LEWIS TROUP (RIGHT). The former Italian consulate, a Queen Anne–style brick building, was used at the turn of the 20th century to assist immigrants. Although the structure is long out of use in formal governmental functions, the current owners of the house still fly the Italian flag, il Tricolore. Augusta Lewis Troup was a typesetter, journalist, union organizer, and suffragist. In her later years, Troup was a philanthropist for multiple causes but particularly as a benefactor to the needs of Italian immigrants, who called her the "Little Mother of the Italian Colony." The Carrara marble bust was presented at the dedication ceremony of Troup Middle School (now Troup Magnet Academy of Sciences) by Mrs. Sylvester Z. Poli in 1926. The artist was Michelangelo Crisafi, who owned the Venice Art Bronze Company in New Haven. (Both photographs by William Sacco.)

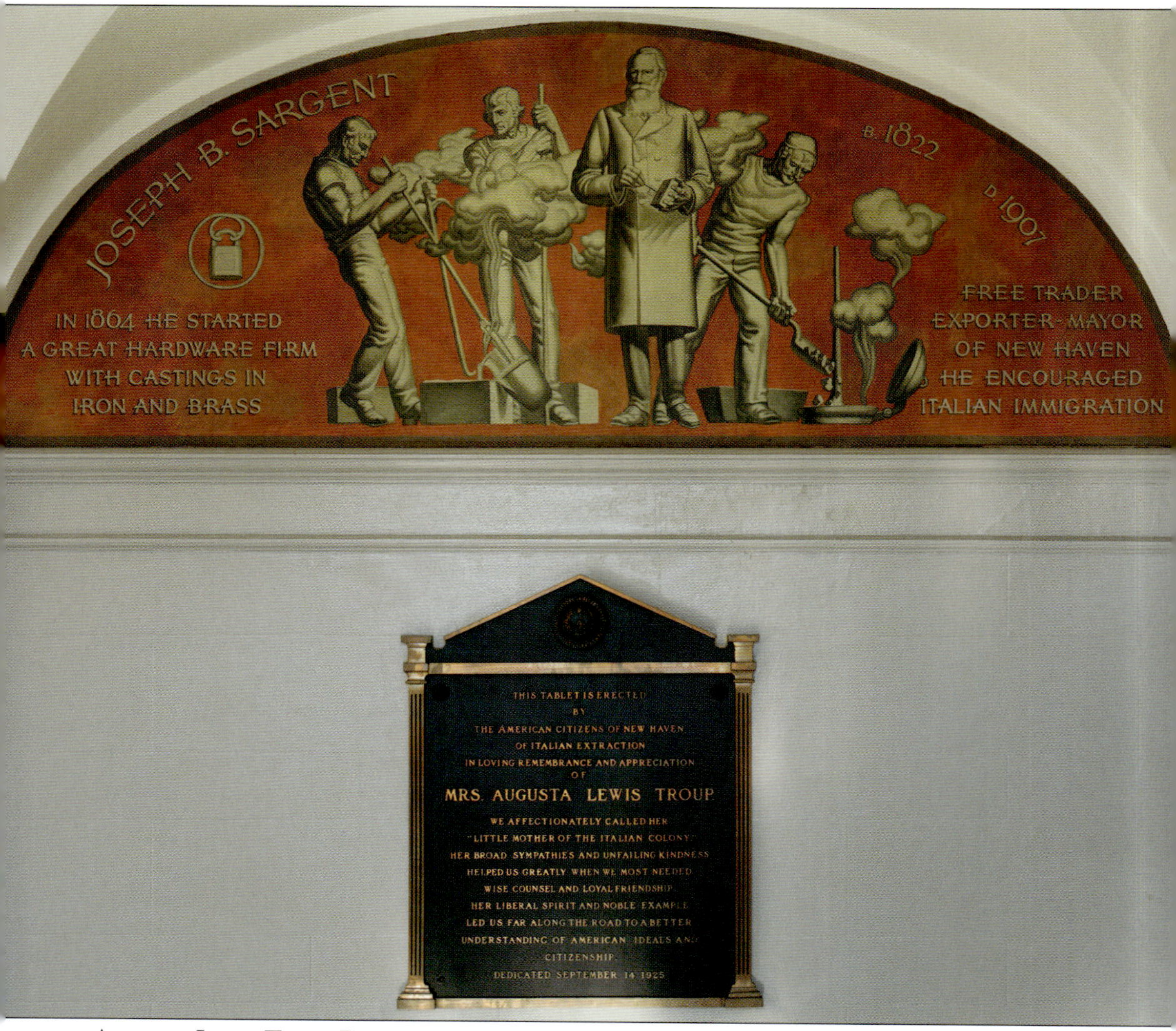

AUGUSTA LEWIS TROUP PLAQUE AND JOSEPH B. SARGENT MURAL. There is a connection between the two, since Troup worked to help the Italian immigrants who came to work in the Sargent Co. factory (as the mural notes, "he encouraged Italian immigration"). The tablet to Troup reads, "This tablet erected by the American citizens of New Haven of Italian extraction in loving remembrance and appreciation of Mrs. Augusta Lewis Troup. We affectionately called her 'Little Mother of the Italian Colony.' Her broad sympathies and unfailing kindness helped us greatly when we most needed wise counsel and loyal friendship. Her liberal spirit and noble example led us far along the road to a better understanding of American ideas and citizenship. Dedicated September 14, 1925." Note the ethnic-looking men in the mural working behind the figure of Sargent. The plaque was installed in 1925, the year the school opened; the mural was painted in 1934 under the city's active Works Progress Administration program. (Photograph by William Sacco.)

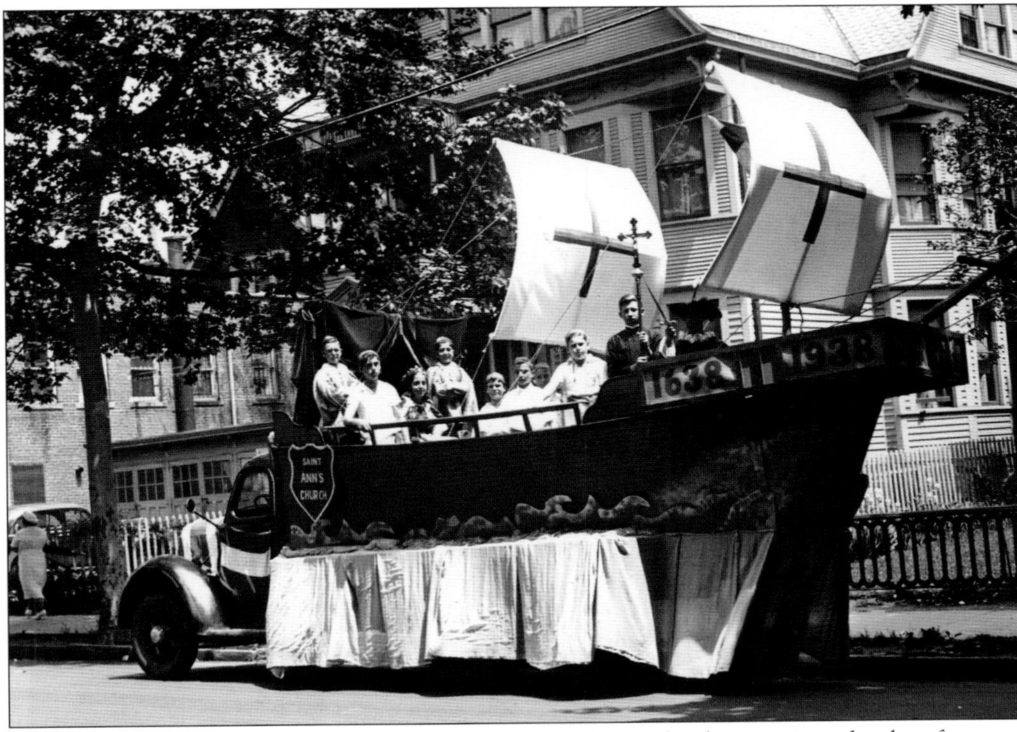

COLUMBUS STAYS RELEVANT. These two images show that Columbus continued to be of interest in New Haven into the 1930s. The image above shows a Columbus-inspired float from St. Ann's Church, with the dates "1638–1938," part of the city's huge 300th-anniversary celebrations: 10,000 of the city's students paraded in the Yale Bowl in front of 35,000 spectators. The image below is a reproduction of a sketch done by Wendell Philips Austin (1896–1966), from Round About New Haven with Pen and Pencil, a syndicated series. Austin was born in New Haven and was drafted in World War I. After the war, Austin lived with his family in Milford, but taught art classes in his own school, the Austin School of Art and Design in New Haven. (Above, New Haven Museum; below, Local History Room of the New Haven Free Public Library.)

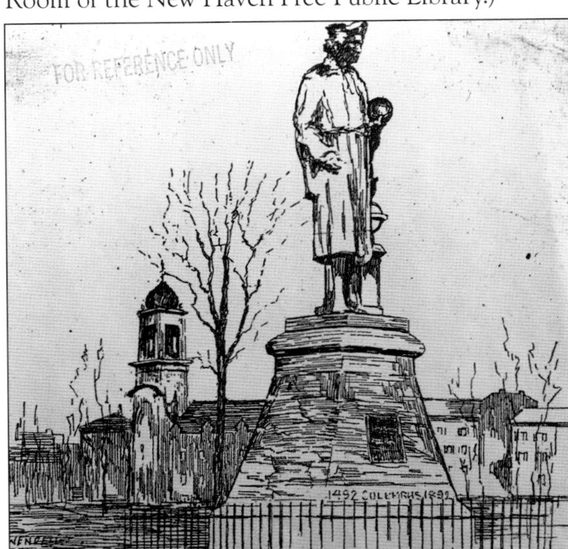

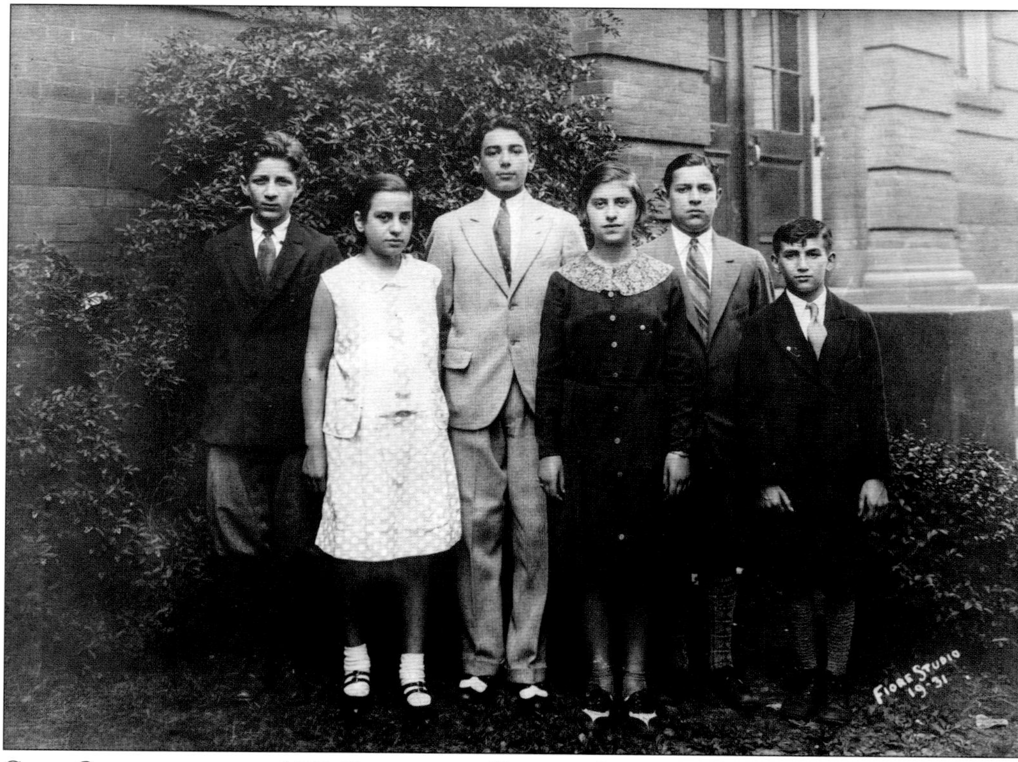

CLASS OFFICERS AND THE 1931 GRADUATING CLASS OF COLUMBUS SCHOOL, NEW HAVEN. There have been multiple schools in New Haven named for Christopher Columbus, including a second school that was built in 1968 and torn down for the current Columbus Family Academy building at 255 Blatchley Avenue (see chapter 4). This Columbus School, an earlier incarnation, is a reflection of city growth from immigration at the end of the 19th century, and of the different ethnicities. The Columbus School class creed stated, "We, the graduating class of 1931, believe that we should go forth to serve . . . we promise to never sully the name of Columbus School by any act of dishonesty or cowardice . . . we pledge ourselves to be loyal, patriotic and law-abiding citizens, and to do our utmost to be worthy of the great privilege of American citizenship." (Both, Italian-American Historical Society of Connecticut.)

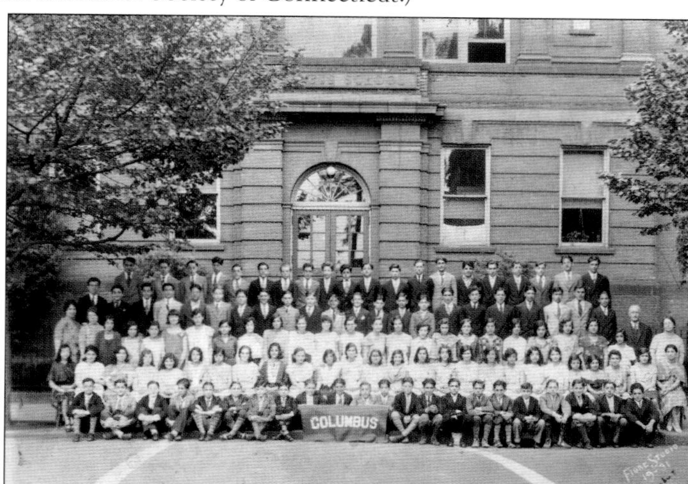

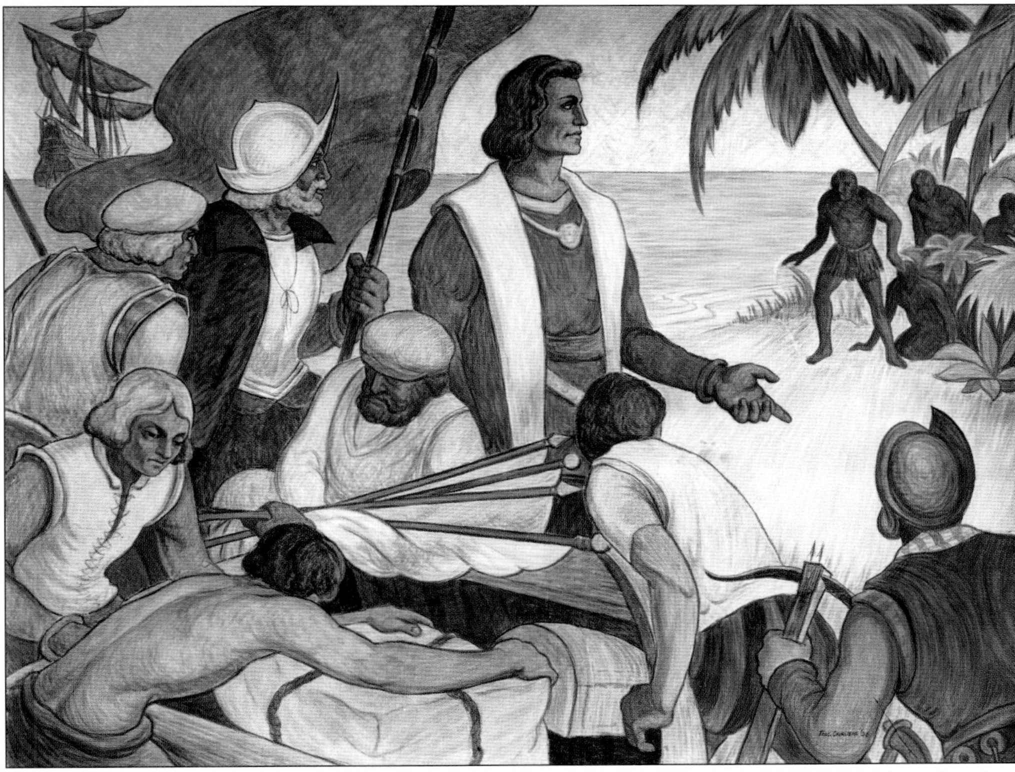

Columbian Art for New Haven Public Schools. Two works of art done for public schools in New Haven included the fresco *Columbus Landing in America* from the American History Series at the Ivy Street School and an untitled triptych, both by Thomas Cavaliere. In the mural, Columbus is the largest figure presented, his men surround him with the tools needed for their work, planting the flag for Spain, and weapons to ensure their safety against the indigenous people, who seem to crawl out from the palm trees to witness the arrival. (Connecticut State Library.)

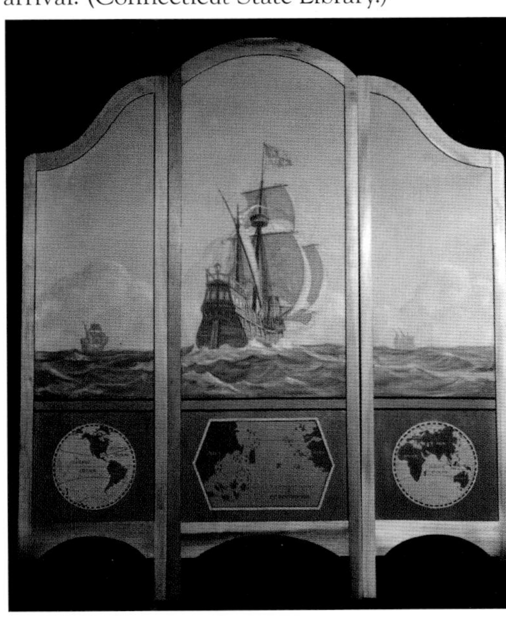

Thomas Cavaliere Triptych. Cavaliere created these works of art for New Haven public schools in the late 1930s, under the Works Progress Administration (WPA) program, part of Pres. Franklin D. Roosevelt's New Deal. These two Columbus-inspired works of art show that, in addition to local heroes Nathan Hale, Eli Whitney, and Roger Sherman (all of whom were the subject of school murals), so, too, was Columbus. Both of these works were destroyed when their schools were closed. (Connecticut State Library.)

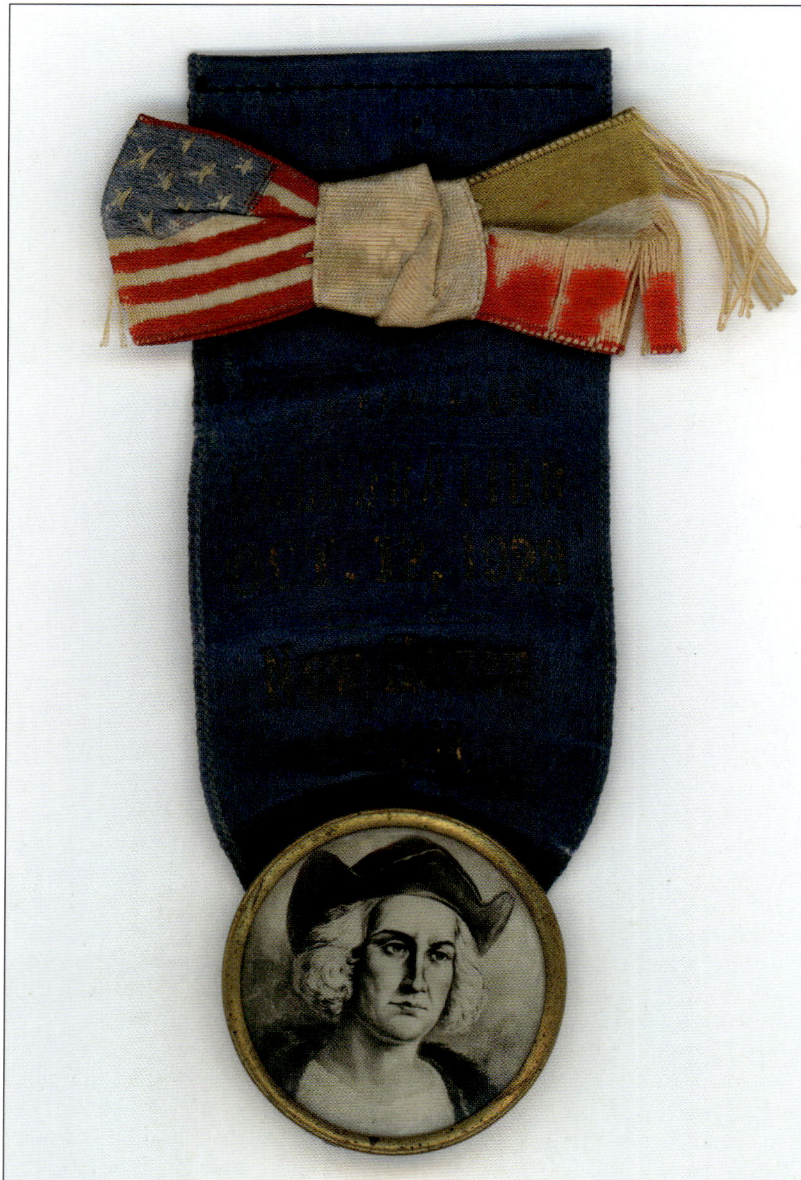

Columbus Celebration Parade Badge, October 12, 1928. Although historical photographs of the Columbus Day Parade from before the 1950s are lacking, this parade badge from 1928 proves its continuation during the first two decades of the 20th century. Comparing the Knights of Columbus parade badges from the very first celebration in 1892 (page 29) with this one reveals how the Italians of New Haven reshaped that event for their own community: the Knights of Columbus badges are red, white, and blue, and emphasize their role as knights (see the depiction of Columbus standing with his sword and flag, just as the Knights of Columbus did in ceremonies and parades); while the Italian version from 1928, where the American and Italian flags come together in the ribbon at the top, shows the blending of two cultures. Before the 1950s, the Columbus Day Parades in New Haven were likely modest affairs sponsored by the Italian American community, but, in the next phase of their life, the parades became an arm of city hall and were huge events, with spectators numbering in the tens of thousands. (Robert Greenberg, Made in New Haven.)

Three

The Revival of the Columbus Day Parade

The year 1945 was a momentous one: the Allies were victorious in Europe and, on the home front, William Celentano became the city of New Haven's first Italian American mayor. For the Italian community, long shut out of political life at city hall (the Irish had their first mayor in 1900), "Now Is The Time" became the slogan for Celentano's race. The funeral home director first ran for office in 1939 but was defeated. Ethnic prejudice still ran high in New Haven, with the city often divided by the wards and their aldermen along ethnic and economic lines. This continued through Celentano's almost 10 years in office, until he was finally ousted in 1953 by Richard C. Lee, the mayor who led the era of urban redevelopment. Although intended to reshape a city in need of transportation and housing projects, redevelopment in New Haven remains nothing less than a dirty word: whole neighborhoods were wiped out for roadways, families were forced to move (many leaving the city for good), and to add insult to injury, some projects were started but never finished.

But in New Haven's postwar years, the 1950s and 1960s, the Columbus Day Parade was revived by the Lee administration, to placate to some degree the injurious projects that destroyed areas of the Wooster Square neighborhood. Lee directed tremendous sums of cash from the federal government to the redevelopment office, which was staffed by neighborhood workers. The New Haven Board of Aldermen provided some funds support to the parade, and the city donated police, public works, and parks department staff to the event. The revival of New Haven's Columbus Day Parade began in 1953 (likewise the revival of the St. Patrick's Day Parade was 1956). In addition, the copper version of the Columbus Monument was replaced by the current bronze version in 1955, likely due to deterioration. During the Lee administration, which lasted from 1954 to 1970, the Columbus Day Parade was a huge success, with reports of up to 60,000 spectators. For the time being, it was the "Mayor's Columbus Day Parade."

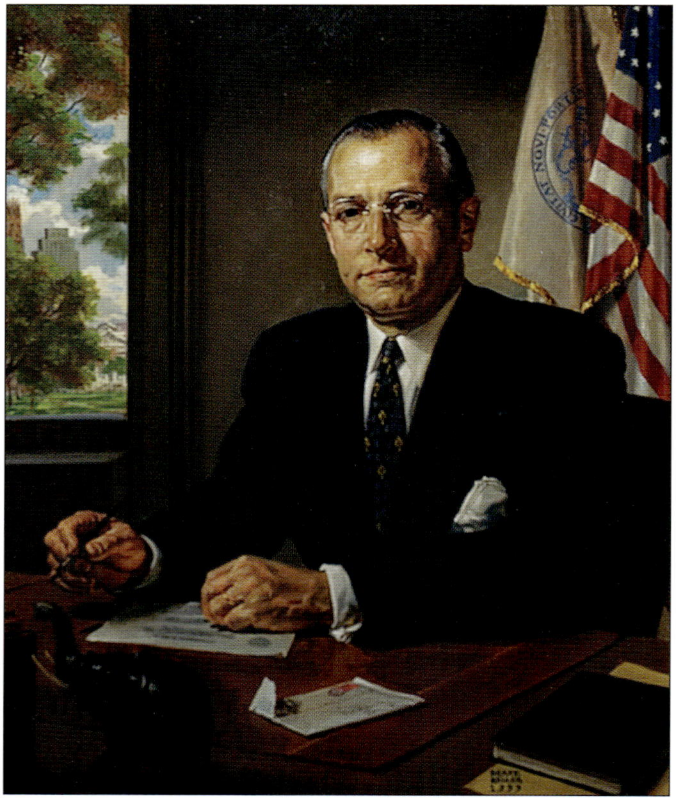

PORTRAIT OF WILLIAM C. CELENTANO, DEANE KELLER, OIL ON CANVAS, 1953. New Haven mayoral portraits are always completed at the end of a mayoral administration. The son of a fruit peddler, Celentano was elected when the Republican Party realized the growing size of the Italian vote, thus becoming the first Italian American mayor of the city. He served on the board of aldermen for 12 years and three terms as mayor. (City of New Haven.)

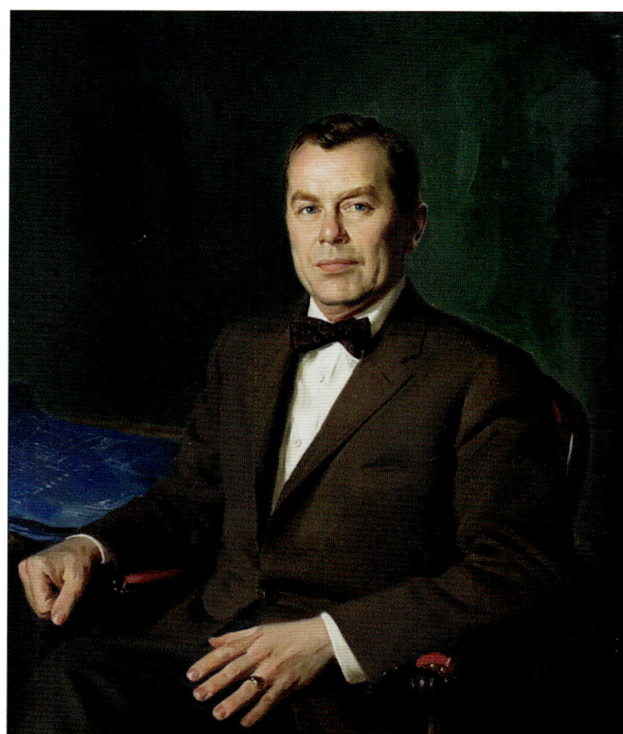

PORTRAIT OF RICHARD C. LEE, RICHARD O. SKEINP, OIL ON CANVAS, 1969. In 1954, Lee was the director of Yale's News Bureau when he began the first of eight terms as mayor—the youngest elected in city history. Under his guidance, urban renewal, called redevelopment in New Haven, was marked by the tearing down, rebuilding, and rehabilitation of downtown and neighborhoods such as Wooster Square. (City of New Haven.)

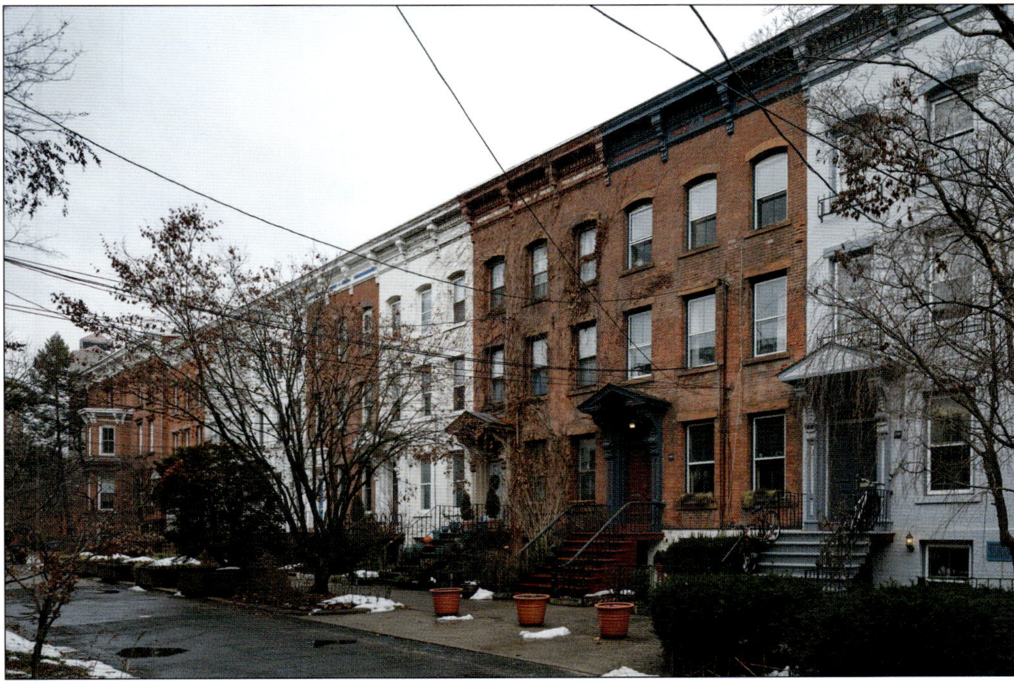

Court Street Row Houses and Green Street Town Houses. These two streets, both connected to Wooster Square, demonstrate the types of redevelopment work that happened under the Lee administration. In the image above, the small brick row houses (built 1869–1870) were rehabilitated in 1961, the street was closed to automobile traffic, and plantings were installed. This largely happened due to the criticism waged against the destruction of historic buildings in the city by the Redevelopment Agency, which helped to spurn the creation of the New Haven Preservation Trust. The photograph below shows the kind of modern architecture urban renewal was equally enamored of in the Town House Apartments, erected in 1963. Lee said of this work, "The new Wooster Square, appropriately the first neighborhood to be settled by Italian pioneers a century ago, will serve as a model which many cities will try to emulate for years to come." (Both photographs by William Sacco.)

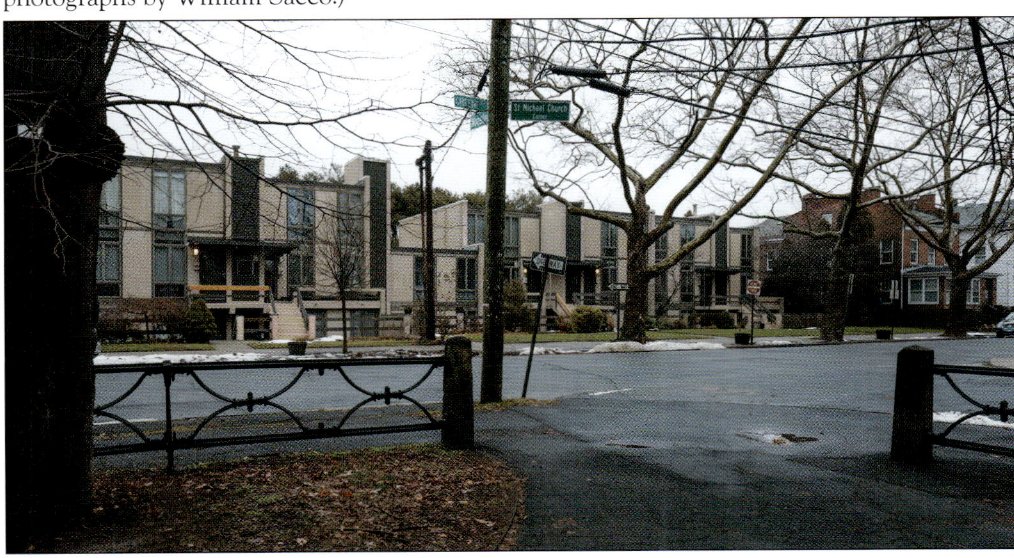

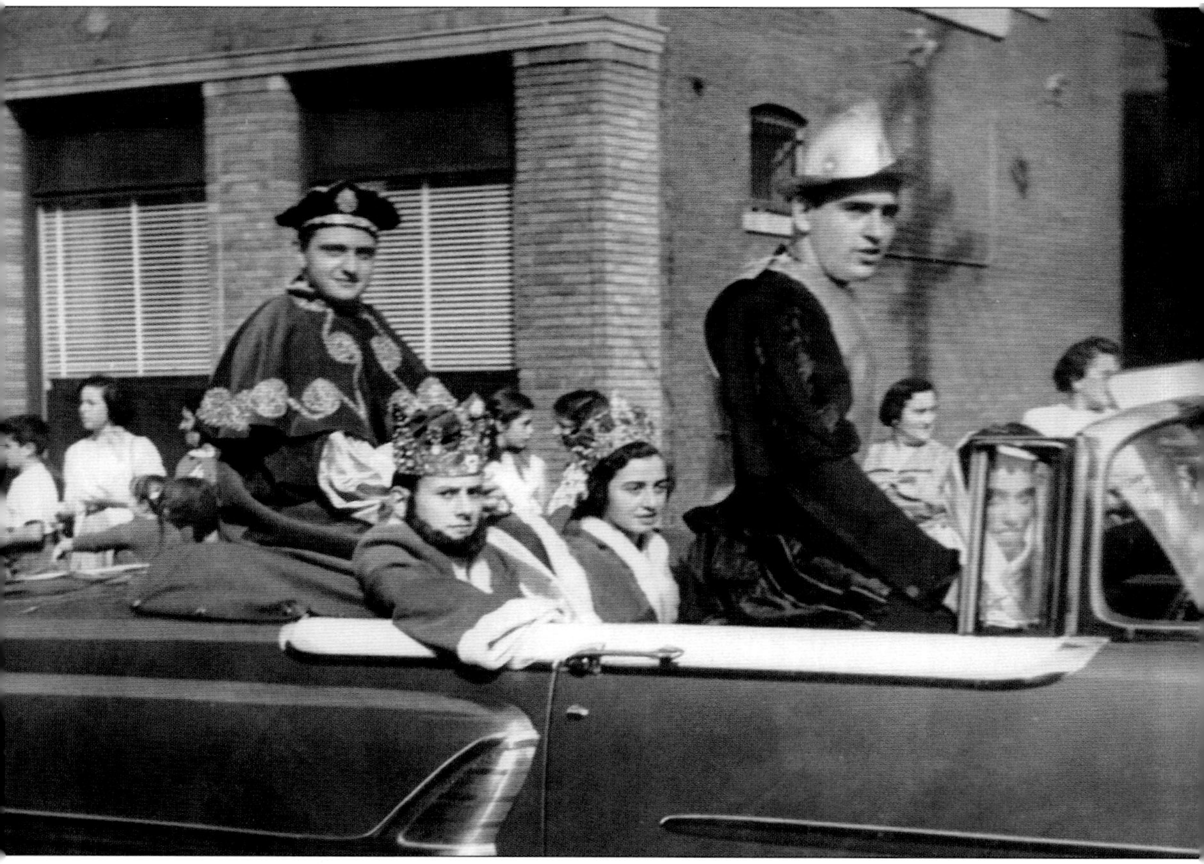

THE COLUMBUS DAY PARADE IN 1955. Frank Grazioso, one of the longest-serving members of the Columbus Day Committee, played Columbus in the parade in 1955, which saw the dedication of the new bronze version of the Columbus Monument. In the car with him is Giulio Passarelli, playing King Ferdinand. The 1955 parade included three tableaux—or decorated cars—a tradition that dated back to the first Knights of Columbus parade in 1892. These were Columbus Setting Foot on Land, Columbus at the Court of Spanish Monarchs, and Columbus at the Helm of the *Santa Maria*. (Frank Grazioso.)

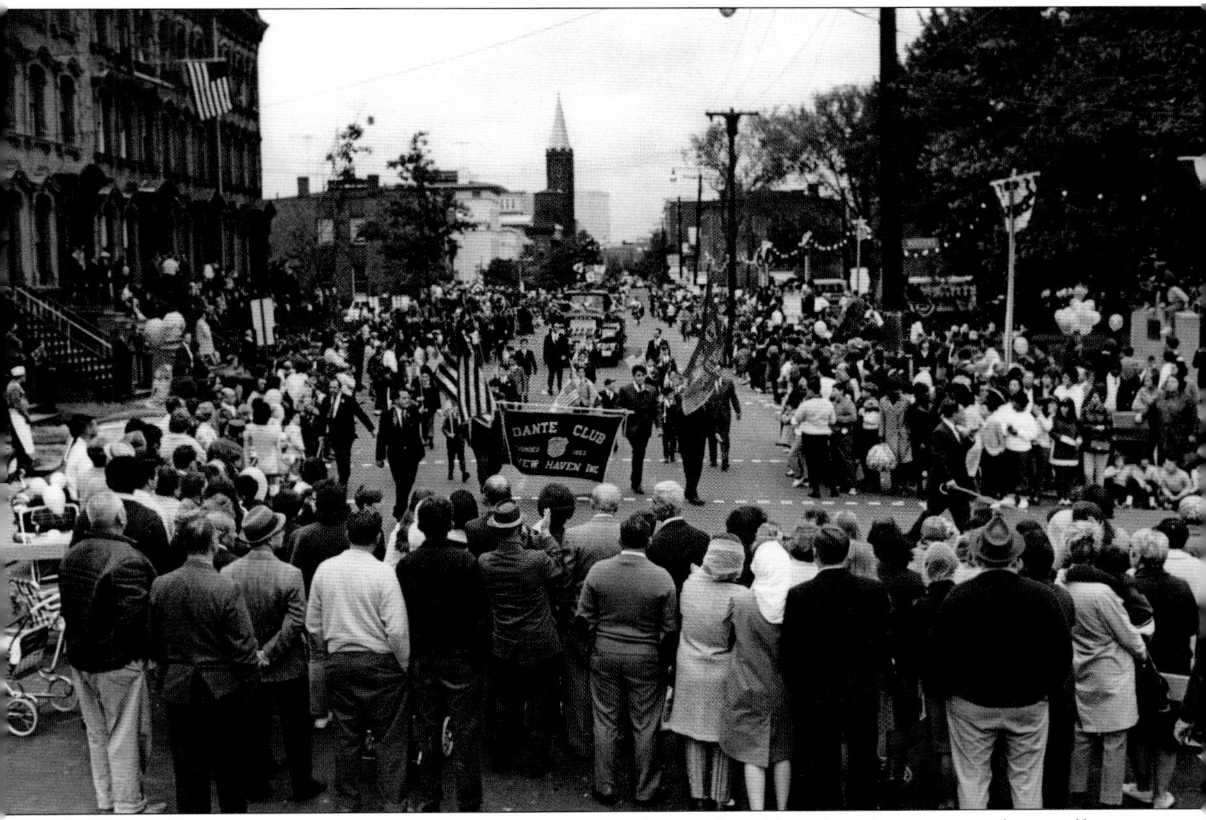

THE COLUMBUS DAY PARADE IN THE 1960S. The Columbus Day Parade route traditionally starts downtown, traveling along Chapel Street to the Columbus Monument and wrapping around Wooster Square. This image shows the Dante Club, founded in New Haven in 1952, in the parade, passing by the 19th-century brownstones to the left and the World War II Veteran's Memorial Monument (installed around 1950; refurbished in 1990 by the Historic Wooster Square Association) to the right. Alphonse Lauro was a member of the Dante Club until its closure; he is also a member of the Santa Maria Maddalena Society. (Alphonse Lauro.)

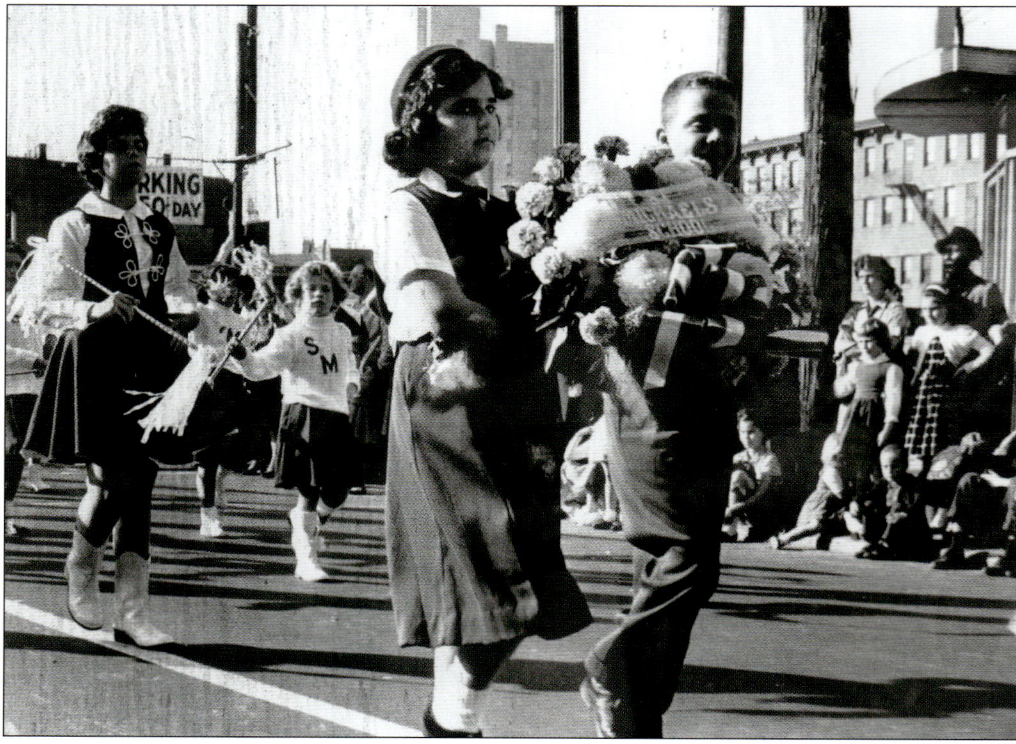

Scenes from New Haven's Columbus Day Parade. Scenes from during the revival years of the 1950s and 1960s include (above) St. Michael's School marching with a wreath to place on the iron fence around the Columbus Monument in 1960, and (below) a common sight for Columbus Day Parades: participants dressed in costumes in boats, heading for the New World. These men are likely from the Knights of Columbus, since they carry the flag of Vatican City with them. A man wearing a Native American headdress is cut off at the far left of the image, showing a lack of awareness many Americans had towards indigenous culture. Columbus, of course, landed in the Caribbean, far away from the Western Plains Indian culture of North America. (Above, Theresa Argento; below, St. Michael's Church, New Haven.)

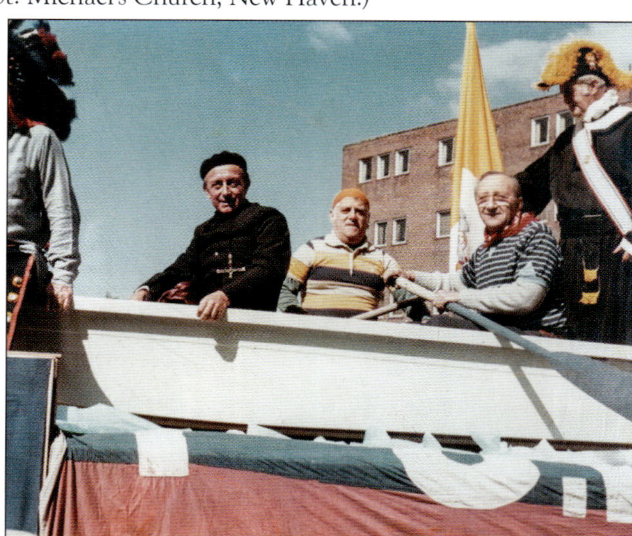

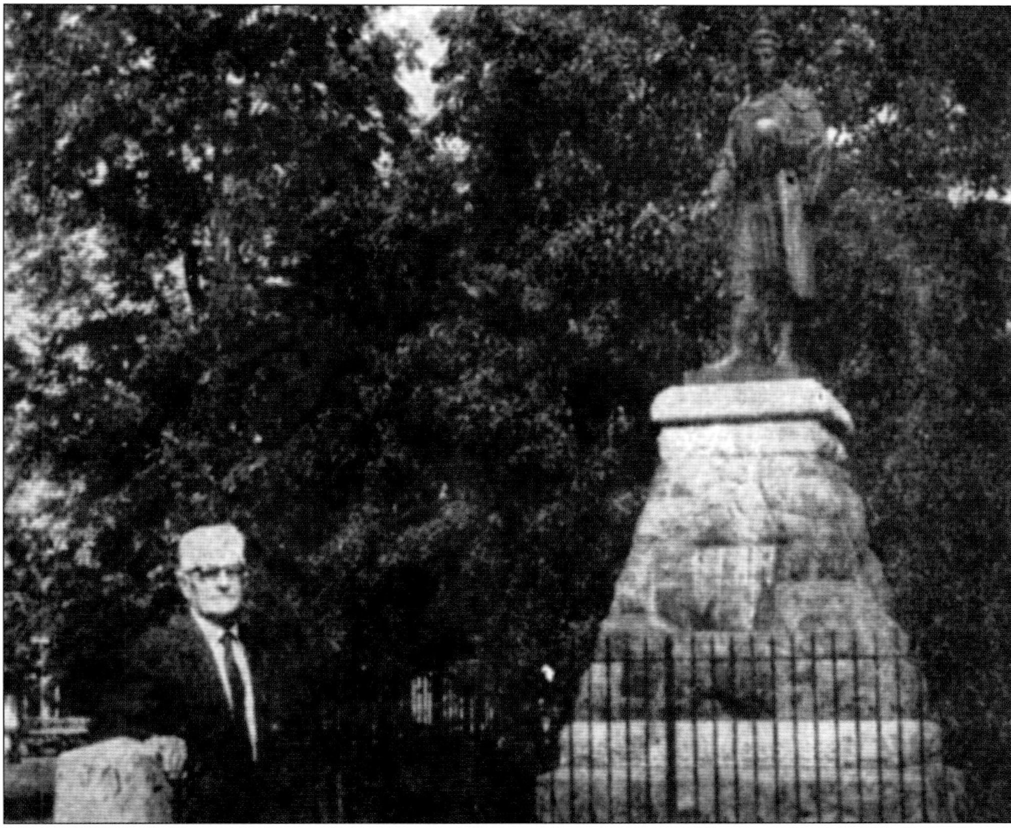

Gagliardi and the Board of Aldermen. Luis Gagliardi (above) pioneered the state of Connecticut's Columbus Day celebrations. Gagliardi was an Italian immigrant who advocated with others from the Elm City—including Paul Russo and Sylvester Poli—for the establishment of a formal Columbus Day celebration. The Connecticut General Assembly in Hartford granted this in time for Columbus Day in 1908. The parade that first year went to Bridgeport, due to the city's deep harbor, according to Gagliardi. The parade then came to New Haven and the following year was held in Waterbury, but the Elm City became its permanent home around 1911. Four members of the board of aldermen (below) are shown bringing their wreath to the Columbus Monument: from left to right are William R. O'Connell, president of the board; Michael DePalma; Louis Ragozzine; and John N. Reynolds. (Both, Local History Room of the New Haven Free Public Library.)

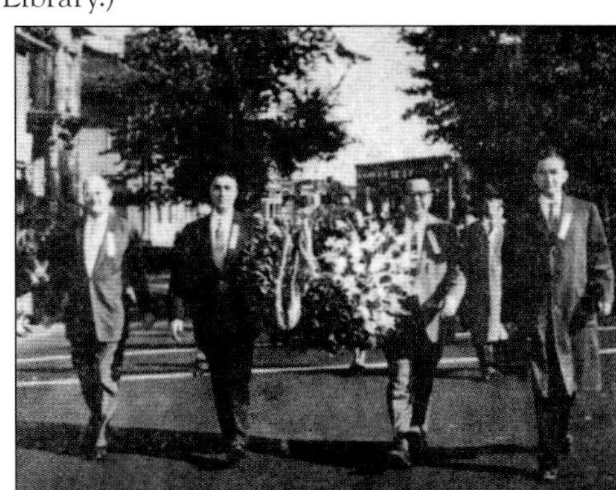

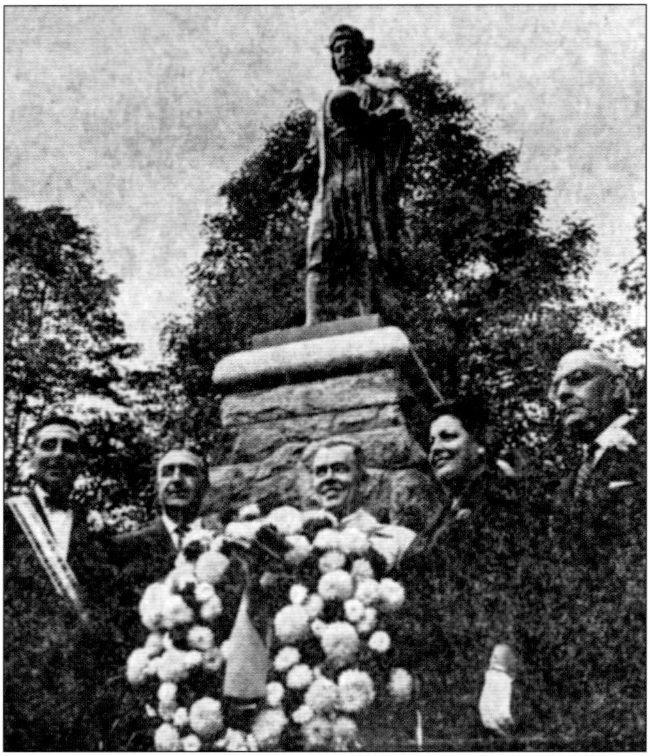

Coordinators of the 1962 Parade. At left, Mayor Richard C. Lee is at the center, surrounded by, from left to right, Anthony Bove, general chairman of the Columbus Day Committee; Michael DePalma, Tenth Ward ambassador; Carmel Scopetta, Eleventh Ward alderperson; and Frank Amato, coordinator of the parade in 1962. The below photograph shows one of the largest Columbus Day Parades in history, around 1961, when thousands of students marched in the parade down Chapel Street. That year, the parade went down Whalley Avenue, to Howe Street, to Chapel Street, and to Wooster Square with Mayor Richard C. Lee leading one and all. (Both, Local History Room of the New Haven Free Public Library.)

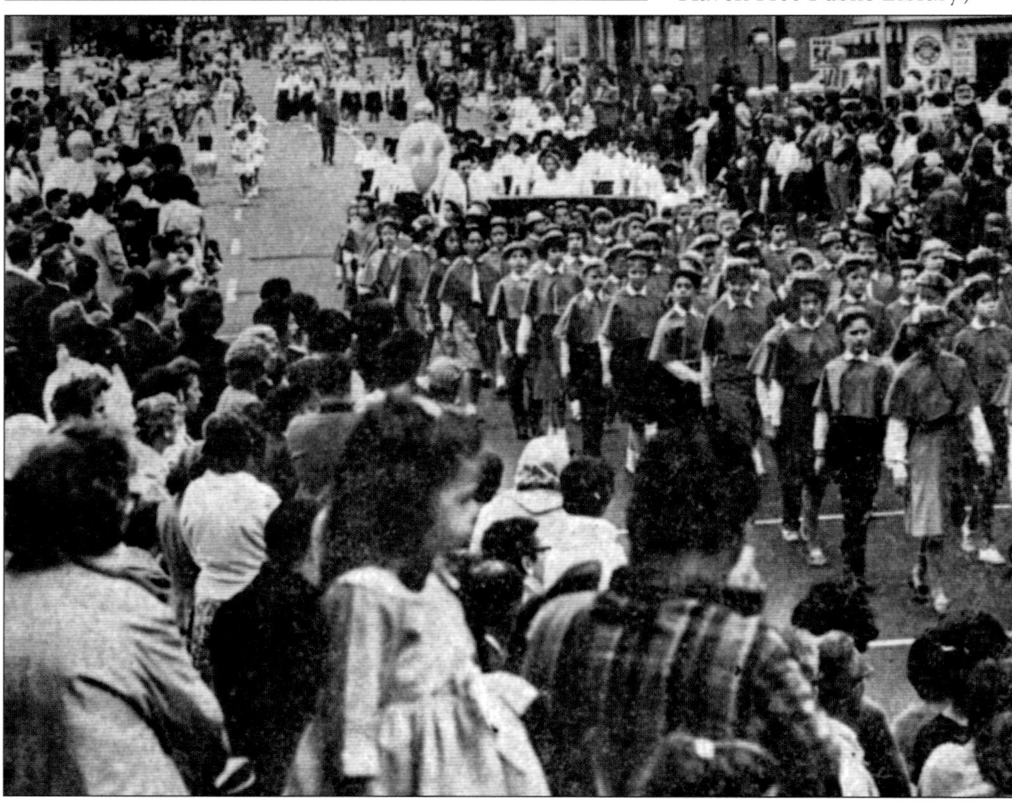

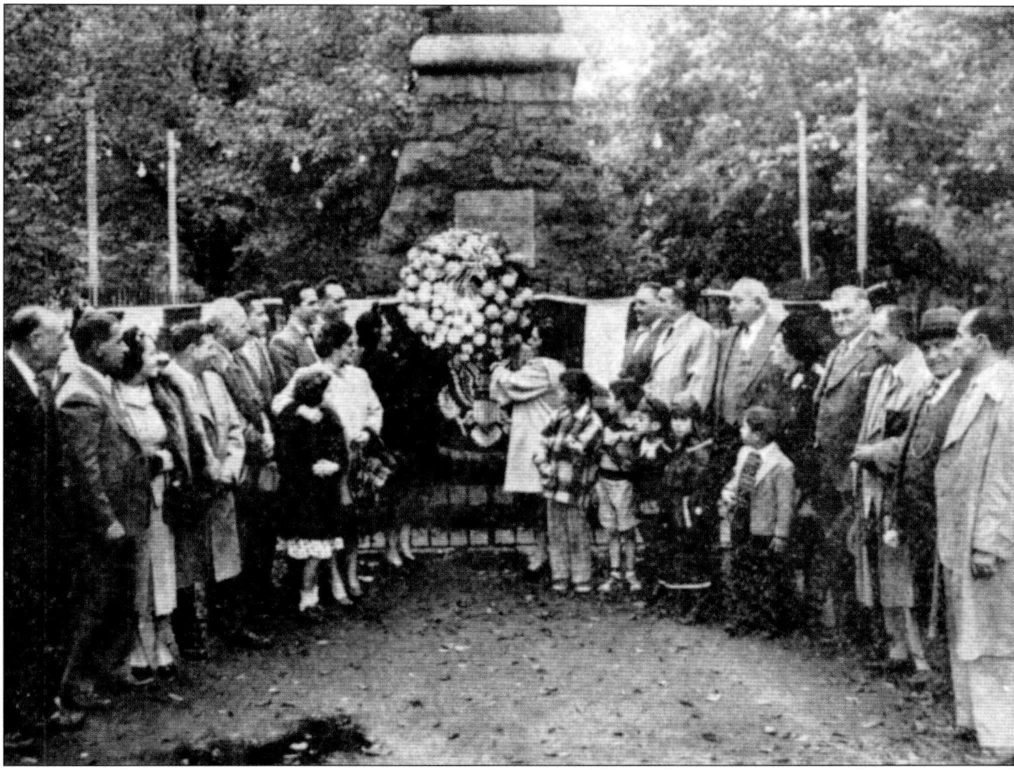

WREATH-LAYING. 1950s. An earlier image of the wreath-laying ceremony at the Columbus Monument is seen here, where a gathering of New Haven's Italian American organizations comes together in the 1950s. Rose LaVorgna and Annette Williams placed the wreath on the iron fence, over a banner with the American eagle. The group had earlier completed a similar ceremony at the World War I Memorial on the green. (Local History Room of the New Haven Free Public Library.)

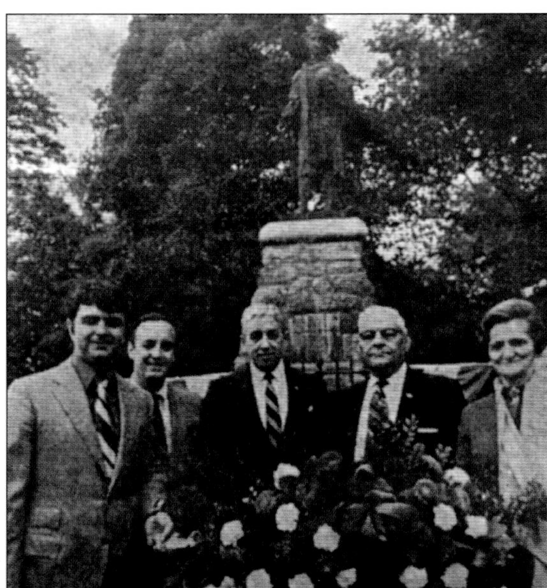

WREATH CEREMONY, 1970. Participating in the wreath-laying ceremony in 1970 are, from left to right, Vincent E. Mauro, aldermanic president; state representative Anthony M. Ciarlone; Mayor Bartholomew Guida (New Haven's second Italian American mayor); Frank Amato, for many years chairman of the event; and alderperson Luisa DeLauro, the longest-serving alderperson in New Haven city history. (Local History Room of the New Haven Free Public Library.)

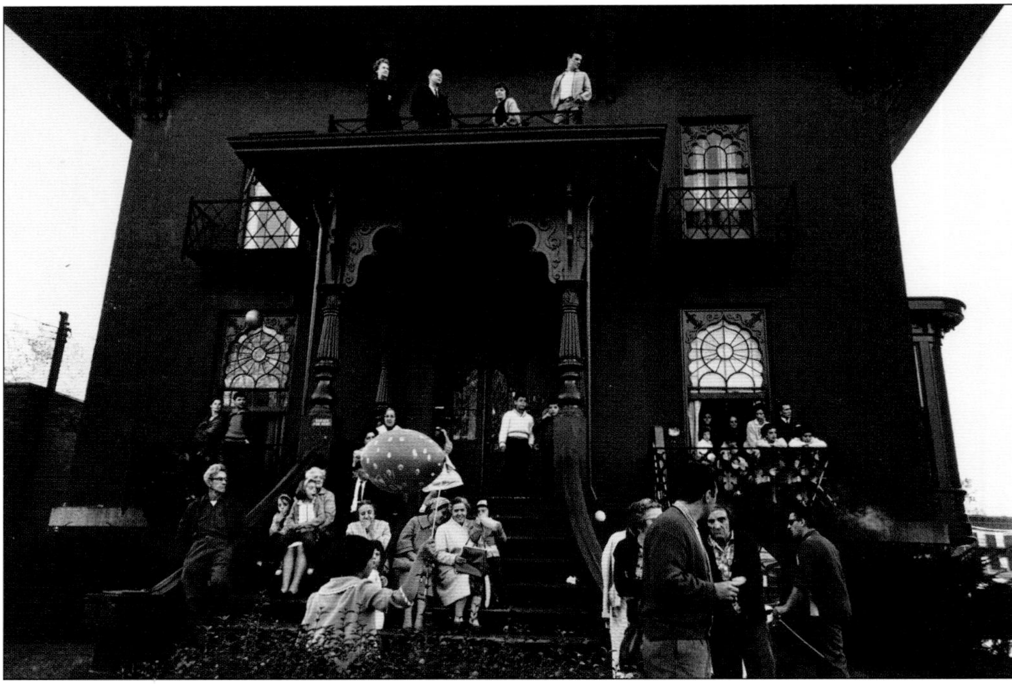

Tony Ray-Jones and the Willis Bristol House. A series of photographs of New Haven's Columbus Day Parade was taken by Tony Ray-Jones, a British student who came to study at Yale University in the mid-1960s. Ray-Jones has placed himself in front of the Willis Bristol House, 584 Chapel Street, in these images. The house faces Wooster Square and the Columbus Monument. The Bristol House was designed by Henry Austin, New Haven's famed 19th-century architect. As shown in these images, the Columbus Day Parade passed directly in front of the Bristol House, thus its staircase made for a great viewing platform. (Both, ©Tony Ray-Jones / National Media Museum / Science & Society Picture Library.)

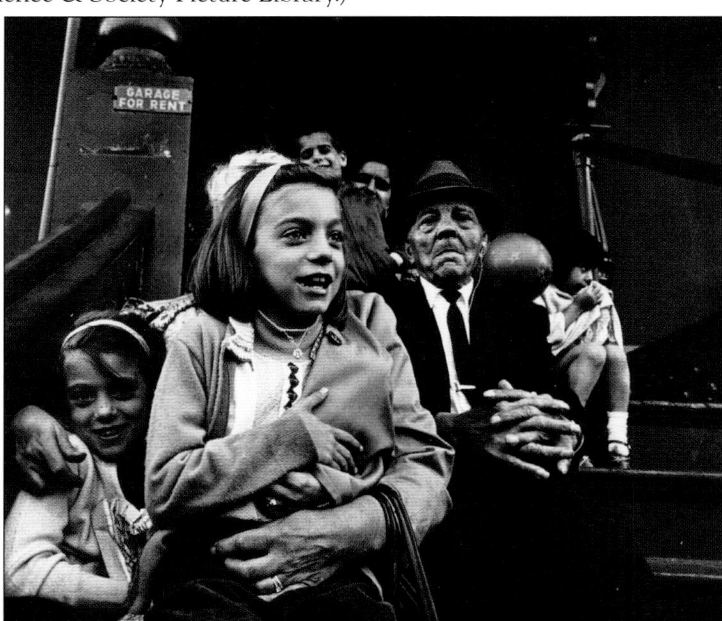

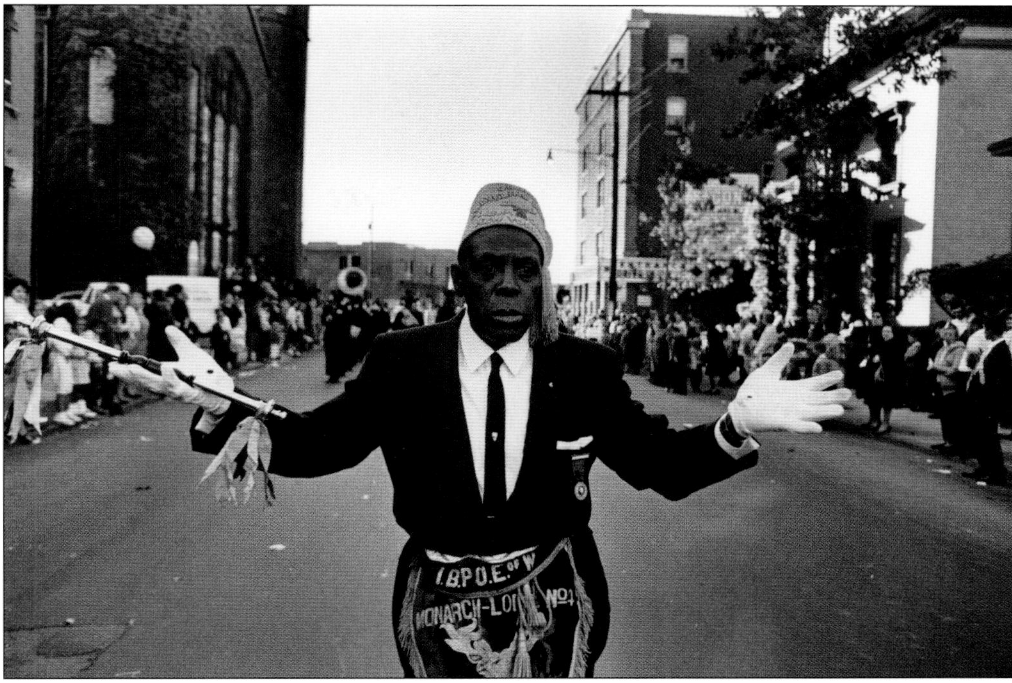

TONY RAY-JONES ON CHAPEL STREET. Here are two more images created by Tony Ray-Jones, who was standing on Chapel Street looking toward downtown from where the Columbus Day Parade was marching. Judging from his hat and apron, this man was a member of the Monarch Lodge No. 4 of New York, part of the Freemasons. The Freemasons belong to a worldwide organization tracing its roots back hundreds of years. In this photograph, the Freemason holding his staff has already passed the Episcopal Church of St. Paul and St. James on Olive Street. The students in the background wear tricorn-style hats with the letter "C"—perhaps they are Columbus School students. (Both, ©Tony Ray-Jones / National Media Museum / Science & Society Picture Library.)

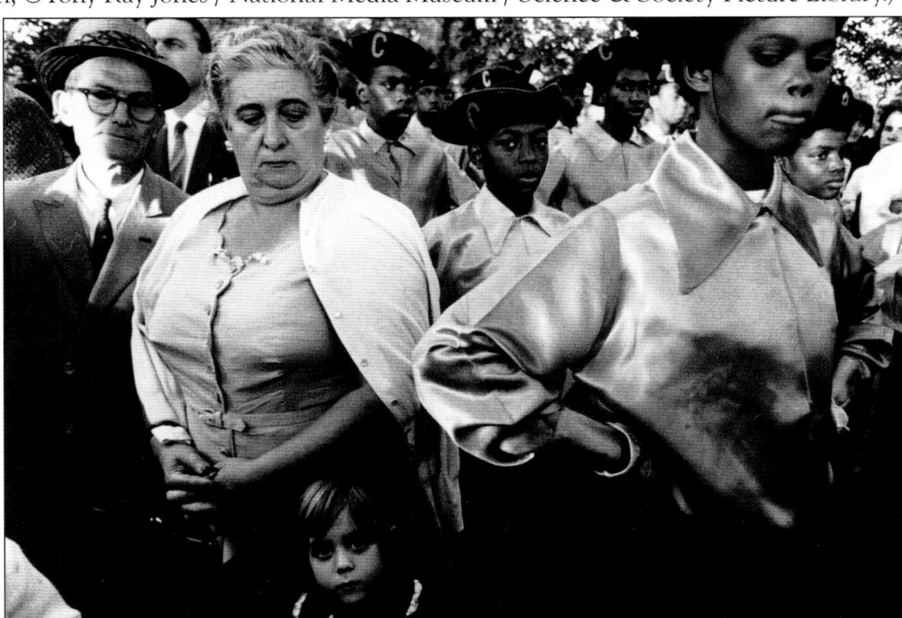

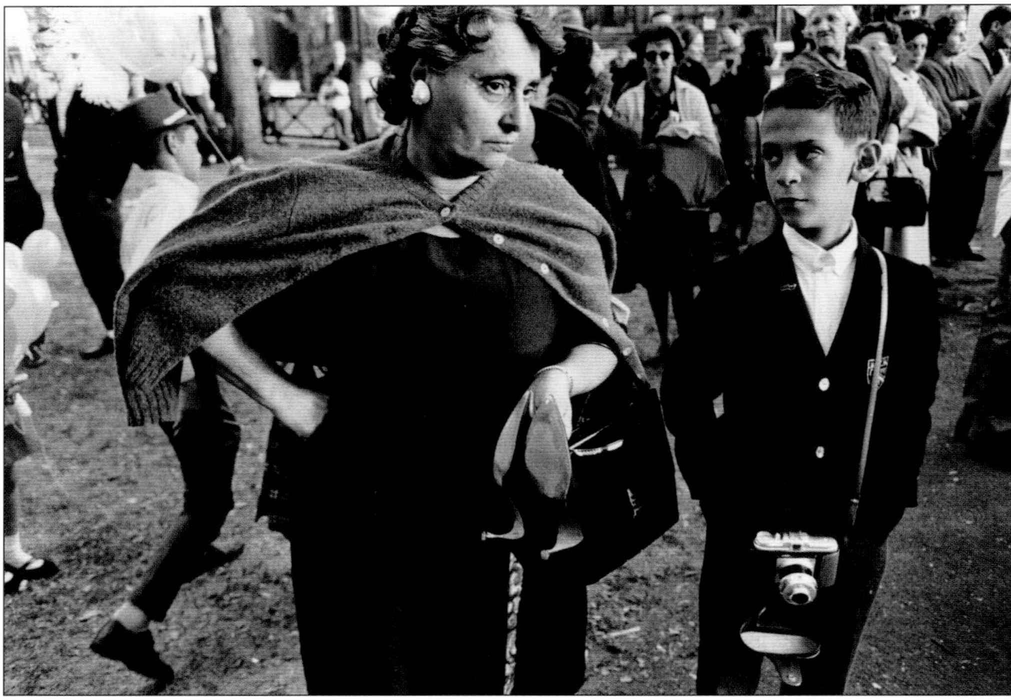

Street Photography. The photographs Tony Ray-Jones took while he was in New Haven, studying at Yale University, went on to influence his life in photography. Ray-Jones (1941–1972) became known for "street photography" that captured people and places with an immediacy that breaks away from formal, traditional portrait photography. Ray-Jones graduated from Yale in 1964 then spent a year traveling the United States taking photographs. He returned to England and lived there (on Gloucester Place, the same street where New Haven's Benedict Arnold lived almost 200 years earlier) until 1970. After a brief time in the United States in 1971, Ray-Jones died from leukemia soon after returning to London in 1972. (Both, ©Tony Ray-Jones / National Media Museum / Science & Society Picture Library.)

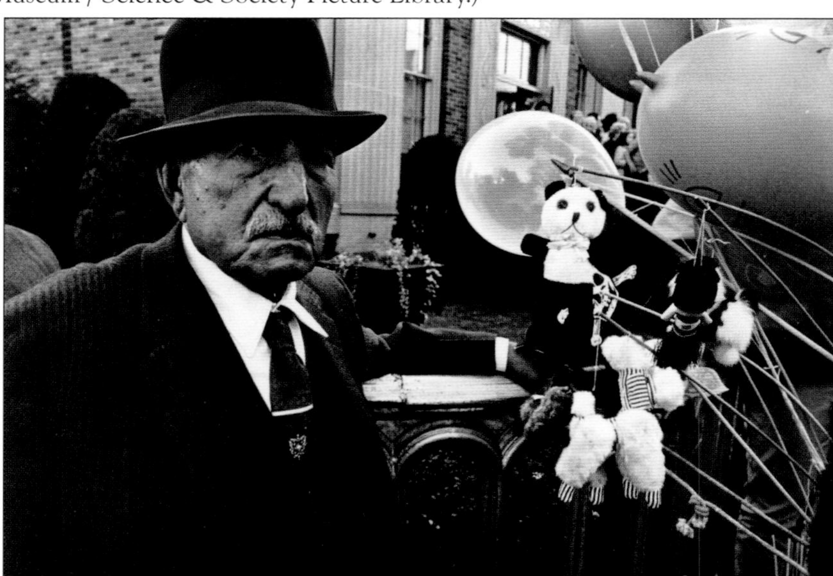

Four

Challenged and Changed

New Haven's Columbus Day Parade continued throughout the last decades of the 20th century, drawing closer to the 500th anniversary of Columbus in the New World in 1992. But as parade committee members geared up to participate in the statewide celebrations, change was also in the air and would become a permanent presence in the Elm City: that of anti-Columbus protest. The 1960s and 1970s had given rise to civil rights movements across the spectrum: women, African Americans, and LGBTQ people and their allies were all fighting for recognition and equal rights—including, pertinent to this history, Native Americans. During this time, under chairman Frank Grazioso and the Columbus Day Committee, the parade was spun out from city hall into its own not-for-profit organization (capable of raising of its own funds) and new elements were added to the Columbus Week events, including an essay and art contest that awarded medals and bonds to students. In partnership with the Knights of Columbus, the Columbus 500 program in New Haven was a robust undertaking, with programming happening across the state and the placement of a granite marker at the foot of the Columbus Monument.

At the same time, protests at the Columbus Day Parade and the Columbus Monument appeared in 1992 and continued throughout the decade, until 2000, when the parade ceased for two years. Americans of a certain age remember September 11, 2001, vividly. Much changed for the nation, and so, too, did things change at the local level. The Columbus Day Committee, struggling with protests and low attendance numbers, did not hold a Columbus Day Parade in 2001, which would have been just one month after 9/11. The following year (2002), there was also no parade, but, in that span of time, the committee realized that although enthusiasm for the parade had dwindled in the Elm City, Italian Americans in the surrounding towns of North Haven, East Haven, Hamden, and West Haven would welcome the parade in their towns—thus a rotation around New Haven County began. Branford, another stronghold for Italian Americans, later joined the circuit. Thus New Haven's Columbus Day Parade was revived yet again.

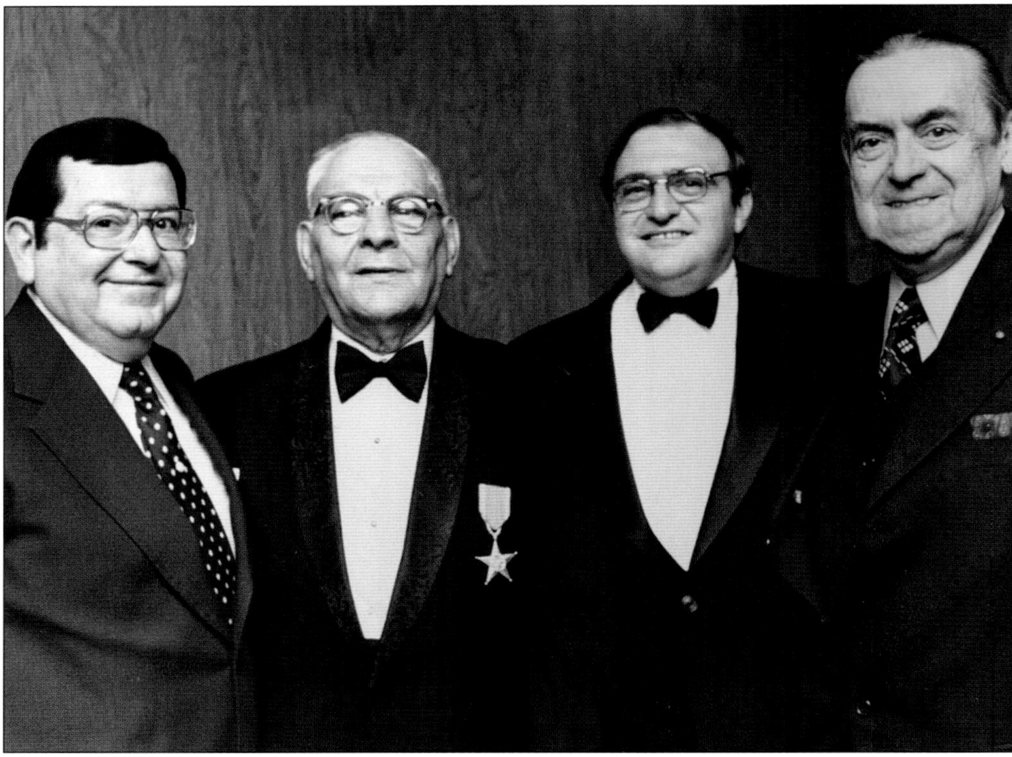

EVENTS THROUGHOUT THE YEAR. The Columbus Day Committee is about Columbus, but it is really about people. In the photograph above are, from left to right, Frank DeLaurentis, Frank Amato, Frank Grazioso, and Louis Siddi at the Columbus Day annual dinner at the Park Plaza Hotel, New Haven, in 1978. In the photograph below, chairman Alfonso E. Panico (first row, third from right) is pictured with members of the Columbus 500 event in New Haven. (Both, Italian-American Historical Society of Connecticut.)

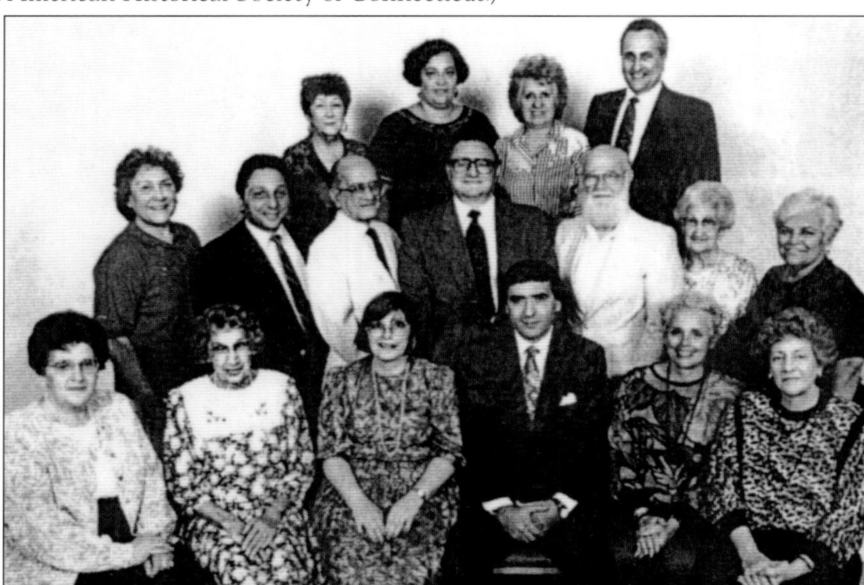

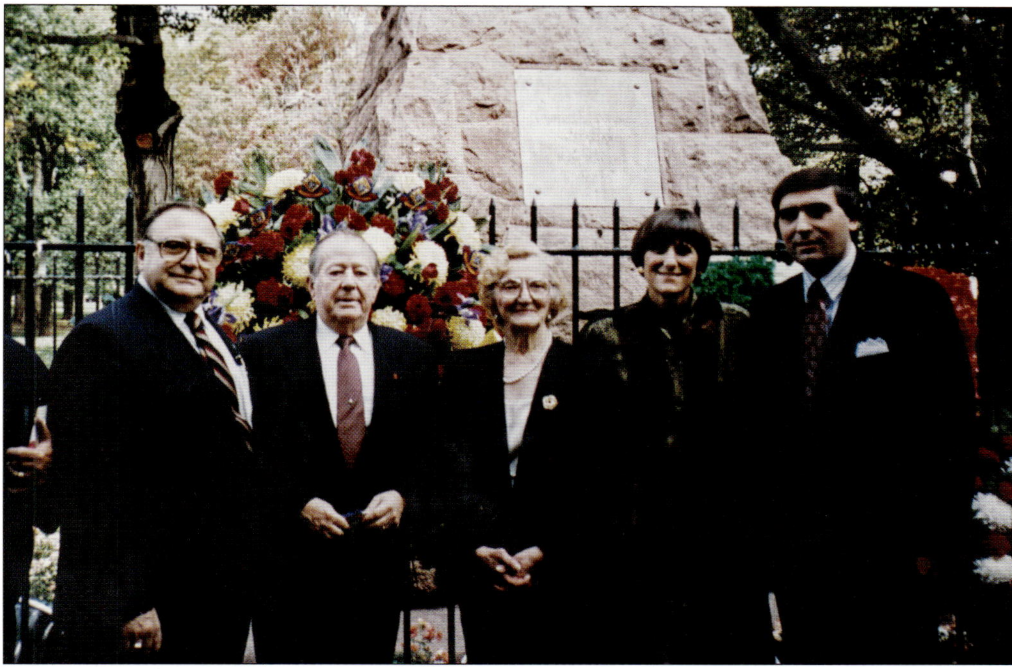

Wreath-Laying, 1992. Frank Grazioso (left) cochaired the annual Columbus Day wreath-laying ceremony held at the Columbus Monument in 1992. Also pictured are, from left to right, William J. Van Tassell, Knights of Columbus; Louise DeLauro, alderwoman; her daughter, Rose DeLauro, then in the second year of her role as US representative for Connecticut's Third District; and Alfonso E. Panico, Columbus Day Committee president. (Italian-American Historical Society of Connecticut.)

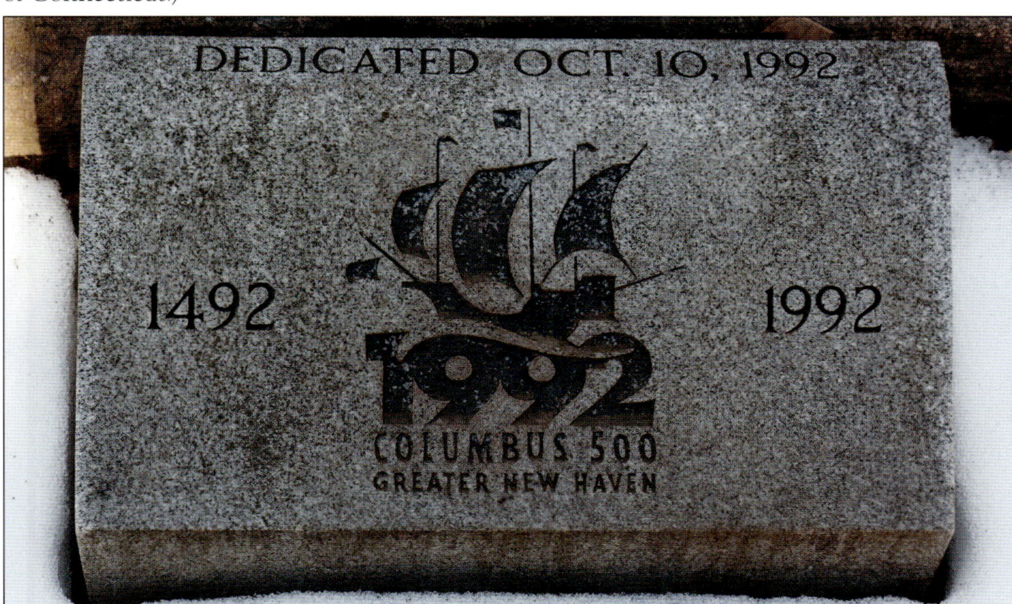

500th Anniversary. This granite marker was placed at the foot of the Columbus Monument in Wooster Square in 1992 to mark the 500th anniversary of Columbus's arrival in the New World. (Photograph by William Sacco.)

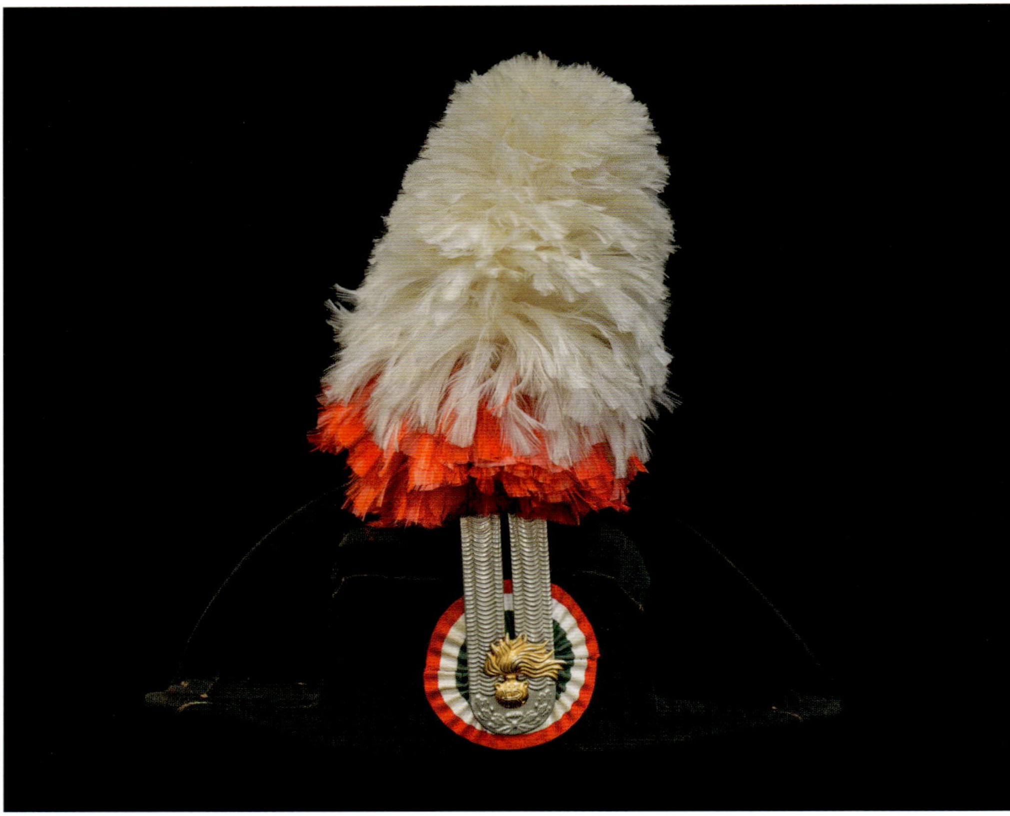

Carabinieri Band. The Carabinieri Band performed in the New Haven Columbus Day Parade in 1985, the year the state of Connecticut celebrated its 350th anniversary. The Carabinieri, first formed in Sardinia in 1814, became a symbol of Italian unification in 1861. The medal commemorates the Battle of Pastrengo in 1848, in which the Carabinieri fought in the first battle for Italian unification. The two-point hat, called a Lucerna, features a plume and a rosette with the colors of the Italian flag. As members of the Italian army, the Carabinieri continue to participate in wars around the world. (Both, Italian-American Historical Society of Connecticut.)

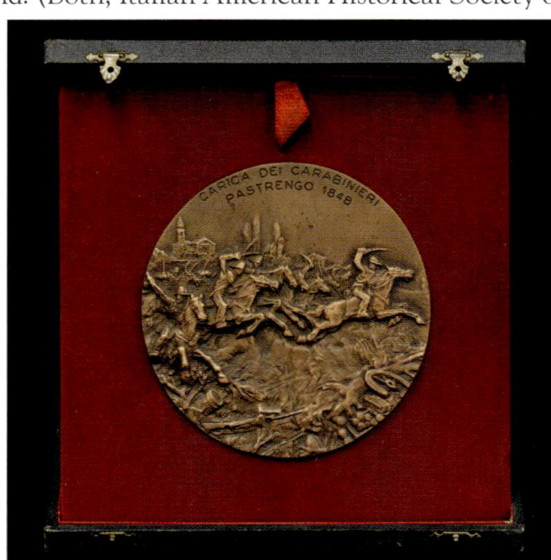

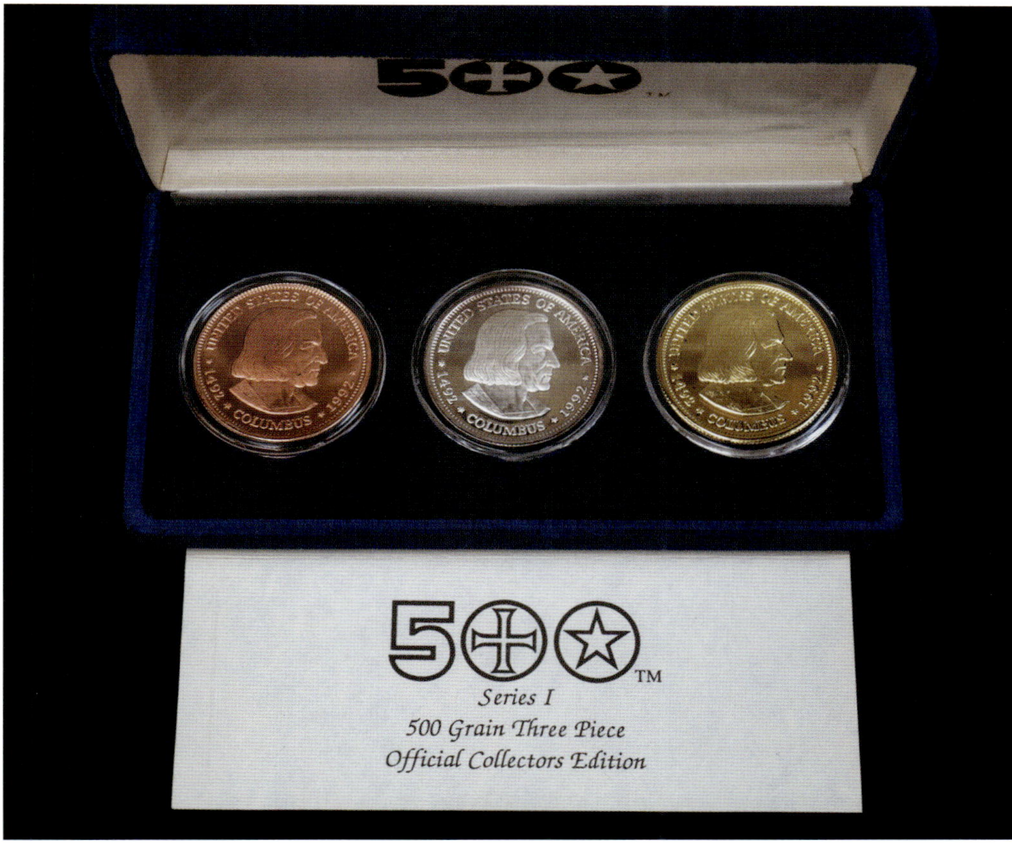

Columbus 500 Souvenirs. Annette Ahlberg of East Haven visits friends and looks through the Columbus 500 T-shirts at the International Celebration held at Moore Field House of Southern Connecticut State University. In addition to inexpensive items such as T-shirts, Columbus 500 also saw the minting of a commemorative coin, much like the coins pictured in chapter 1. (Above, photograph by William Sacco, Italian-American Historical Society of Connecticut; below, photograph by Melanie Stengel, *New Haven Register*.)

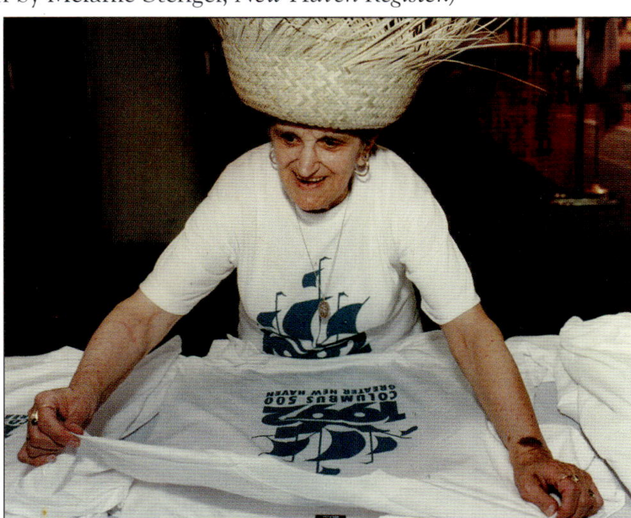

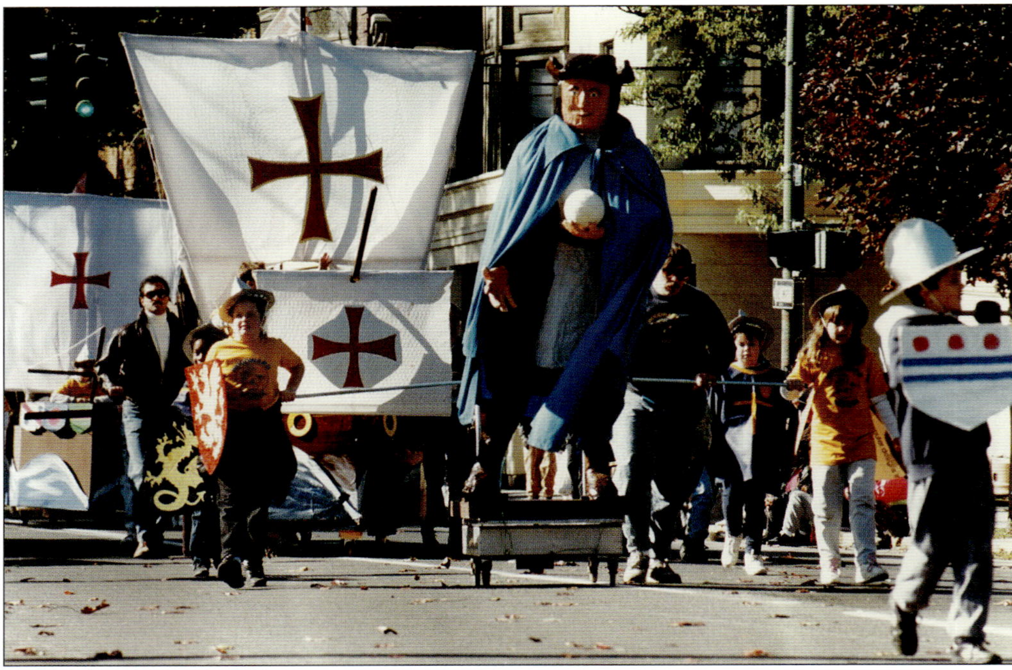

WOODWARD SCHOOL STUDENTS MARCH. Woodward School students march in the 1993 Columbus Day Parade with the figure of Christopher Columbus and the *Niña, Pinta*, and *Santa Maria*, made by school principal Frank Palmeri. The First Company, Governor's Foot Guard has been marching in New Haven parades since its formation in 1771. (Above, photograph by Jeanette Glicksman, *New Haven Register*; below, photograph by Kirby Kennedy, *New Haven Register*.)

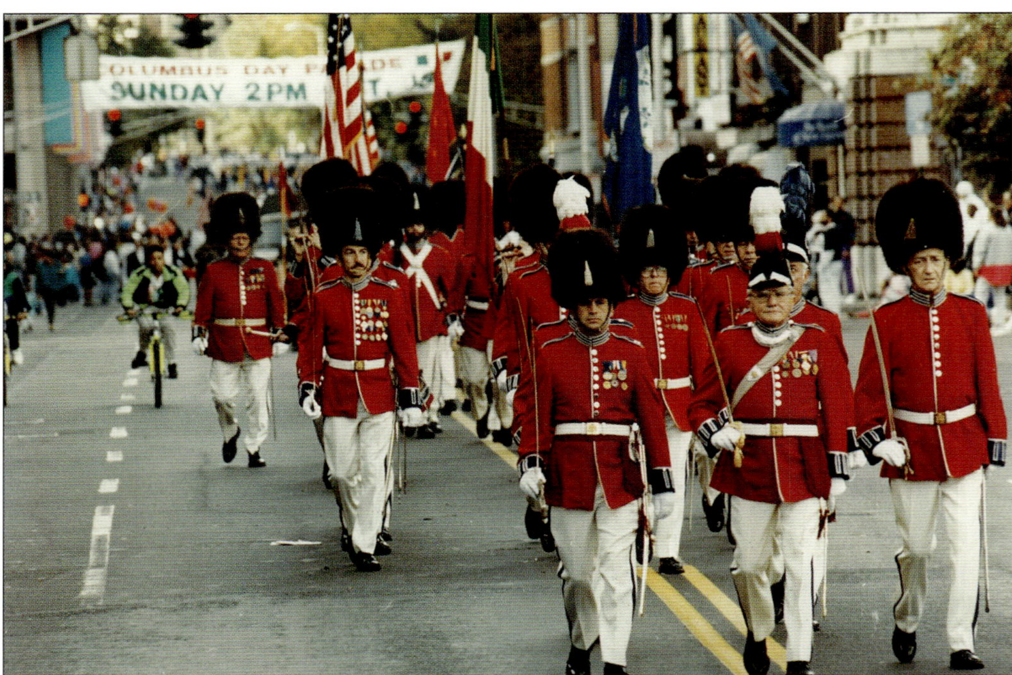

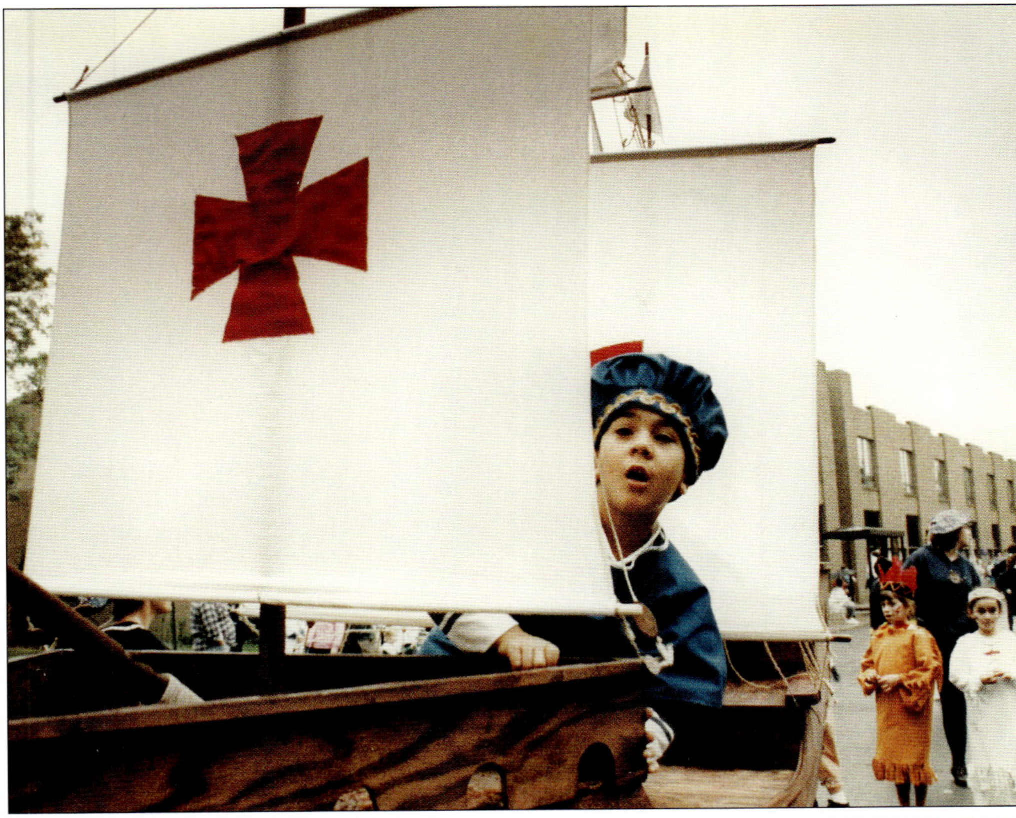

Sailing down Chapel Street. Michael Celentano, age 4, of New Haven, peers around his sail as he travels down Chapel Street. Celentano played Columbus for the St. Francis School float in the 1992 Columbus Day Parade. Note the children dressed as Native Americans behind the float. After finishing walking in the 1992 Columbus Day Parade, Ray Borelli of North Haven takes photographs of the other Columbuses behind him. (Both photographs by Melanie Stengel, *New Haven Register*.)

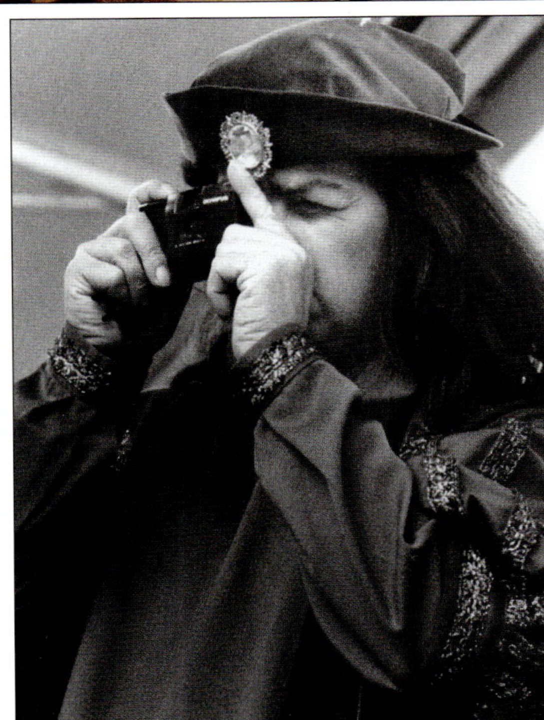

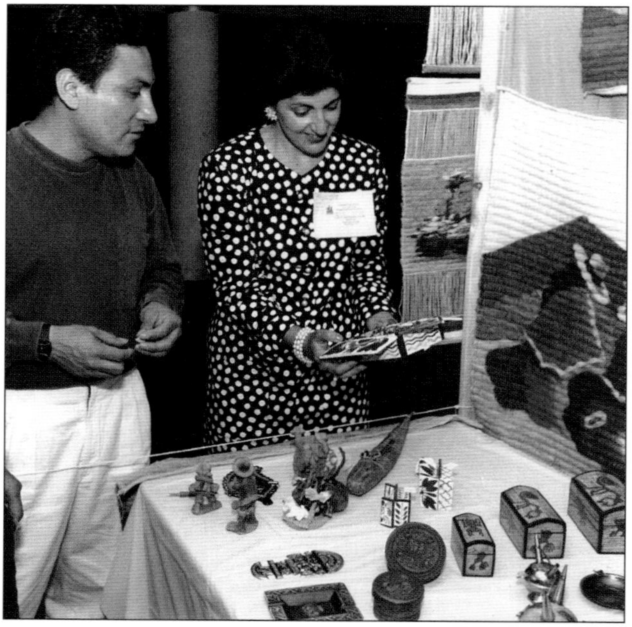

INDIGENOUS CULTURE AND COLUMBUS. In the image at left, Mary Lou DiPaola of North Haven examines the materials on display created by the Peru Club of New Haven as club member Jaime Mori explains their significance. The Peru Club and many others were part of the International Celebration hosted by Moore Field House on the campus of Southern Connecticut State University during the Columbus 500 event. Children dressed in Native American costumes sit under palm trees in a float seen during the Columbus 500 parade in New Haven. (Left, *New Haven Register*; below, Italian-American Historical Society of Connecticut.)

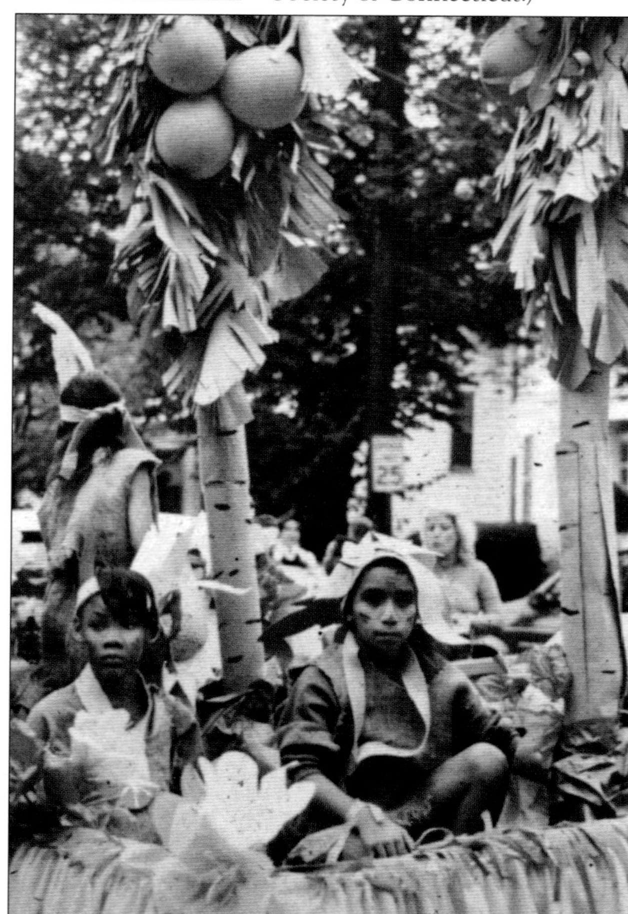

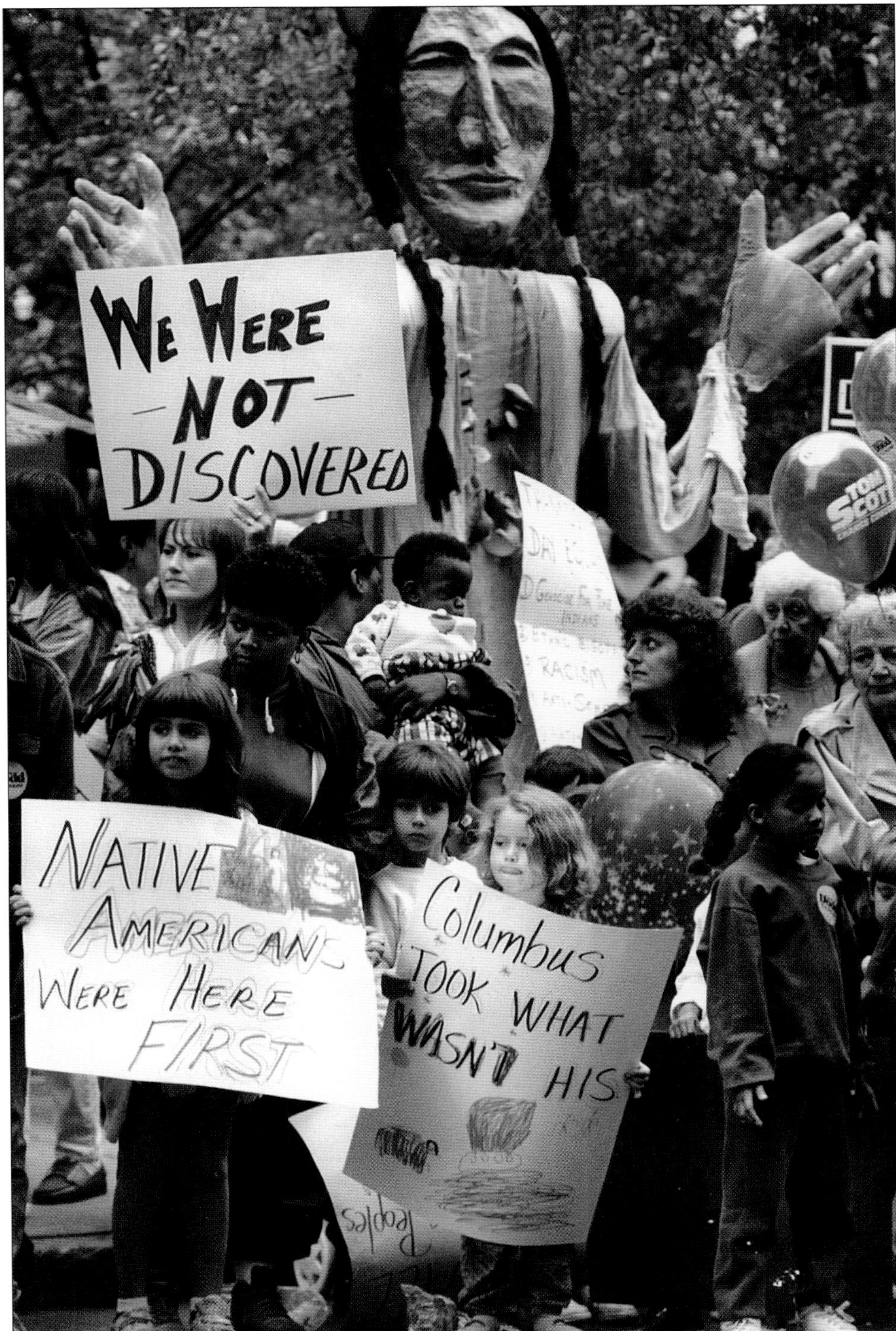

PROTESTING COLUMBUS. Protesters from several different groups gathered on Chapel Street at the green and made their feelings about Columbus Day known to all. (Photograph by Melanie Stengel, *New Haven Register*).

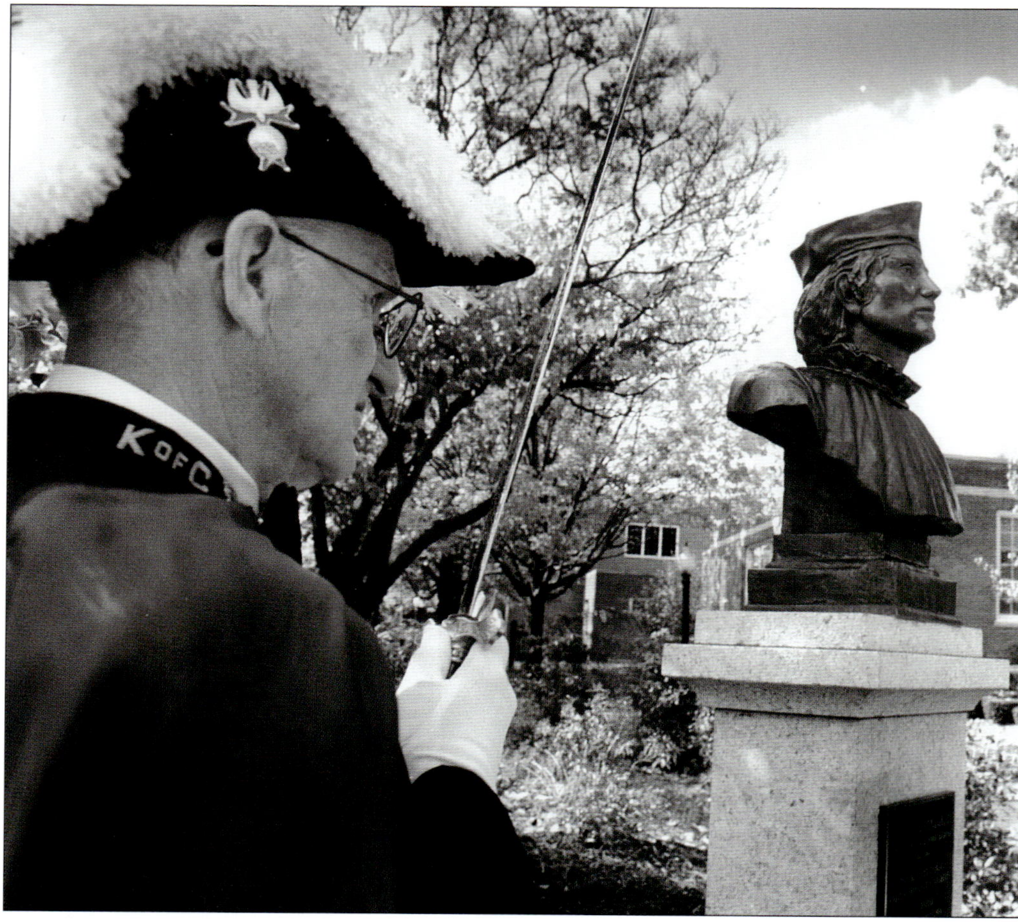

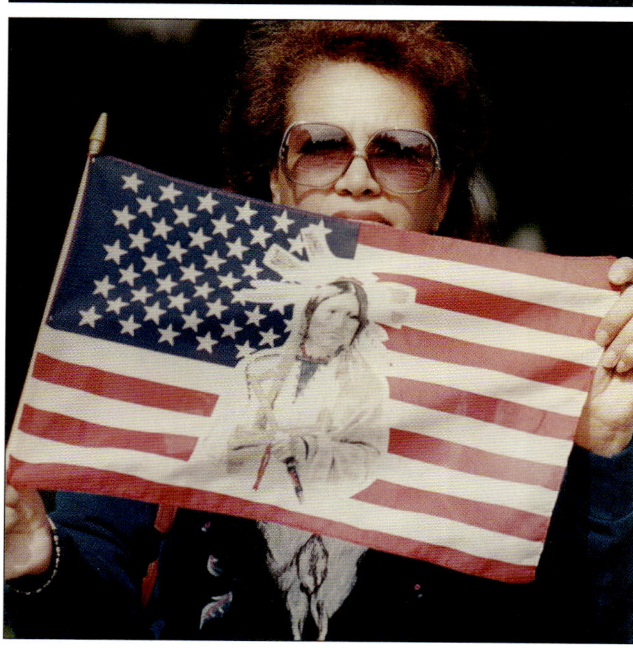

Commemorations across Connecticut. During the Columbus 500 statewide celebrations, cities and towns across Connecticut marked the quincentennial by hosting events and erecting monuments, such as this bronze bust in Milford. Knights of Columbus member and Milford resident John Wickun and protestors such as Johnette LaConte, whose ancestors were Schaghticoke, gathered in the Parsons Government Complex in Milford for the dedication. (Both photographs by Melanie Stengel, *New Haven Register.)*

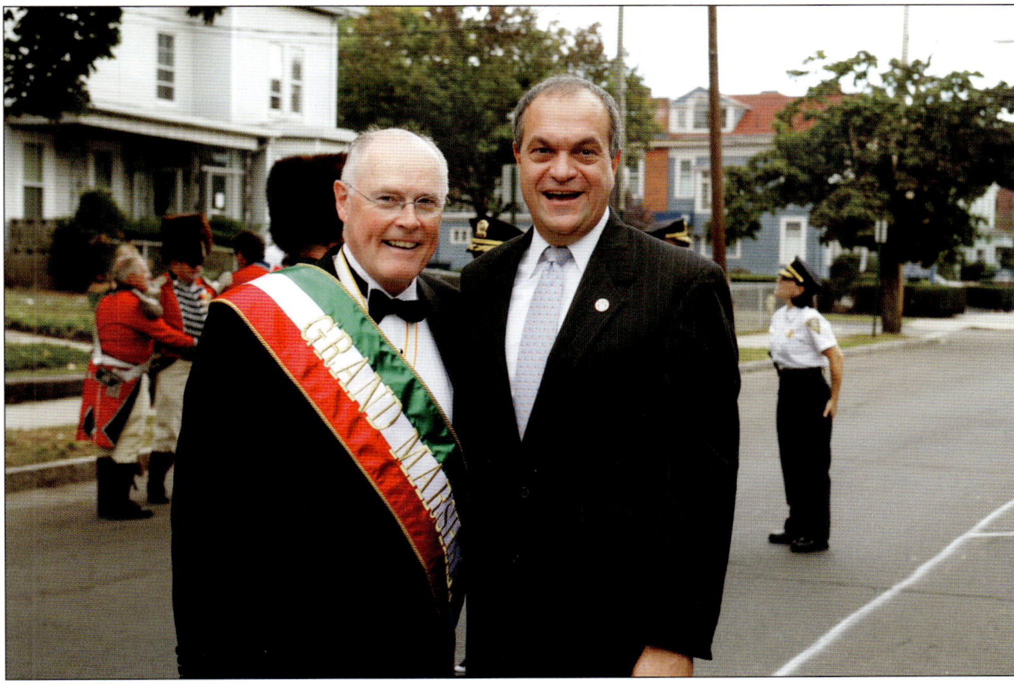

Familiar Faces at Many Columbus Day Parades in New Haven. Above, former Knights of Columbus secretary Robert Lane (left) poses with Mayor John DeStefano. Below, Lane is seen with US senator Richard Blumenthal. Lane was honored as the grand marshal in 2007. (Both, Knights of Columbus.)

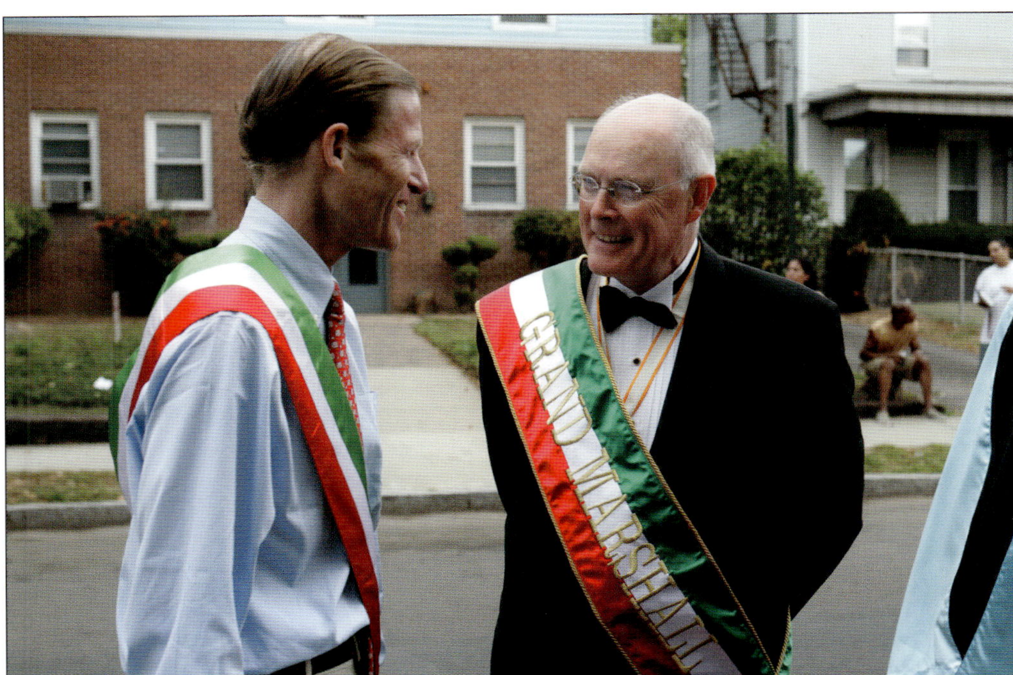

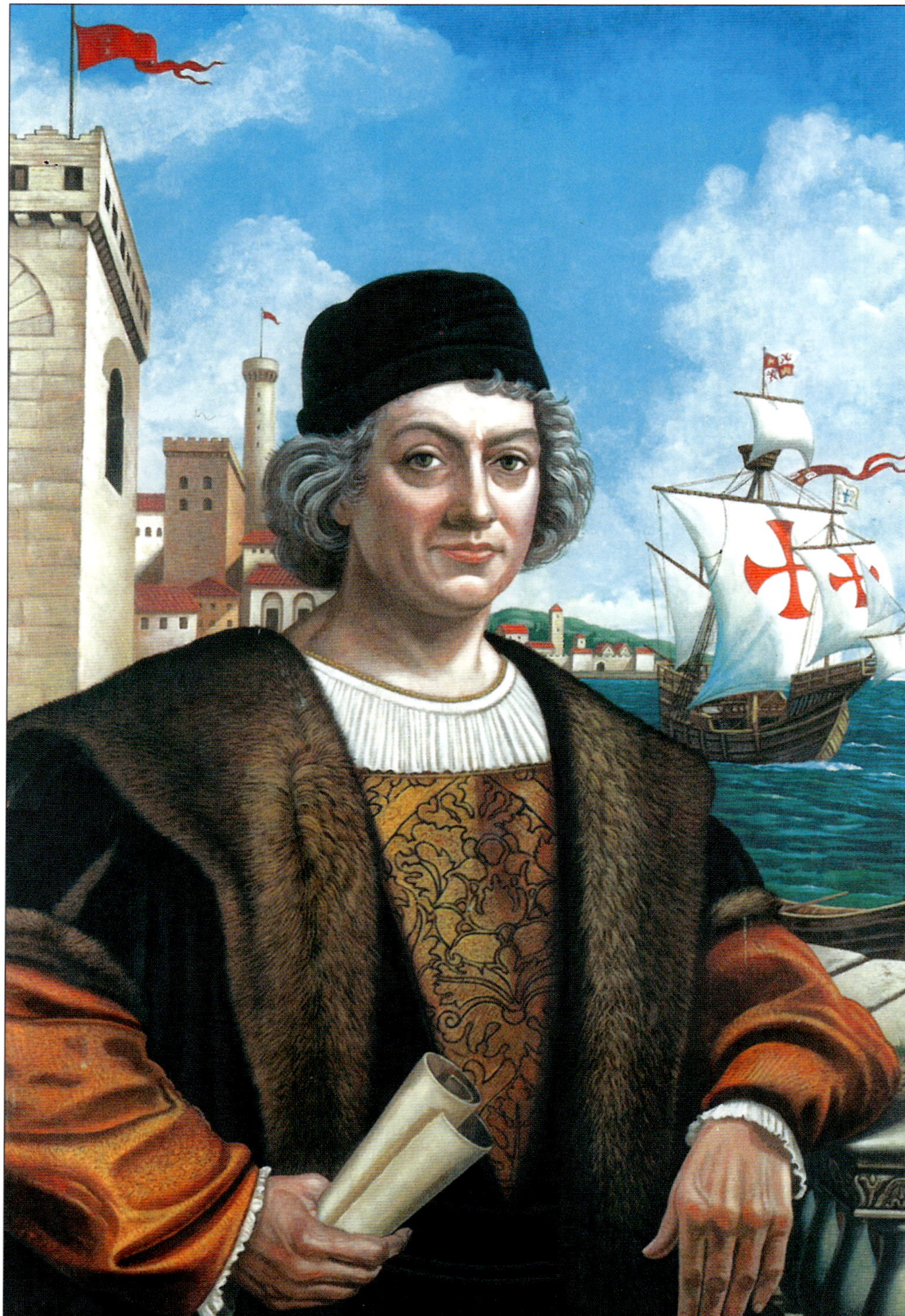

A Portrait of Columbus. The Knights of Columbus commissioned artist Teresa Fasolino to paint this portrait of Christopher Columbus in observance of the 500th anniversary in 1992. (Knights of Columbus.)

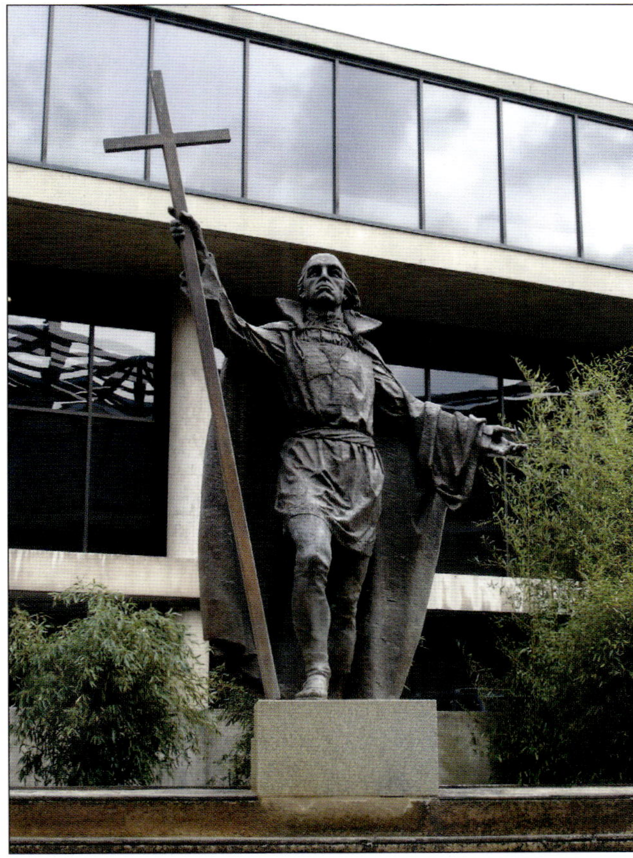

Knights of Columbus Museum. When the Knights of Columbus opened their new museum in the rehabilitated City Services Building, they commissioned Weston, Connecticut, artist Stanley Bleifeld to create a nine-foot-tall bronze statue of Columbus for the courtyard. Bleifeld was already known to the Knights of Columbus due to his work on the multiple Michael McGivney statues placed at the headquarters building and the cancer center of Yale New Haven Hospital. (Both photographs by Mike Ross, Knights of Columbus.)

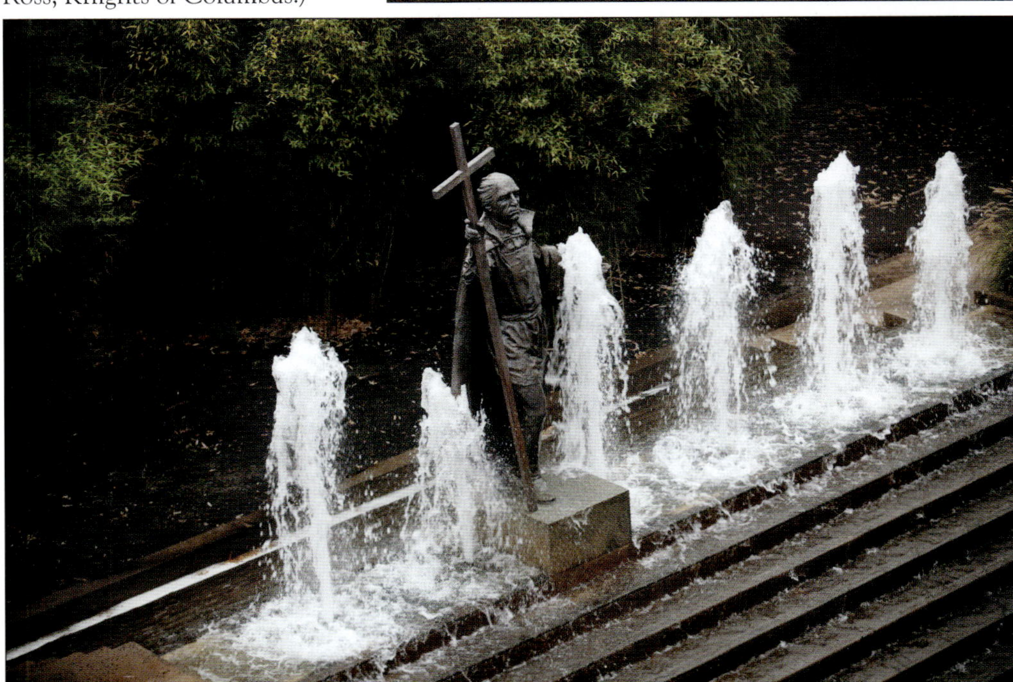

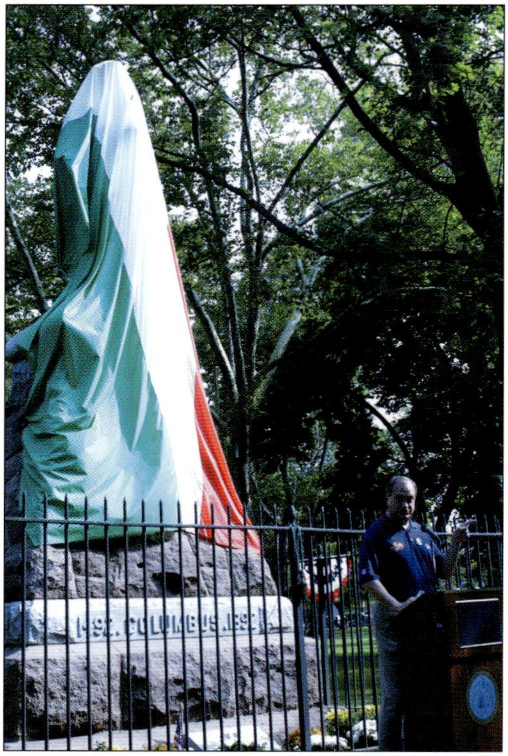

RESTORED MONUMENT. The restored Columbus Monument was unveiled in Wooster Square in 2004. The Knights of Columbus, partnering with City of New Haven agencies, worked to conserve the monument. In the image at left, Mayor John DeStefano is speaking at the unveiling. Jean B. Migneault, Deputy Supreme Knight, also spoke at the ceremony, saying, "We are happy to have been able to help make this restoration possible, as it enhances the beauty of our community, celebrates our cultural heritage, and pays tribute to Columbus, the discoverer of America and namesake of our organization." (Both, Knights of Columbus.)

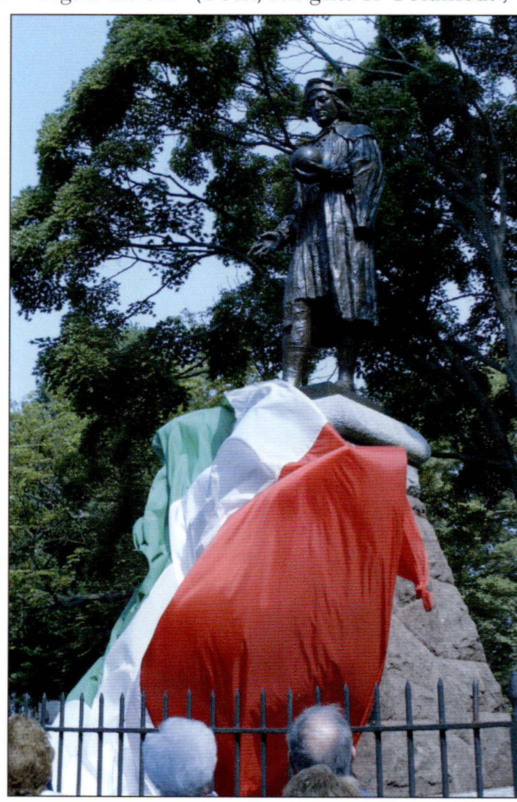

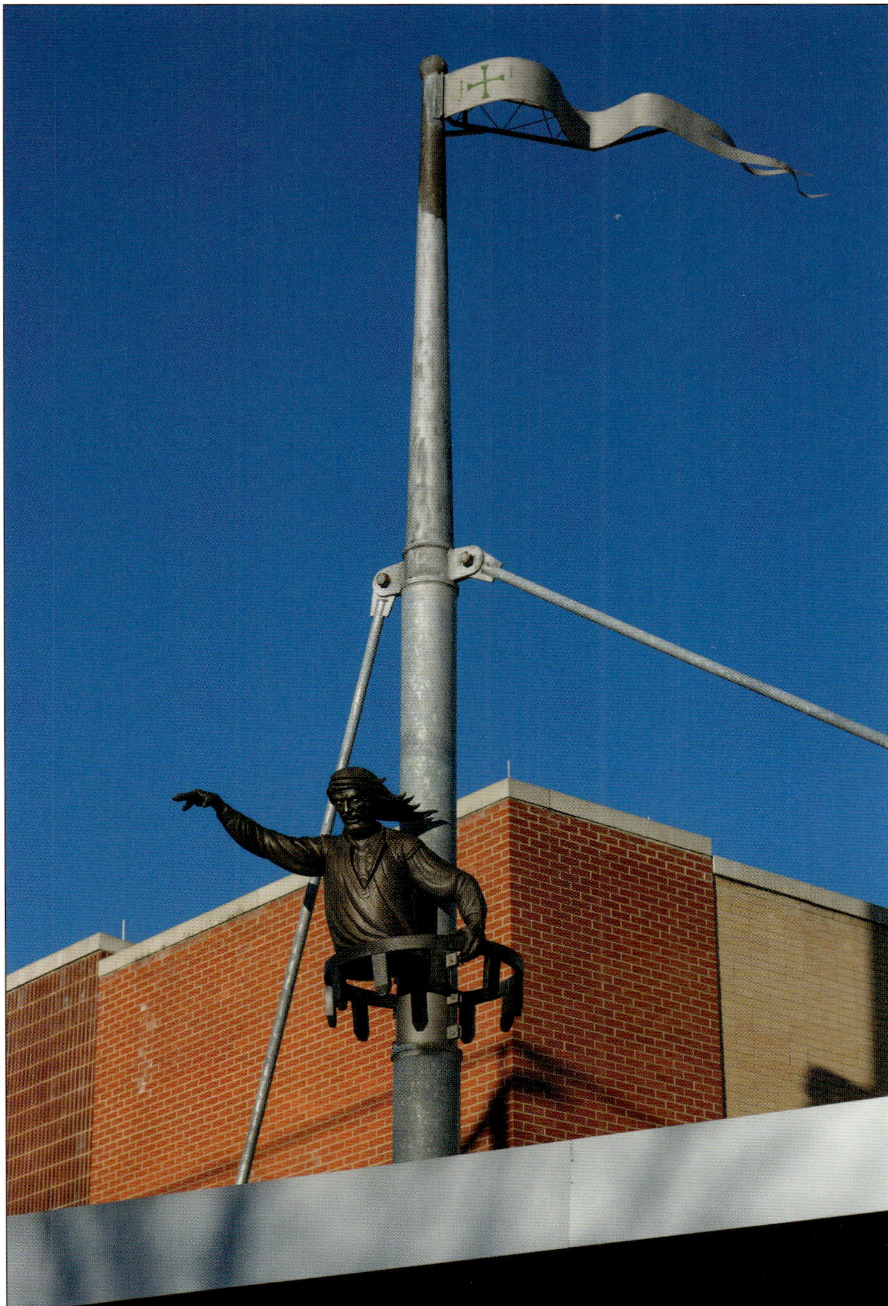

Columbus Family Academy. The bronze figure of Rodrigo de Triana, the Spanish sailor who first saw land while standing in the crow's nest of the *Pinta*, was installed at the entrance to the refurbished Columbus Family Academy in 2008, one of the city's Percent for Art projects. The artist José Buscaglia chose to feature one of the crew members to demonstrate the many people who assisted in Columbus's accomplishments. The subject chosen also speaks to the neighborhood shift, from an Irish and Italian makeup to a now heavily Latino population. (Photograph by William Sacco.)

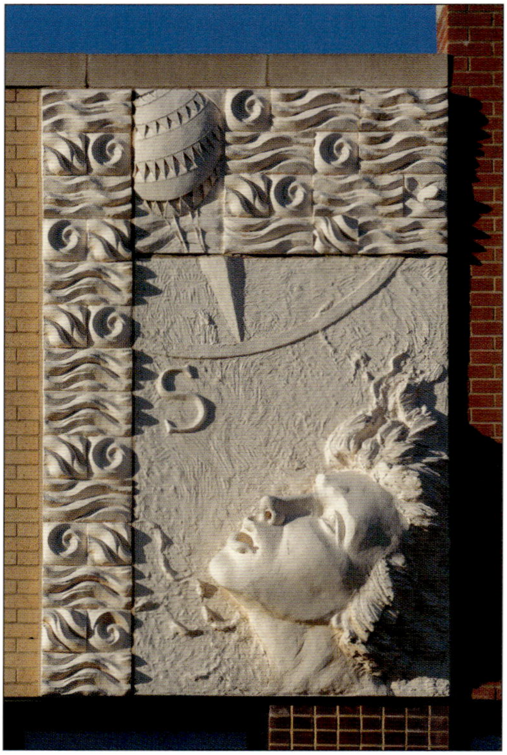

Winds of Discovery. New Haven–based architect Barry Svigals & Partners designed a series of plaster relief sculptures for the exterior of Columbus Family Academy, working with the theme presented in the name of the school and the installation of the *Rodrigo de Triana* bronze over the entrance. Svigals calls these bas-reliefs *Winds of Discovery*, with the south wind shown here. (Both photographs by William Sacco.)

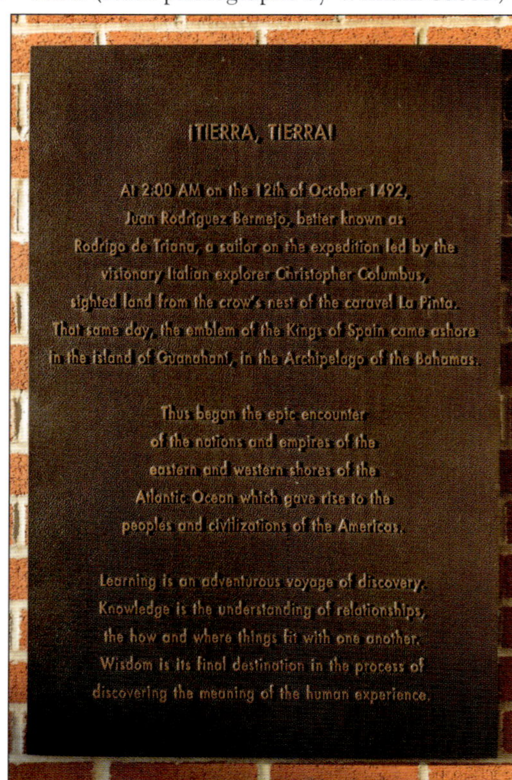

Five

Columbus in the 21st Century

Well into the new century, the Columbus Day Committee of Greater New Haven continues to share the story of Columbus in New Haven, through its many activities, some of them, such as the wreath ceremony, dating back more than 50 years, and others, such as the parade, dating back more than 100 years. In collaboration with others, the Columbus Day Committee sponsors a heritage dinner, walking tours of Wooster Square, a "Festa Italiana," the wreath ceremony, and the parade. Many of these events have been photographed by committee member Arthur Giulietti, and a selection of his photographs, taken between 2006 and 2015, appears in this last chapter. Another group of photographs was provided by Richard Biondi, a teacher and now author who has done great work collecting oral histories and photographs of Wooster Square and beyond.

Some elements of these Columbus Day Parade photographs would be recognizable to a parade spectator in 1955 or even 1905, such as men dressed in Columbus costumes on floats or rows of marching bands with their colorful uniforms. Antique cars and fire trucks lend a flavor of the past, too, as does the wearing of sashes and the presence of a grand marshal. One thing is certain about the Greater New Haven Columbus Day Parades: the American flag is always featured, demonstrating how members of the Italian American community worked hard to remember their own ethnic heritage while at the same time embracing the colors of their now native country. The most unique feature of the Greater New Haven Columbus Day Parade is the continued presence of the many Italian societies and clubs. Although many clubs have faded away with time, new ones are also formed in the spirit of community and love for heritage.

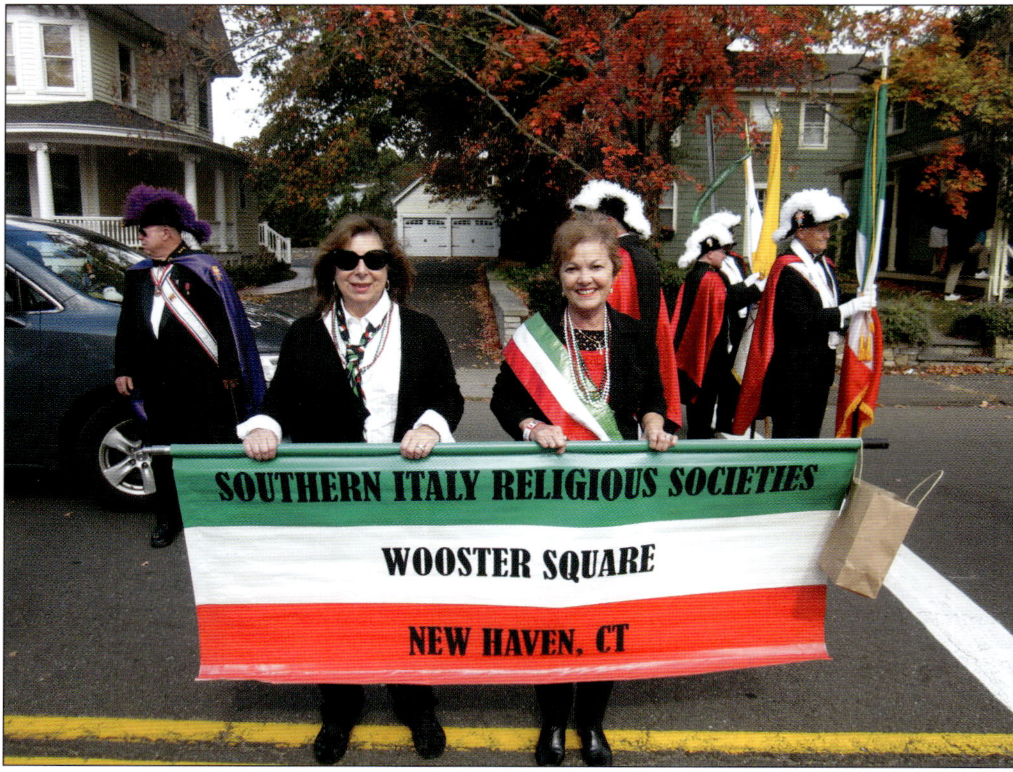

Southern Italian Religious Societies (SIRS). SIRS was formed in 1987 out of the Wooster Square religious societies: S. Maria Maddalena, S. Andrea Apostolo, S. Trifomena, S. Maria delle Vergini and S. Catello. These Italian societies work to care for each other, and for their Italian heritage. Each has a statue of its patron saint in the chapel at St. Michael's Church. (Photograph by Richard Biondi.)

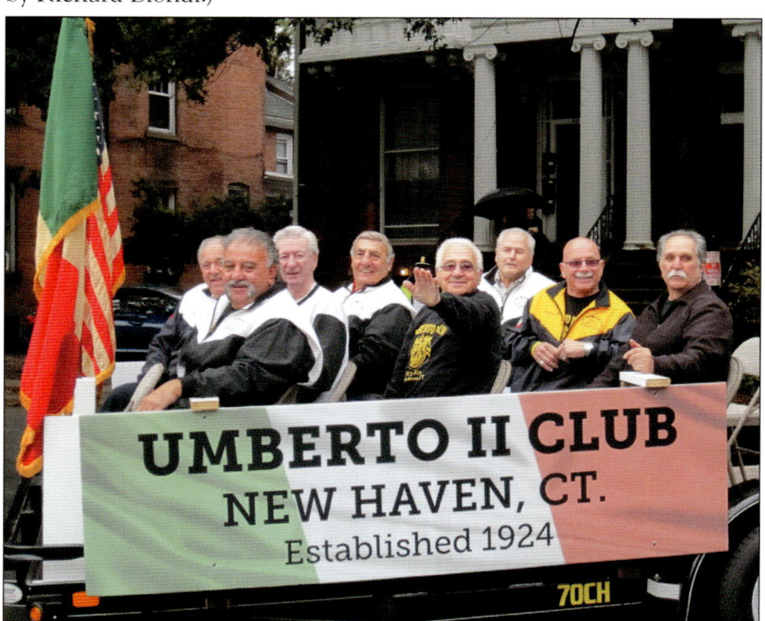

Umberto II Club. Founded in 1924, the club was named for King Umberto II (1904–1983) of the House of Savoy, who ruled Italy at the end of World War II. The current members pictured include Guy Bimonte, Sal Mauriello, Art Tuttle, Mike Giovanni, Mike Massomino, Egisto Fillipelli, Frank Pisano, and Louis Giametti. (Photograph by Richard Biondi.)

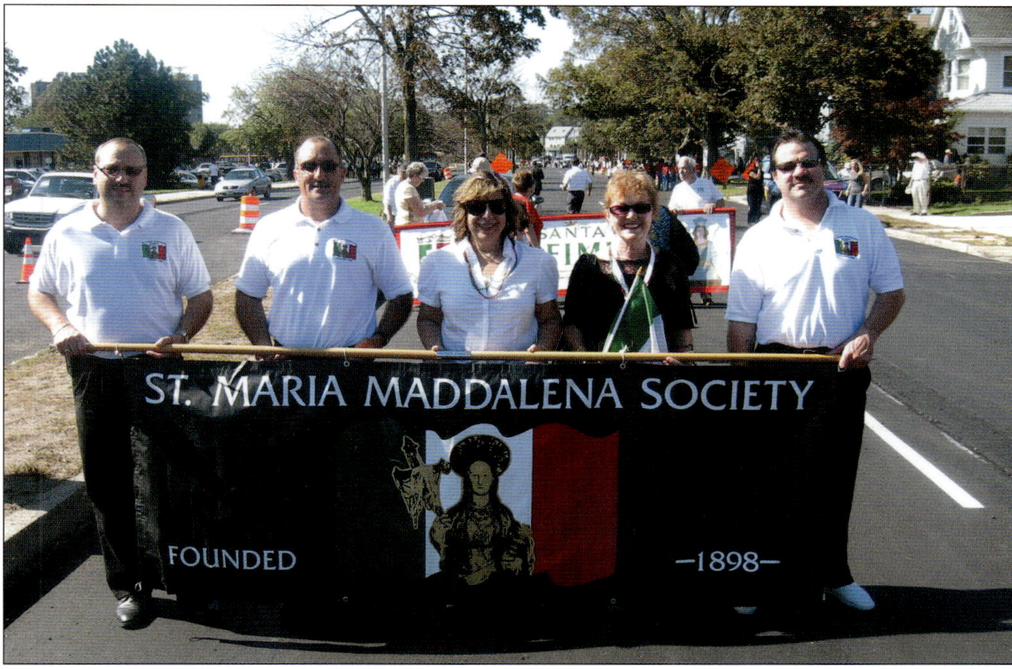

Santa Maria Maddalena Society. The Societá Santa Maria Maddalena di Mutto Socorso was founded May 1, 1898, in New Haven, making it the oldest surviving Italian fraternal organization in the state of Connecticut. Like most of the Italian societies, S.S.M.M. has both the main male organization and a female auxiliary, founded in 1925. (Photograph by Richard Biondi.)

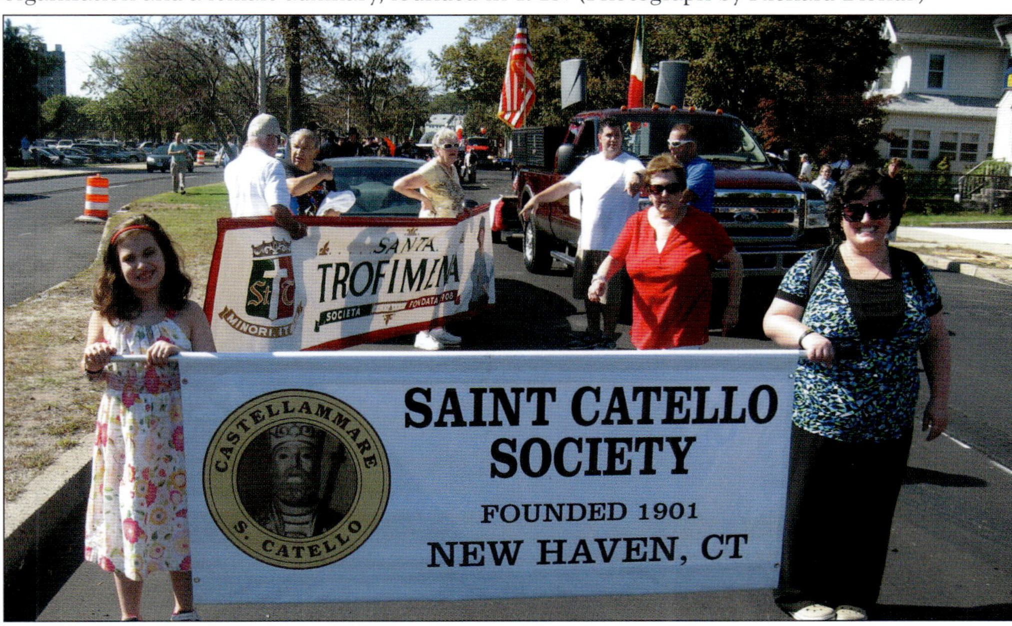

Saint Catello Society and Santa Trifomena Society. The Saint Catello Society was founded on November 3, 1901, by immigrants from Castellammare di Stabia. Although founded by men, today the St. Catello Society has almost 200 male and female members. The Societá Santa Trifomena di Minori was founded in 1908 by immigrants from Minori, a small seaside town on the Amalfi Coast. (Photograph by Richard Biondi.)

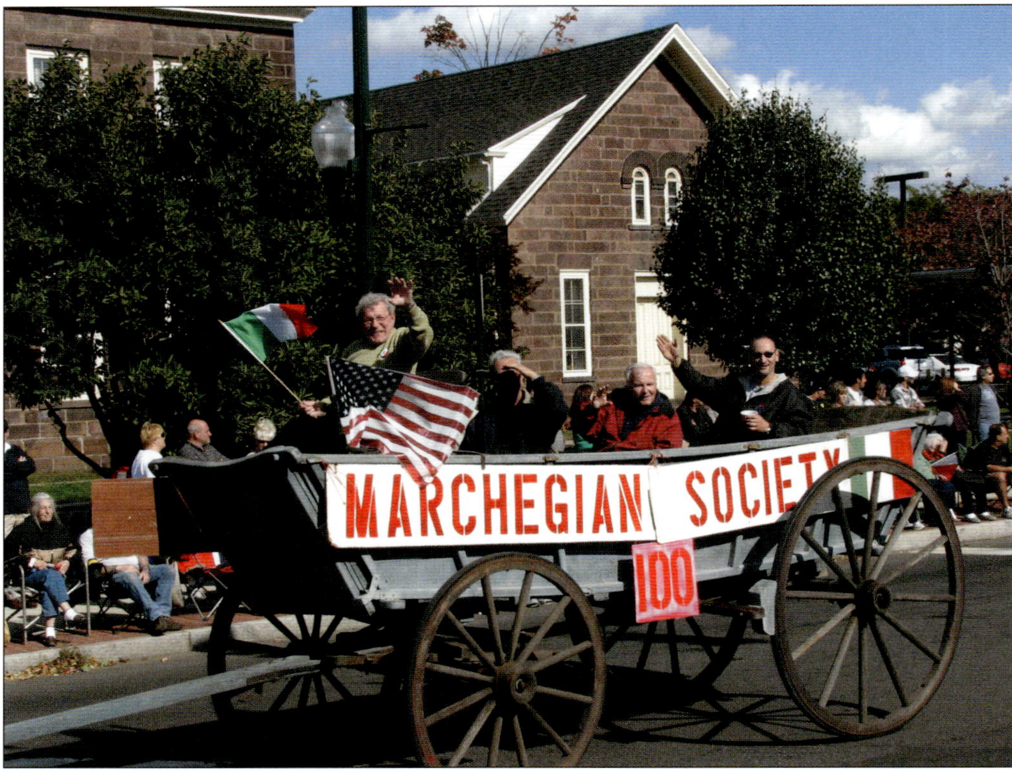

Marchigian Mutual Benefit Society. This group celebrated 100 years of existence at the 2009 Columbus Day Parade in East Haven. Members of the Marchigian trace their family roots to Le Marche, a region in central Italy on the Adriatic coast. Club members continue to meet in their 1938 clubhouse on the corner of Cedar and Minor Streets in New Haven. (Photograph by Arthur Giulietti.)

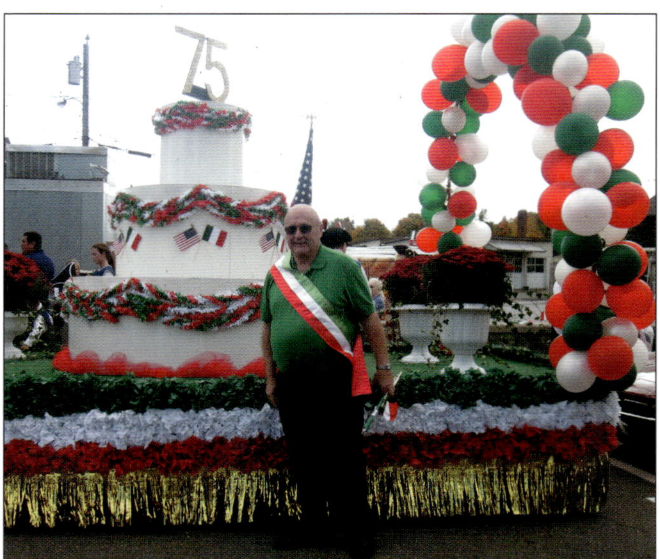

Paul Criscuolo. Criscuolo acted as general chairman of the 2013 Columbus Day Parade in Branford. Criscuolo has served in numerous capacities in the Greater New Haven area, including volunteering for the Branford Italian American Club and serving as president of both the Columbus Day Committee of Greater New Haven and the St. Catello Society (founded in 1901). Criscuolo stands in front of the Branford Italian American Club float. The club celebrated its 75th anniversary in 2013. (Photograph by Richard Biondi.)

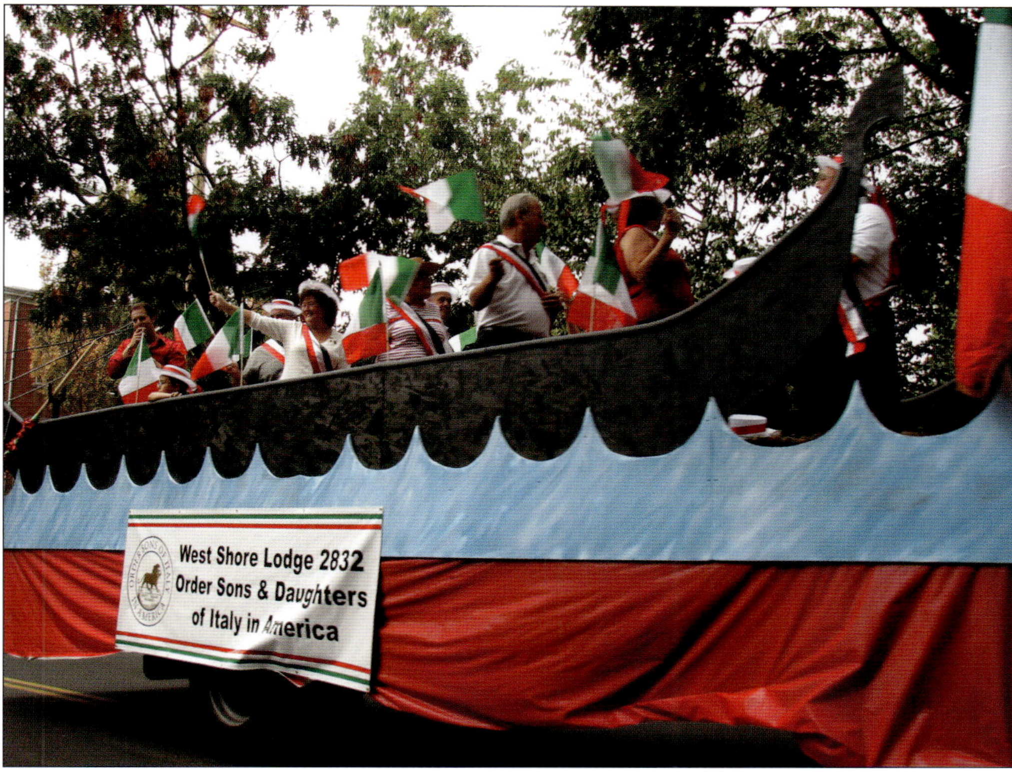

WEST SHORE LODGE 2832 ORDER SONS & DAUGHTERS OF ITALY IN AMERICA. The group celebrates Columbus in the 2007 parade in New Haven. The Order Sons and Daughters of Italy is a national organization for Italian Americans—and the oldest in the United States—with chapters from coast to coast, representing 26 million Americans of Italian descent. The West Shore Lodge 2832 is named for Sylvester Z. Poli, an early-20th-century theater impresario from New Haven. (Photograph by Arthur Giulietti.)

PROVINCES OF LE MARCHE, PESARO-URBINO FLOAT. The float depicts "Il Mercato" in the 2007 Columbus Day Parade in New Haven. Pesaro and Urbino are two historic urban areas of Le Marche, in central Italy. This float is demonstrating the agricultural products that come from the Pesaro-Urbino region, including wine, suggested by the water fountain seen in front. (Photograph by Arthur Giulietti.)

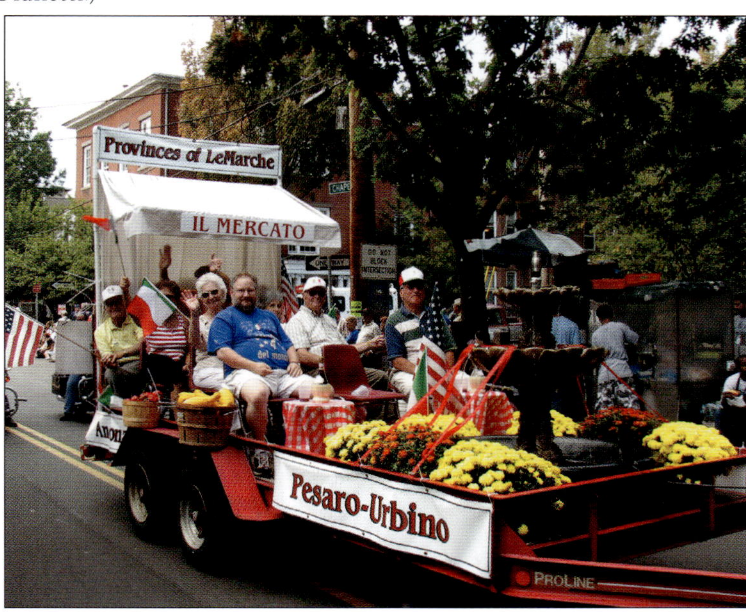

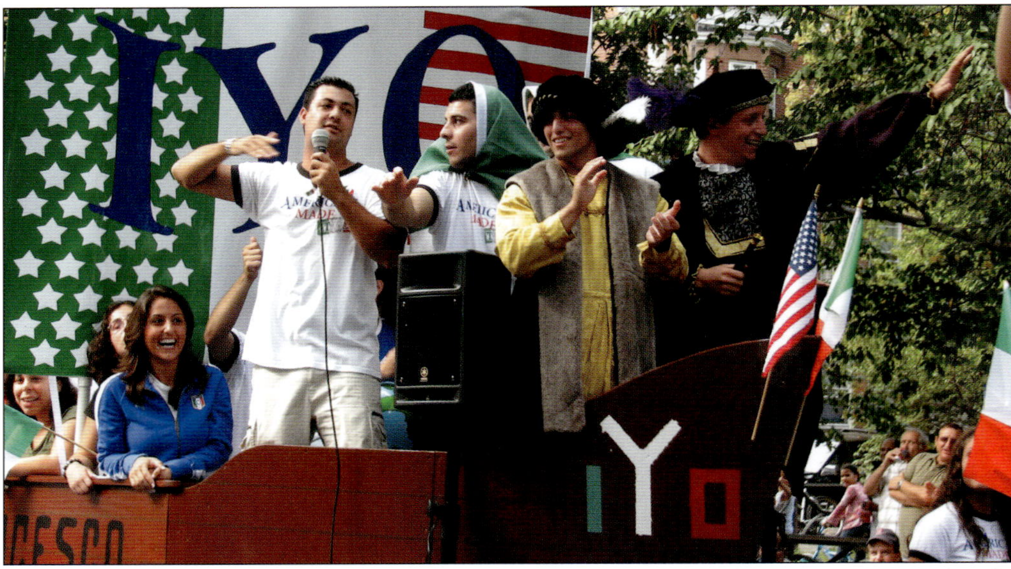

Italian American Youth Organization. The Italian American Youth Organization was founded on November 10, 2004, to celebrate, promote, and maintain Italian and Italian American culture among young people. Its mission is philanthropic in supporting Italian and Italian American culture and education in the Greater New Haven community. (Photograph by Arthur Giulietti.)

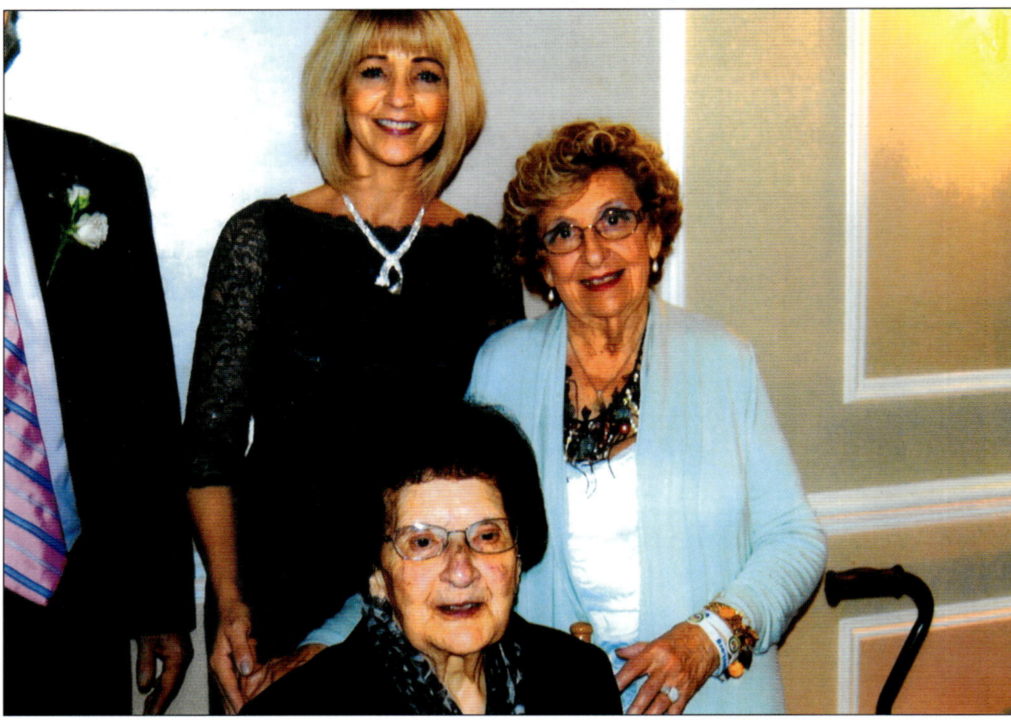

Columbus Day Dinners, a Long Tradition. Ann Nyberg (left), Frances Calzetta (right), and Theresa Argento (seated) enjoy each other's company at the 2013 Columbus Day dinner. Calzetta and Argento are longtime members of the Columbus Day Committee of Greater New Haven. Nyberg has been a news anchor at WTNH for many years. She loves the Columbus Day Parade and took over 300 photographs of the 2013 event in Branford, where she lives. (Frances Calzetta.)

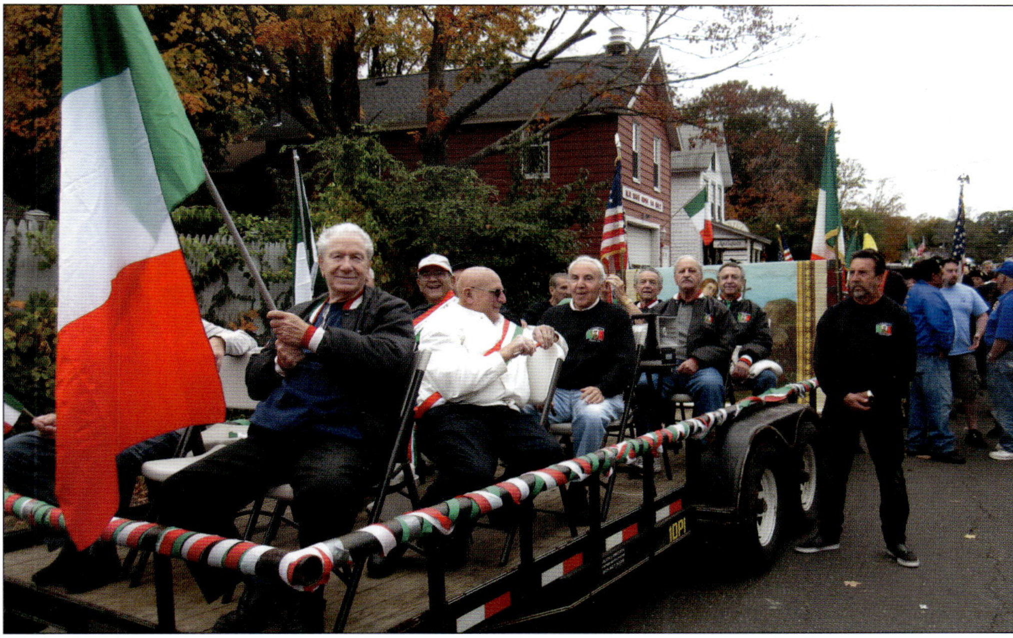

Santa Maria Maddalena Society, 2013 Columbus Day Parade, Branford. The society members shown here include, from left to right, Paul Pagliaro (holding the Italian flag), Alphonse Ruocco-White, Michael LaBonia, Frank Fronte, Anthony Giordano, Michael Novella, and Kessler Bailey (standing). (Photograph by Richard Biondi.)

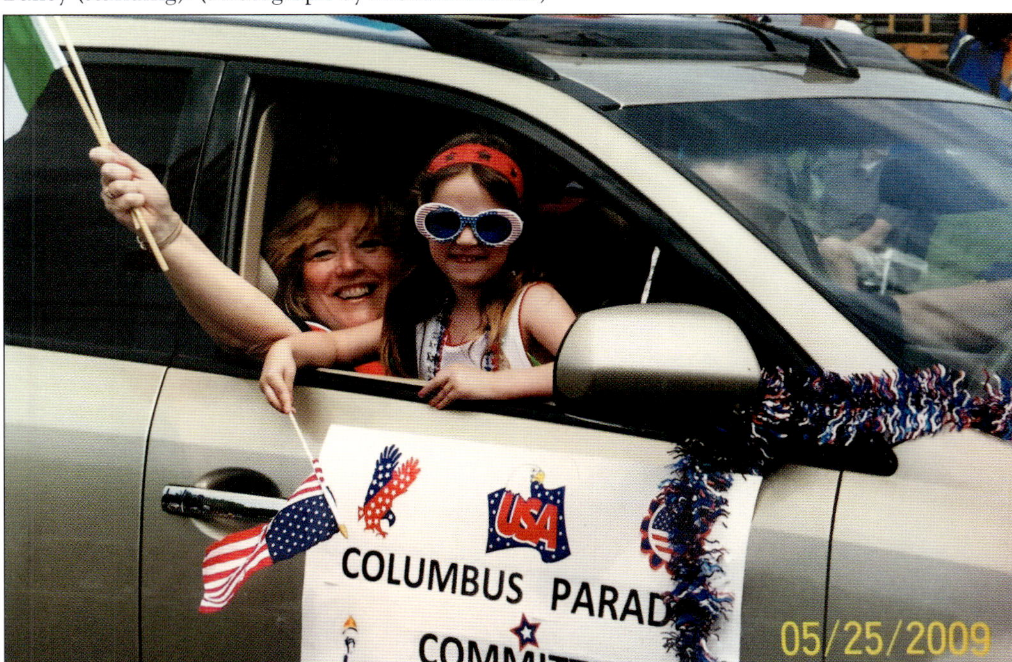

Rita Barbieri-George with Isabella Martinez, 2009. Riding in the Columbus Day Committee car is a privilege reserved for those who work at the upper committee level—or are especially cute, as was the case with Isabella. Rita is waving both American and Italian flags. (Rita Barbieri-George.)

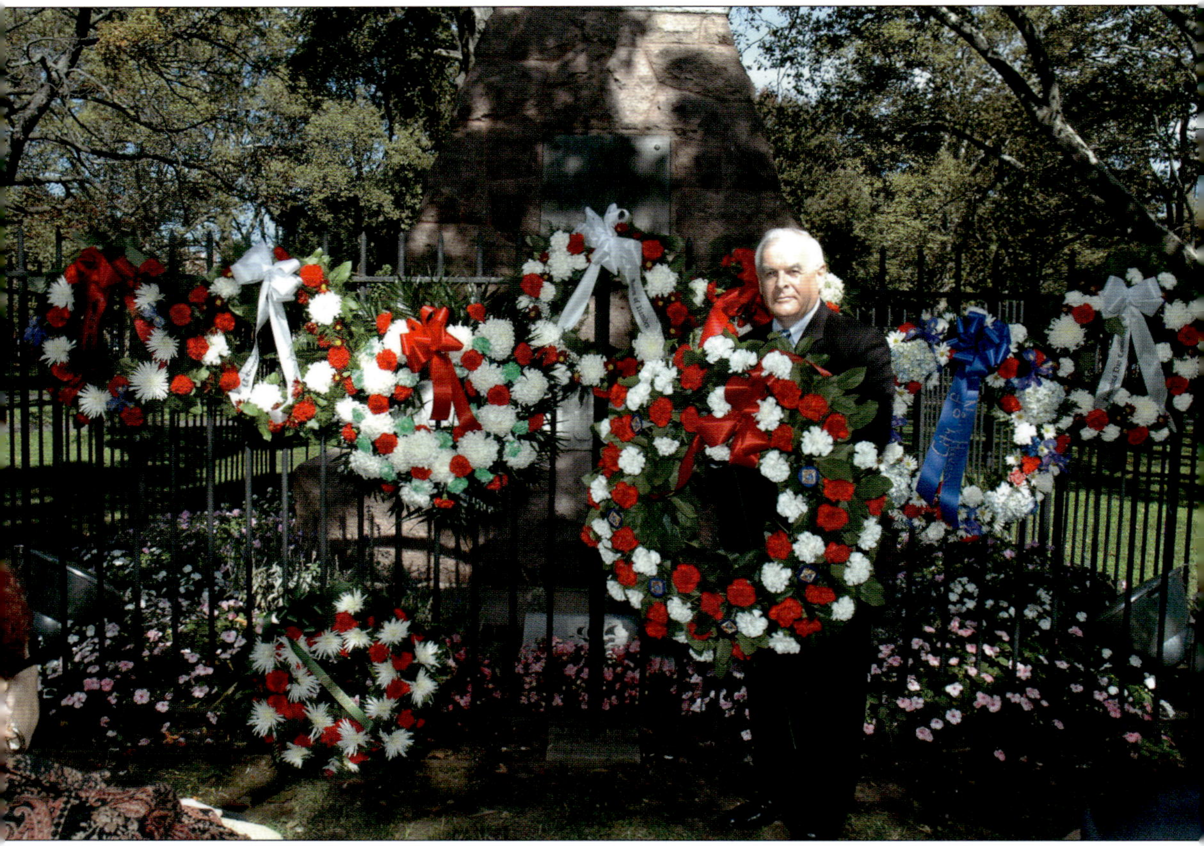

Knights of Columbus in Wooster Square. They march in the parade, sponsor a wreath every year, and also helped sponsor the conservation treatment of the Columbus Monument in Wooster Square. Here, Deputy Supreme Knight Dennis Savoie lays a wreath at the foot of the Columbus Monument in 2006. (Knights of Columbus.)

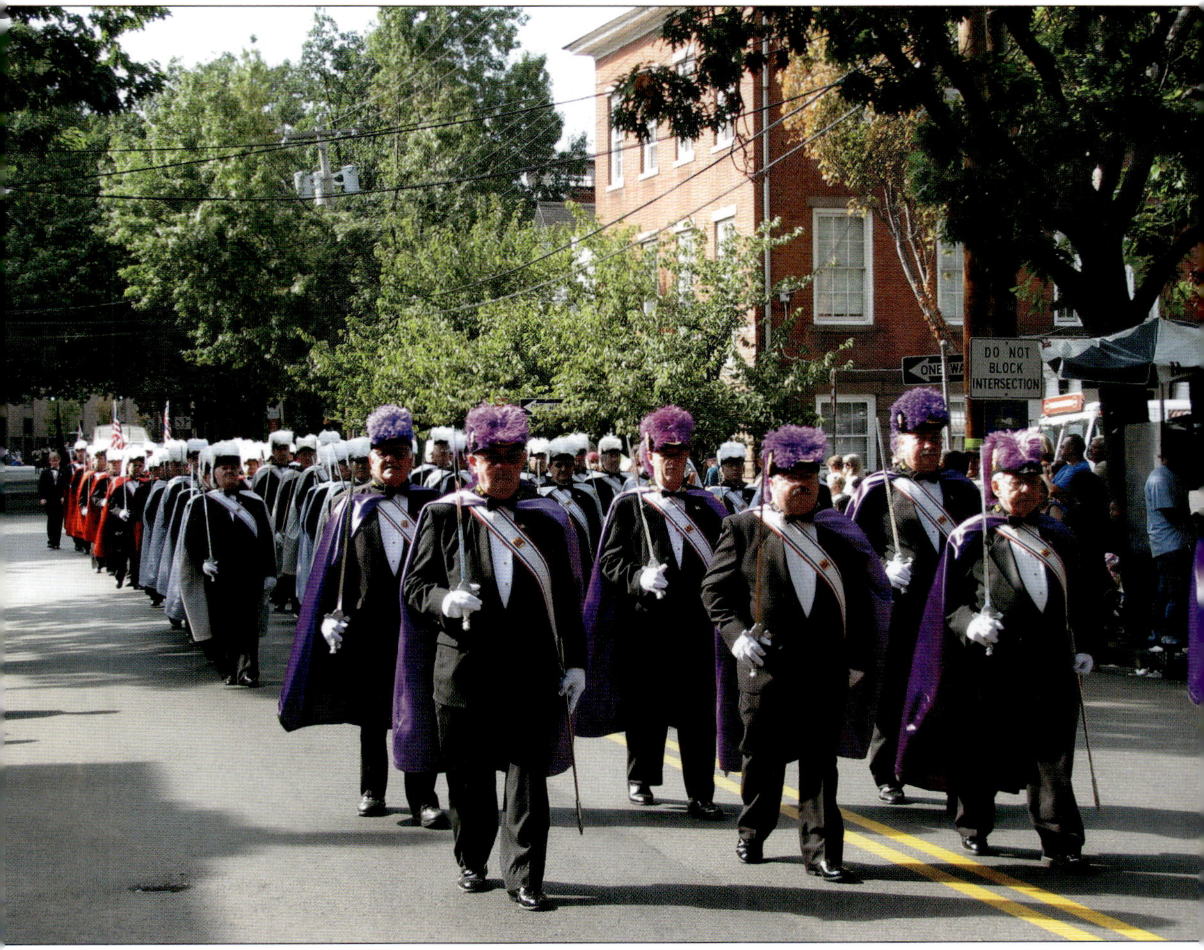

Knights of Columbus in Living Color. Men who have passed to the fourth degree of their knighthood can choose to join the Color Corps, wearing a cape and chapeau and carrying a sword. The colors shown here in the 2007 Columbus Day Parade in New Haven relate to their respective roles in the organization. (Photograph by Arthur Giulietti.)

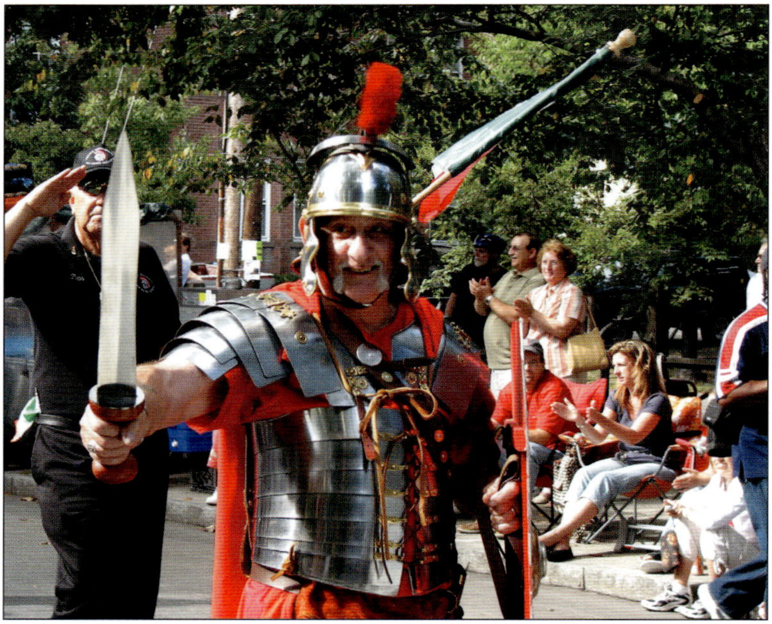

Roman Centurion. The New Haven County Police Order of Centurions, an Italian American group, was cofounded by Harry DeBenedet. Calling upon their Italian heritage, members of the group use the Roman centurion image to remind spectators of their roles as warriors—although they mostly raise funds to help others. (Photograph by Arthur Giulietti.)

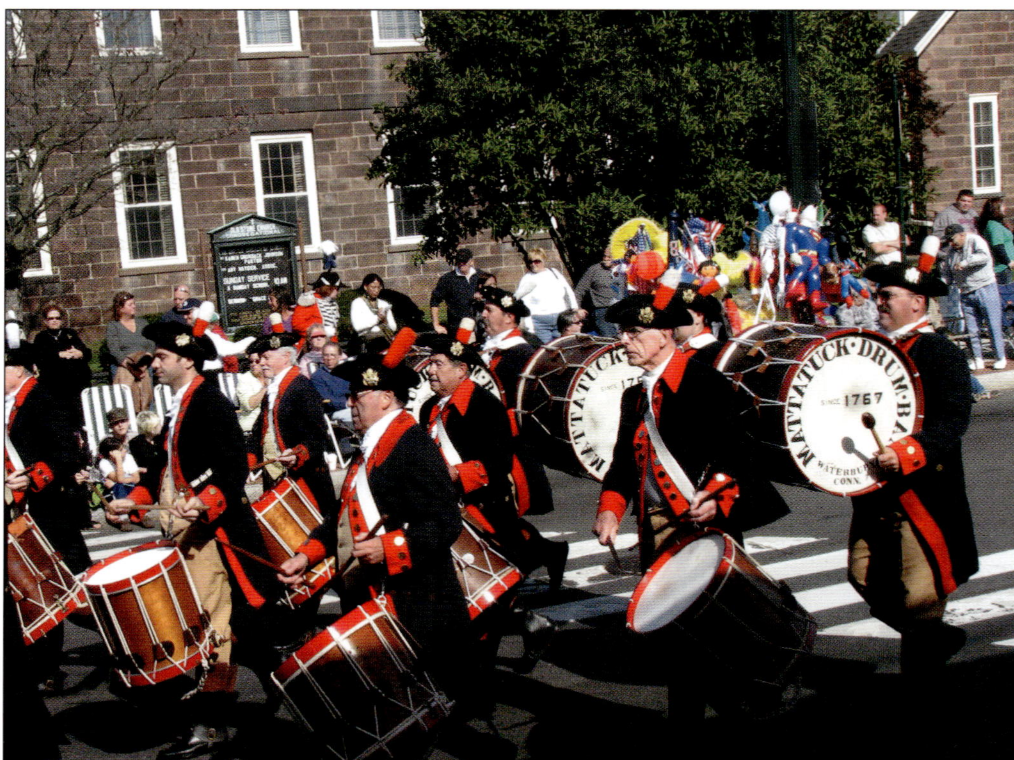

Mattatuck Drum Band from Waterbury, 2015. The Mattatuck Drum Band is seen in the Columbus Day Parade in East Haven. The group was founded in 1767, making it the oldest band with continuous membership in the United States. Marching bands such as the Mattatuck Drum Band come from other cities across Connecticut and beyond to participate in the Greater New Haven Columbus Day Parade, creating a mix of old and new. (Photograph by Arthur Giulietti.)

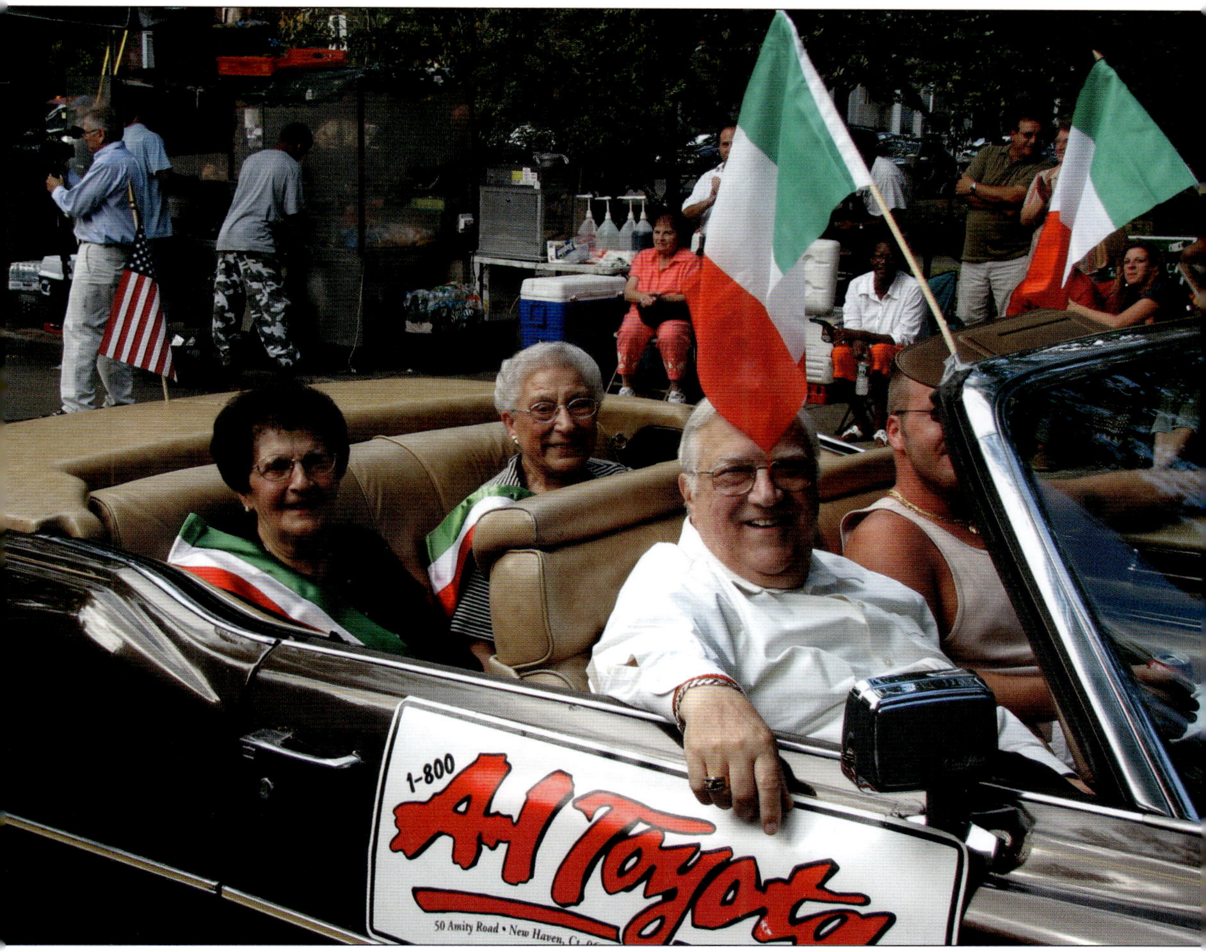

Columbus Day Committee Parade Car, 2007. Seen in the backseat are Theresa Argento (left), who has been an active member of the Columbus Day Parade committee and of the St. Andrew Society for more than 70 years, and Ann Proto, another longtime member of the committee, who passed away in early 2017. In the front seat is Dominic Garladi, who loved New Haven and was a great supporter of the Columbus Day Parade. (Photograph by Arthur Giulietti.)

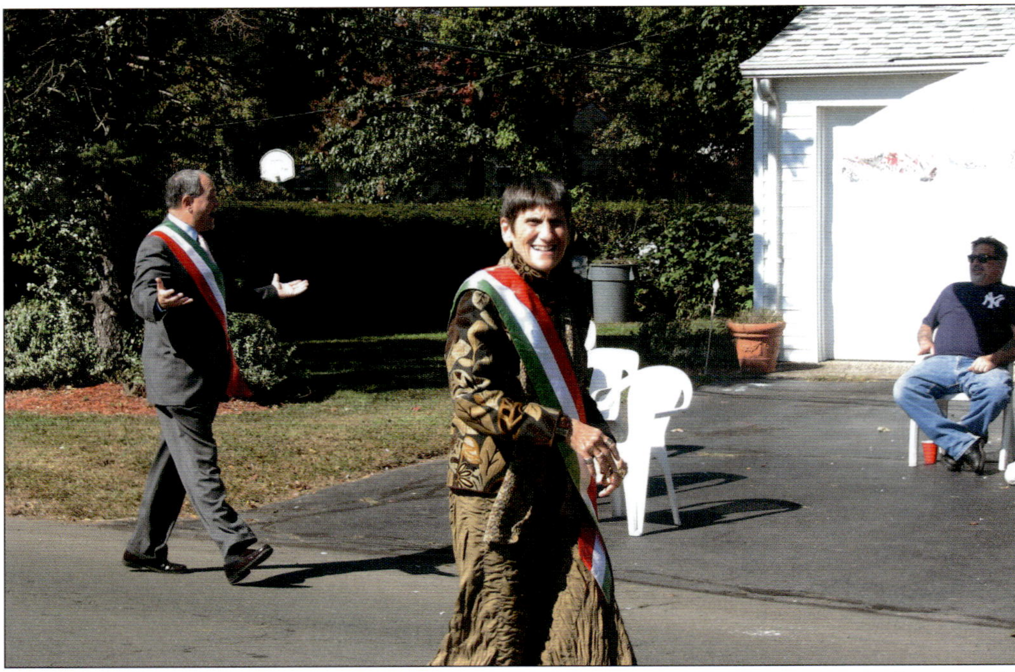

Rep. Rosa DeLauro with Mayor John DeStefano, 2008, North Haven. DeLauro is the daughter of Luisa DeLauro, the daughter of an immigrant from Amalfi who opened Canestri's Pastry Shop on Wooster Street. Both Luisa and her husband, Ted, were active in community advocacy, giving their daughter Rosa a taste for working in public service. DeStefano is the son of a New Haven police officer and became the longest-serving mayor in New Haven history. (Photograph by Arthur Giulietti.)

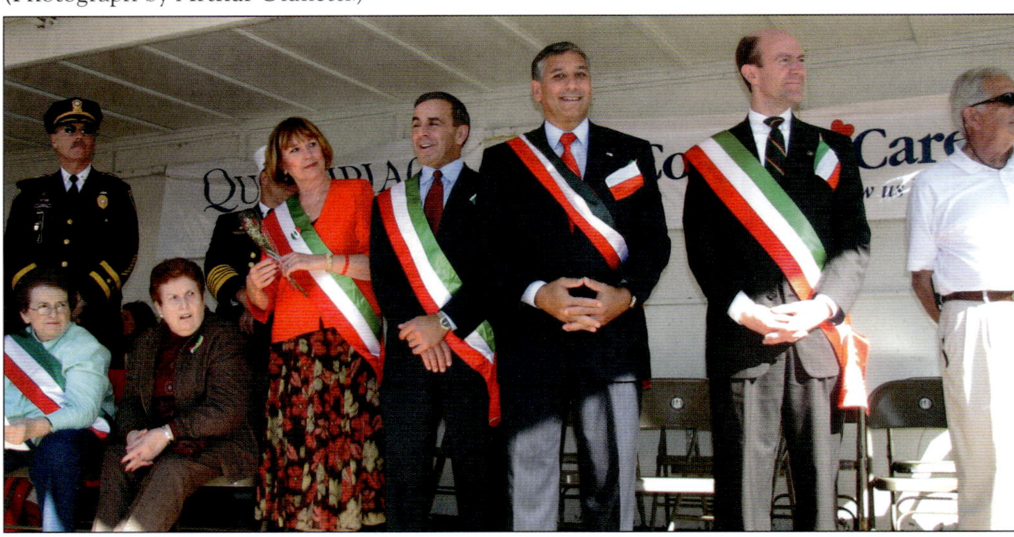

Reviewing Stands. Dignitaries gather at the reviewing stand with, from left to right, Magdalen Sparaco, Patricia Zampa, Janet McCarthy, Mike Freda, Len Fasano, Steve Fontana, and Peter DeBrino in North Haven in 2008. Reviewing stands are a long tradition in parade culture, giving a formal stamp of approval from the event's honored onlookers. The first parade review stand for Columbus Day can be seen in the 1892 photograph of the Knights of Columbus and city officials standing on a dais in front of city hall in New Haven. (Photograph by Arthur Giulietti.)

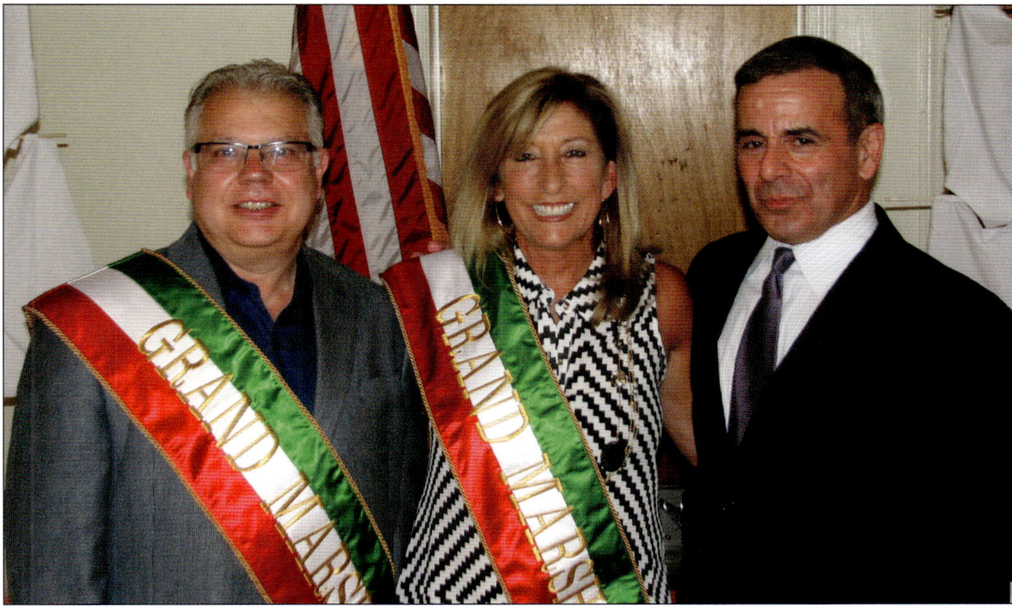

Grand Marshals, 2008, North Haven. Luigi Nuzzolino (left) and Phyllis Turriccio Havens were honored to serve as grand marshals during the parade. They are pictured here with Mike Freda, first selectman of North Haven. Freda participates in many Columbus Day activities and is a member of the S. Maria Maddalena and St. Andrew Societies. (Photograph by Arthur Giulietti.)

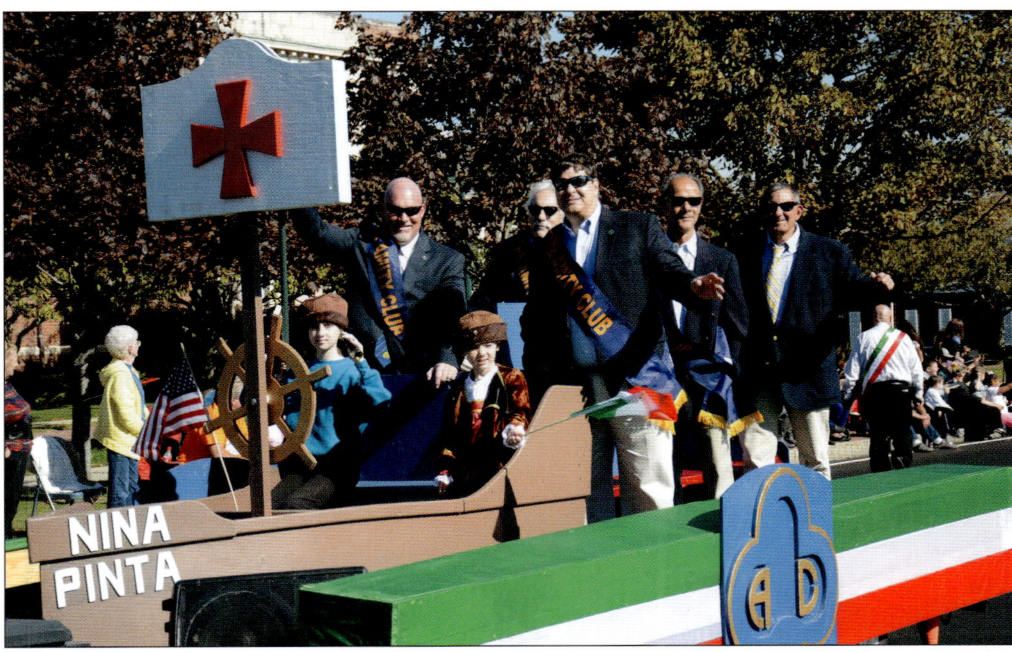

The Amity Club Float, 2015. The Amity Club was formed in 1936 by a group of Italian American men from New Haven who wanted to create their own service club outside of those already in place for the established Yankee population. Amity Club members continue to raise funds for many philanthropic purposes, and remember their heritage with an annual wine and Italian cuisine event. (Photograph by Arthur Giulietti.)

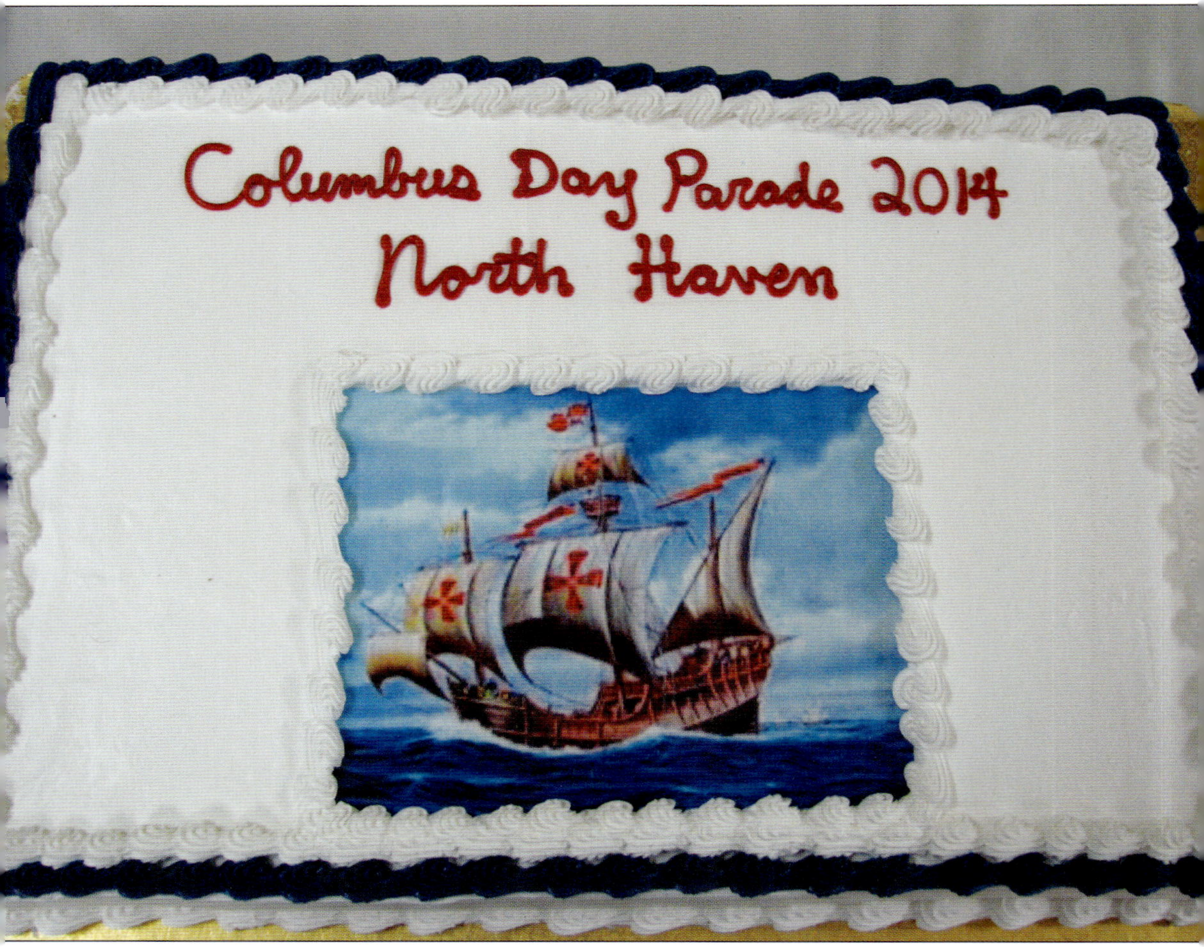

COLUMBUS DAY CELEBRATORY CAKE, 2014. Italians are known for their great desserts that are reflective of region—*cannoli* from Sicily, *biscotti* from Prato, and the endless array of *le paste* from Italy, including *sfogliatella*, *zeppole*, *gelato*, and *tiramisu*. Sheet cake with decoration seems a distinctly American idea—it is practical and serves many—but here, with the picture of Columbus's ship, Italy and the United States join together once again. (Photograph by Arthur Giulietti.)

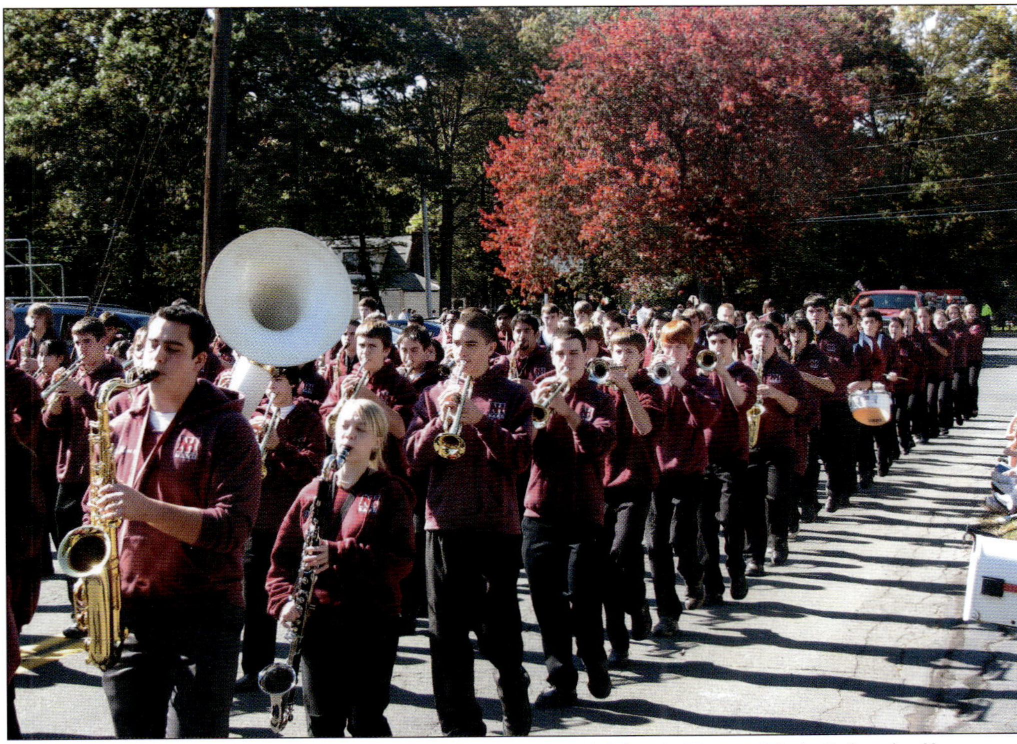

North Haven High School Marching Band, 2015. North Haven High School offers many opportunities for performance for musically inclined students; the marching band attends football games, concerts, the Memorial Day Parade, and musical performances farther afield, such as in Boston. (Photograph by Arthur Giulietti.)

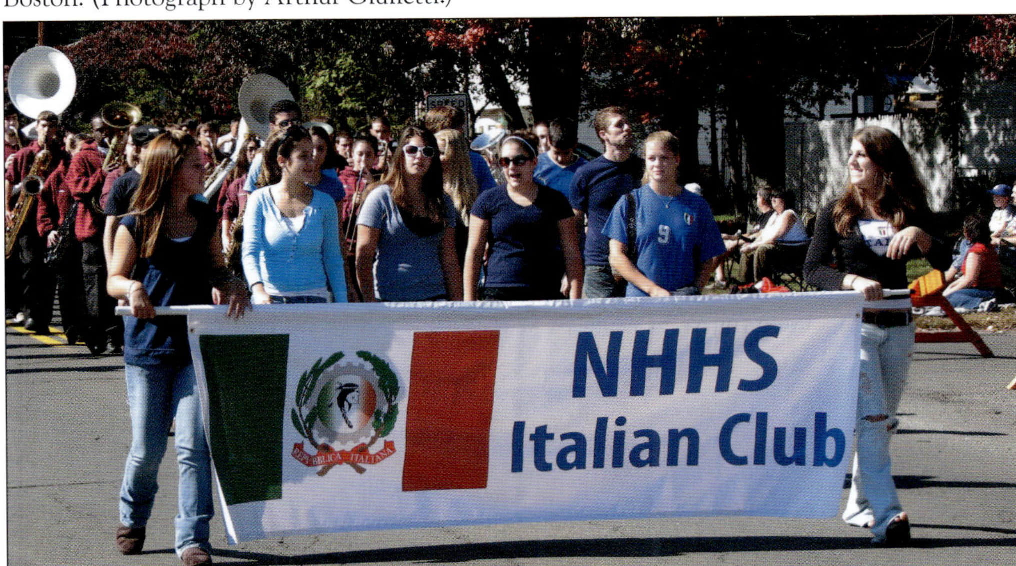

North Haven High School Italian Club, 2008. The New England states of Connecticut and Rhode Island have the highest percentages of people who trace their heritage to Italy in the country, thus making the study of *la lingua italiana* possible at the high school level, which is not true in many other parts of the country. (Photograph by Arthur Giulietti.)

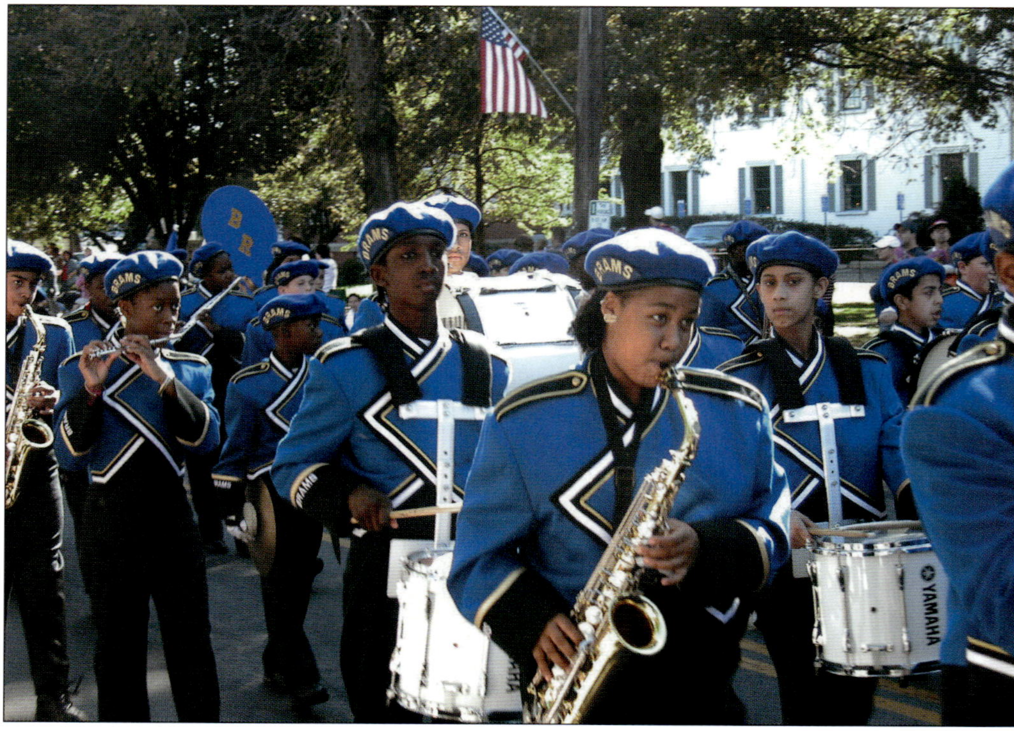

Betsy Ross Arts Magnet School, 2006, West Haven. It is no surprise that students from BRAMS should appear in the Greater New Haven Columbus Day Parades. Students at the school study dance, music, theater, and the visual arts at an advanced level with certified teachers and professional artists. (Photograph by Arthur Giulietti.)

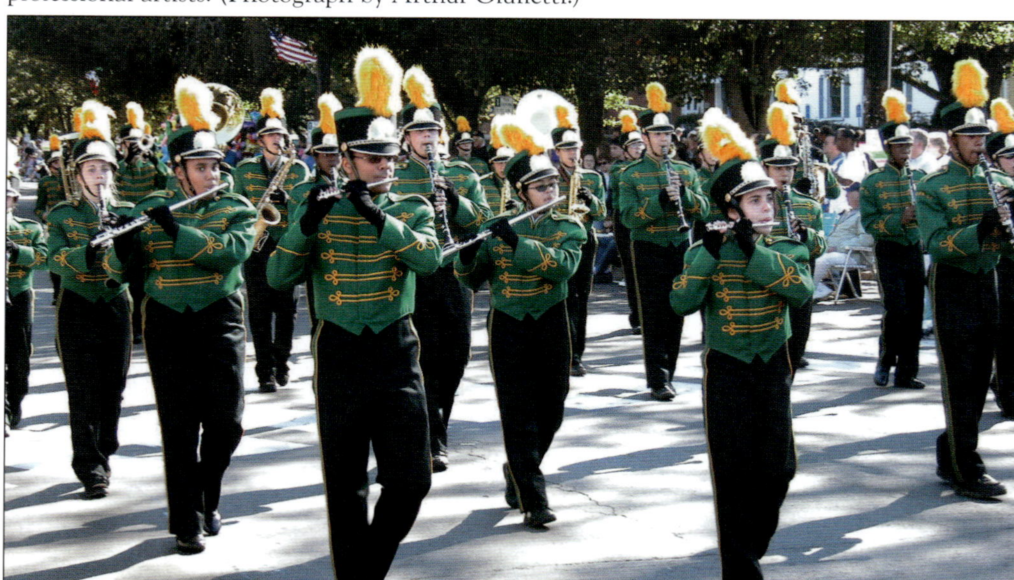

Hamden High School Marching Band, 2006, West Haven. Hamden High School is a powerhouse of musical opportunity for students: in 2016, the Music Department won a silver medal at an international competition. In addition to the marching band, Hamden High has a jazz band and a chorus. (Photograph by Arthur Giulietti.)

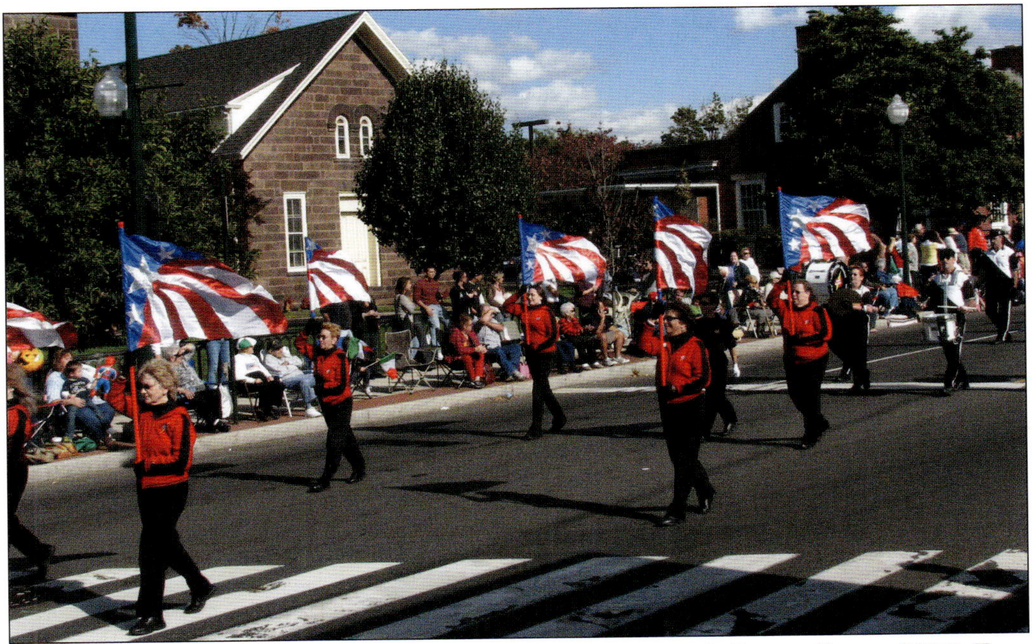

Flag Bearers of the Connecticut Alumni Senior Drums & Bugle Corps, 2009, East Haven. Based in Seymour, Connecticut, the corps was developed out of an earlier organization called the Connecticut Hurricanes. Wearing distinctive black/white and black/red uniforms, this large group of musicians practices and performs in parades across the state. (Photograph by Arthur Giulietti.)

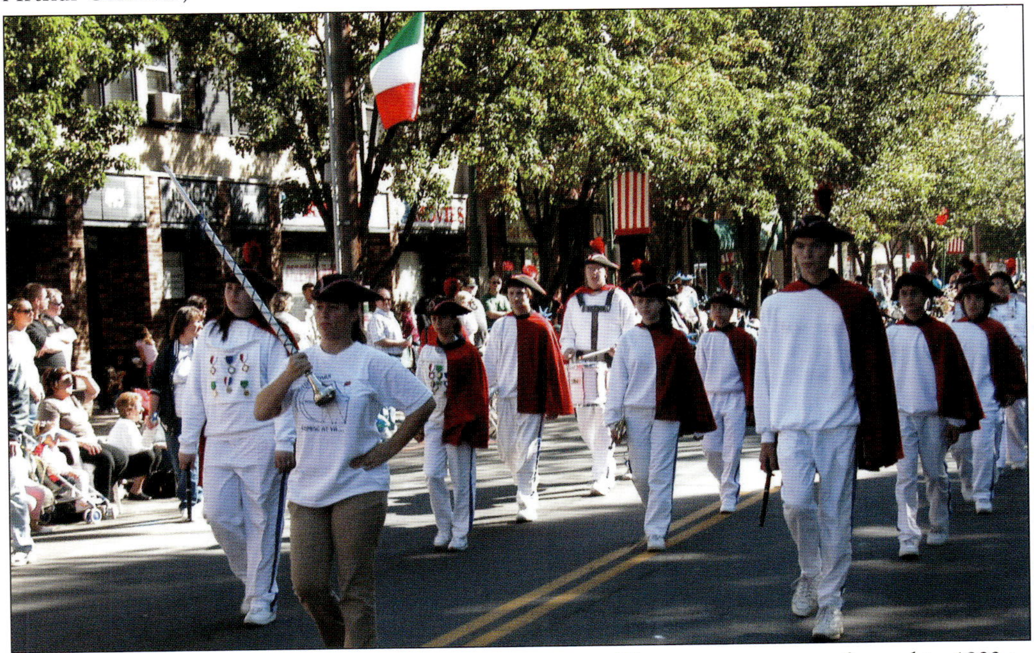

Washington Park Drum Corps, 2006, West Haven. This civic group was formed in 1933 in Meriden, Connecticut, for young people between the ages of 8 and 21. Encouraging musicianship and participation in competition is challenging in the 21st century: technology has seized the attention of many youths. (Photograph by Arthur Giulietti.)

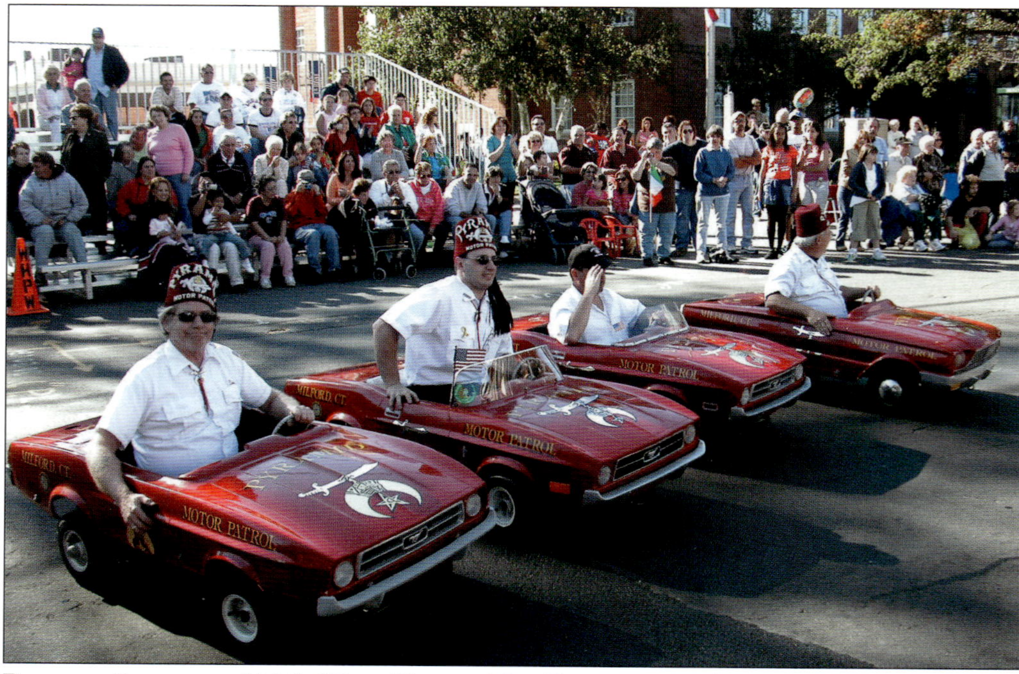

PYRAMID SHRINERS, 2006, WEST HAVEN. The Shriners, seen here in their distinctive red fezzes, have been a feature of American parades since their founding in 1872. This group from the nearby Pyramid Shrine Temple in Milford, Connecticut, loves cars so much that members organize a classic car show every year to raise funds for their philanthropic mission. (Photograph by Arthur Giulietti.)

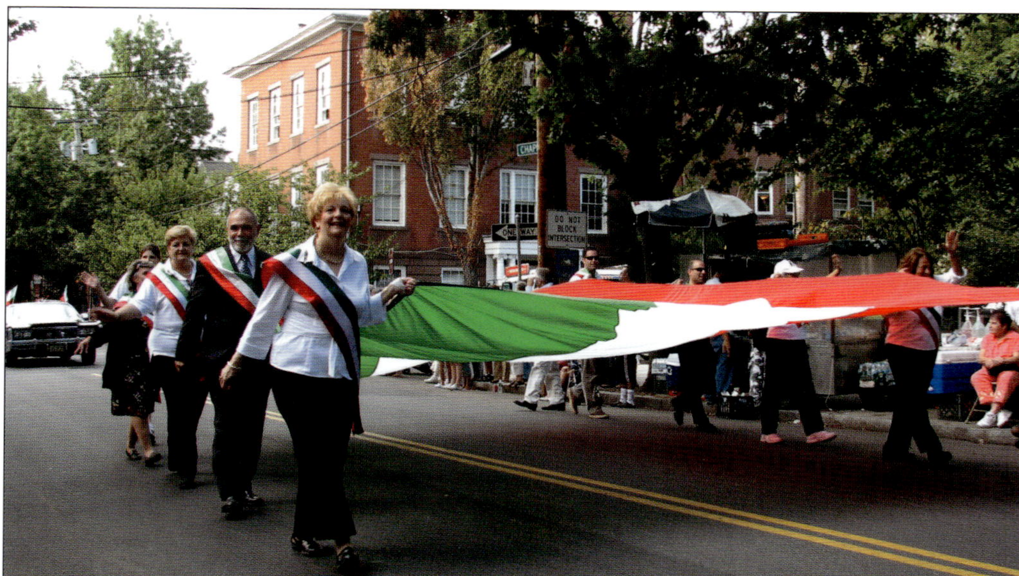

IL TRICOLORE. The Columbus Day Committee of Greater New Haven members carry "il Tricolore" in the 2007 Columbus Day Parade in New Haven. This oversize Italian flag was another parade idea from Theresa Argento. Former members and friends of the Columbus Day Committee are seen here, including Carmel Suntino, Vanna Francia, Natalie Guiliano DeRosa, Mike Quoka, and Mario Coppola. (Photograph by Arthur Giulietti.)

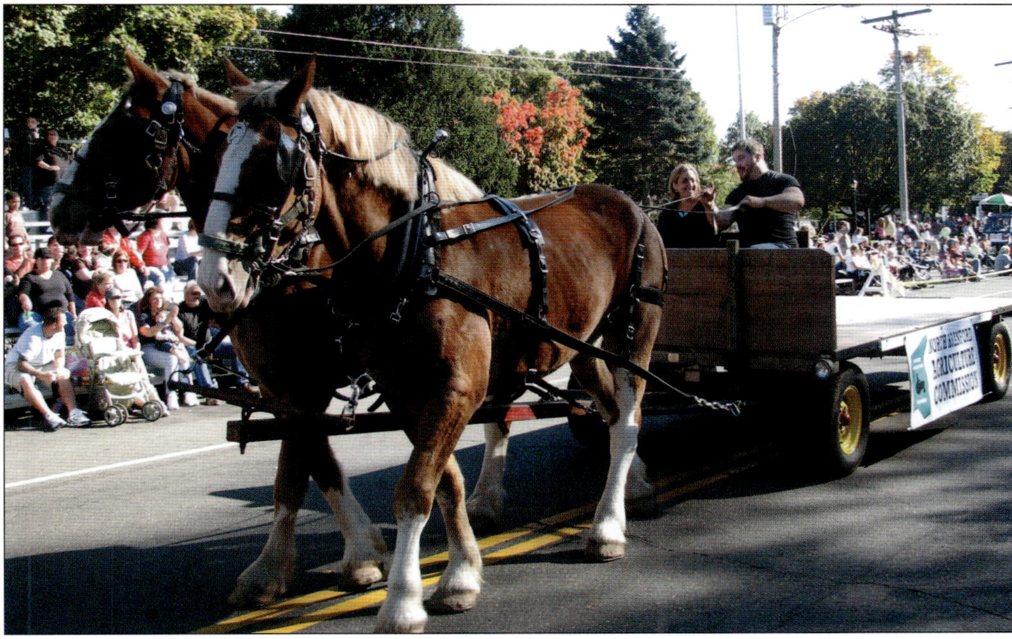

North Branford Agricultural Commission, 2013, Branford. Connecticut has a long and rich agricultural history—even in urban areas such as New Haven, crops were grown when the city was first founded in the 17th century. The North Branford Agricultural Commission is a reminder of the region's economy, which included agriculture and continues to do so today. Agriculture and gardening are also important parts of the histories of Italy and Italian Americans. (Photograph by Arthur Giulietti.)

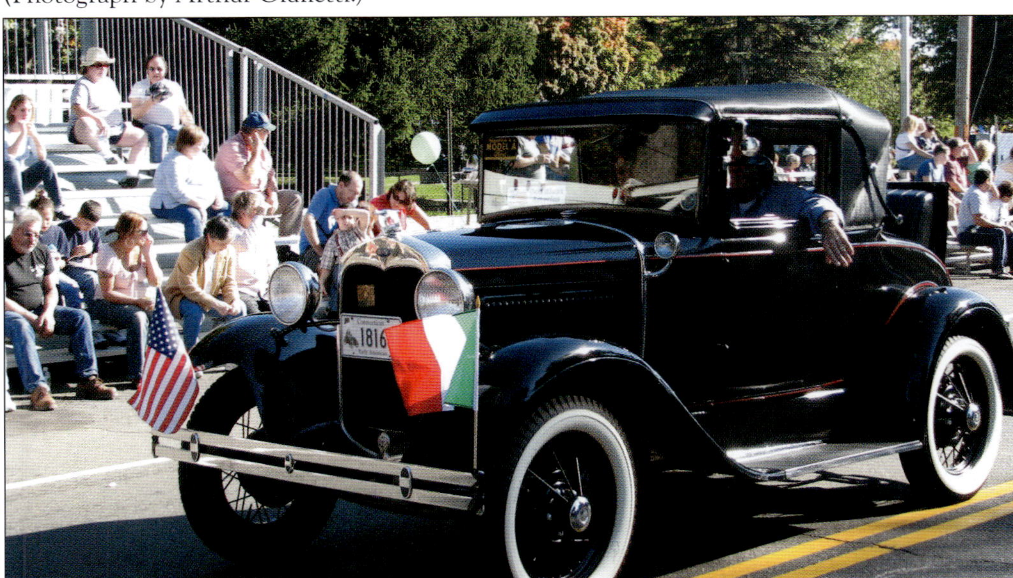

Ford Model A. Antique cars are a fixture in many American parades, including the Greater New Haven Columbus Day events. Antique car club owners have the opportunity to show off their meticulously restored and maintained automobiles, while spectators wonder at the ways in which their great-grandparents purchased their first cars in the early decades of the 20th century. (Photograph by Arthur Giulietti.)

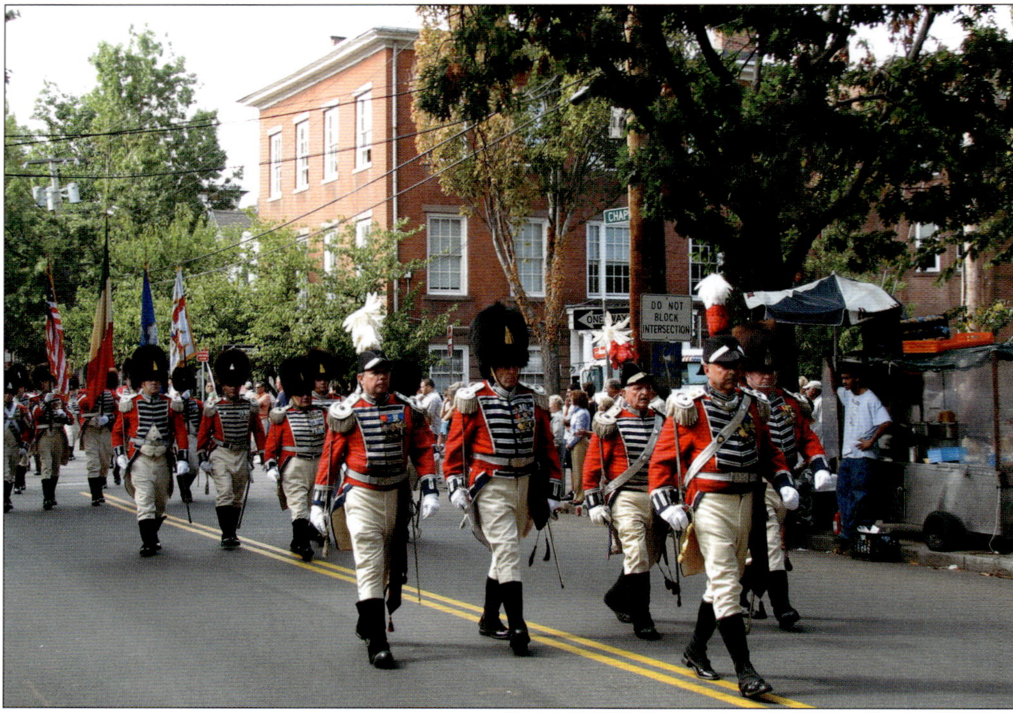

SECOND COMPANY, GOVERNOR'S FOOT GUARD, 2007. The Second Company, Governor's Foot Guard has been in existence since 1775, when the militia unit was formed under Capt. Benedict Arnold. A parade in New Haven would not be the same without them. Every April, the Foot Guardsmen remembers their own history with Powder House Day, a reenactment held on the steps of New Haven City Hall. (Photograph by Arthur Giulietti.)

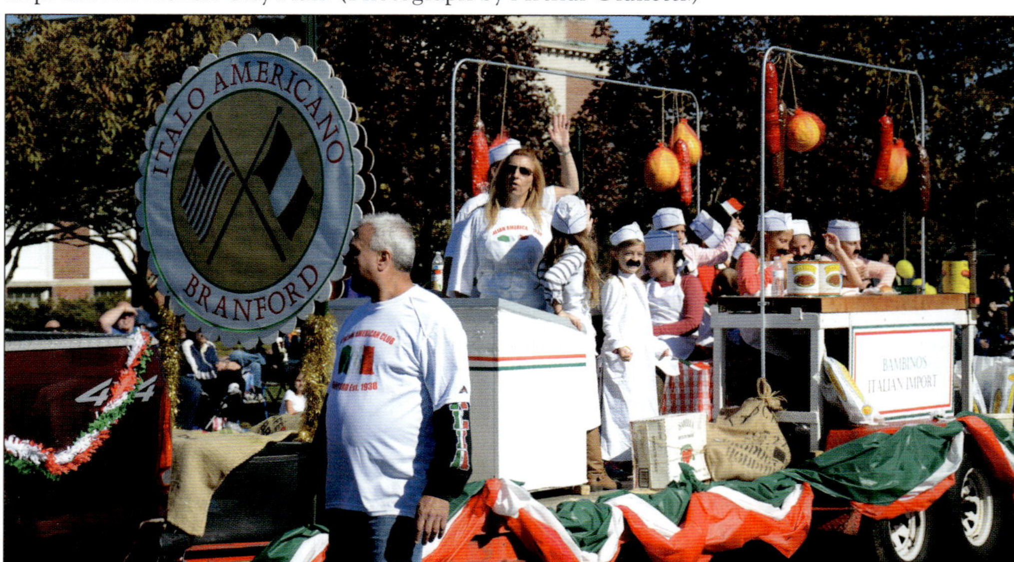

BRANFORD ITALO AMERICANO CLUB, 2016, EAST HAVEN. On a clever float called "Bambinos Italian Market," children and friends of club members—wearing black mustaches—sell their meats and cheeses from the market stand. Cans of Roma tomatoes are ready to be turned into red sauce for pasta. (Photograph by Arthur Giulietti.)

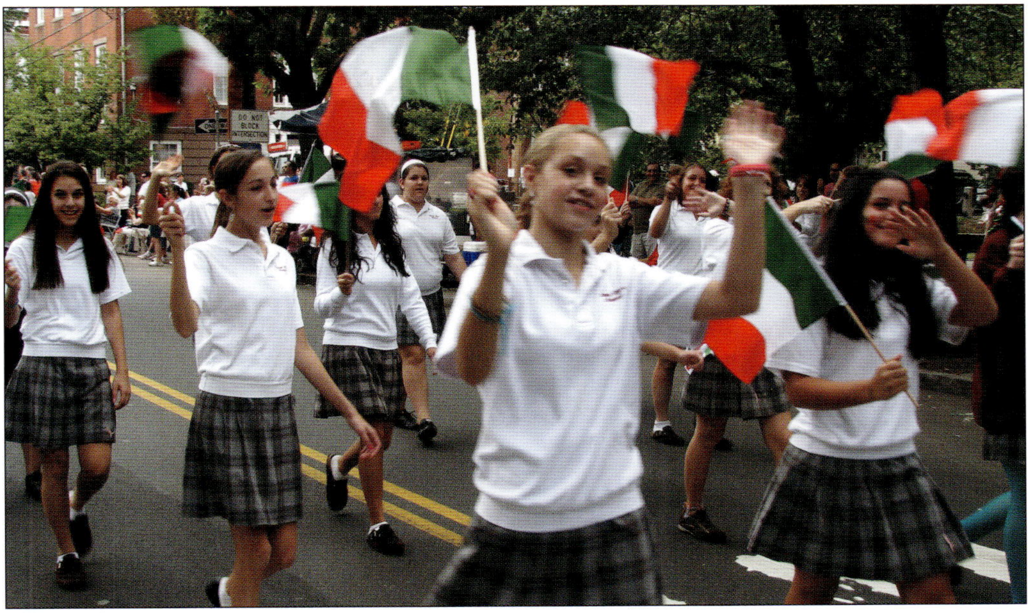

Sacred Heart Academy Students, 2007. Sacred Heart is a survivor in the 21st century, as many Catholic primary and secondary schools have closed. The all-girls high school was founded in 1946 in New Haven, but moved to nearby Hamden in 1953. (Photograph by Arthur Giulietti.)

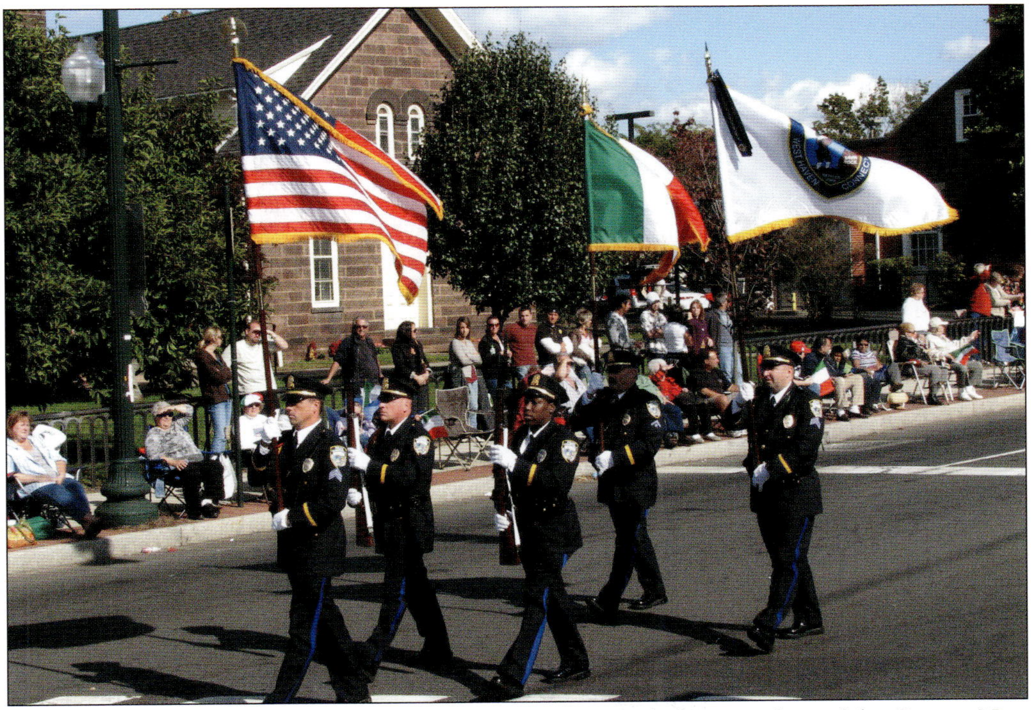

West Haven Police Department, 2009, East Haven. Including members of the Greater New Haven community in blue is a tradition in parades going back to the 19th century. Here, members of the West Haven Police Department wear patches on the left shoulder and carry a flag showing a man with a spyglass looking at Savin Rock, a famous landmark in the town. (Photograph by Arthur Giulietti.)

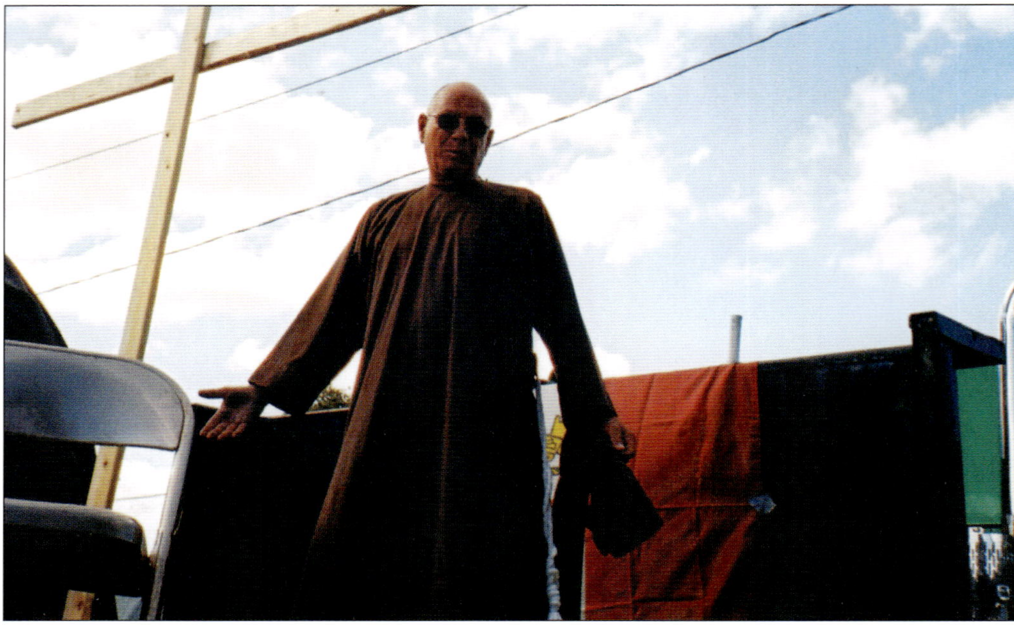

ANTHONY PAOLILLO. Paolillo is a longtime member of the Societá di Sant'Andrea Apostolo (St. Andrew Society). Here, he is in Catholic missionary clothing standing with a wooden cross; in the Columbus story, the cross is a symbol of evangelization—that is, bringing faith to the New World. (Photograph by Richard Biondi.)

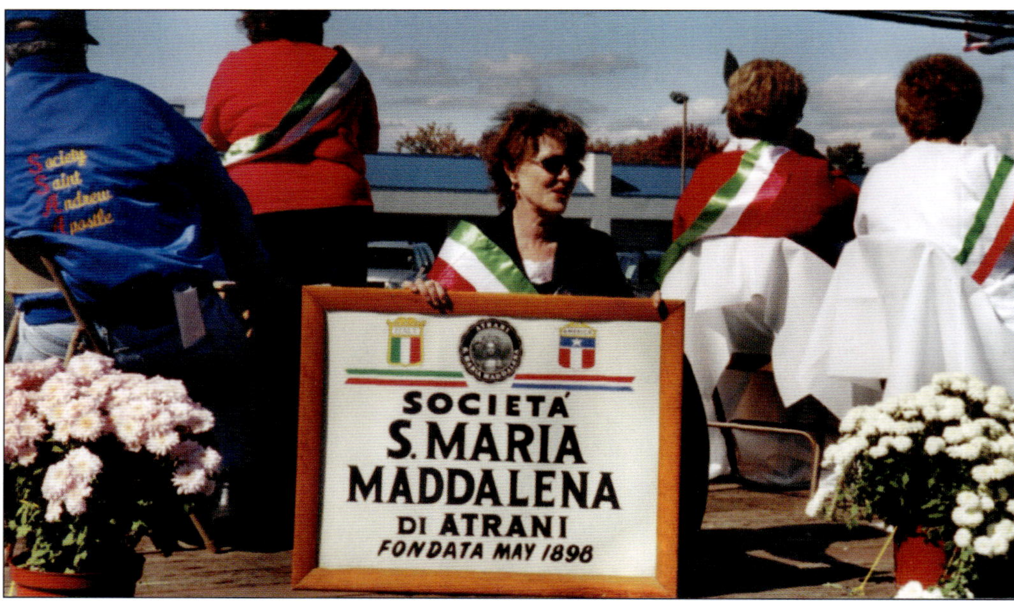

SANTA MARIA MADDALENA. As noted earlier, the Santa Maria Maddalena is the oldest Italian fraternal organization in the state of Connecticut. The sign, held by Rheta DeBenedet, reminds viewers that members are descendants of immigrants from Atrani, in southern Italy. DeBenedet is the president of the S.S.M.M. Women's Society. The organization maintains a building and a clubhouse on Wooster Street with a statue of Santa Maria Maddalena outside. (Photograph by Richard Biondi.)

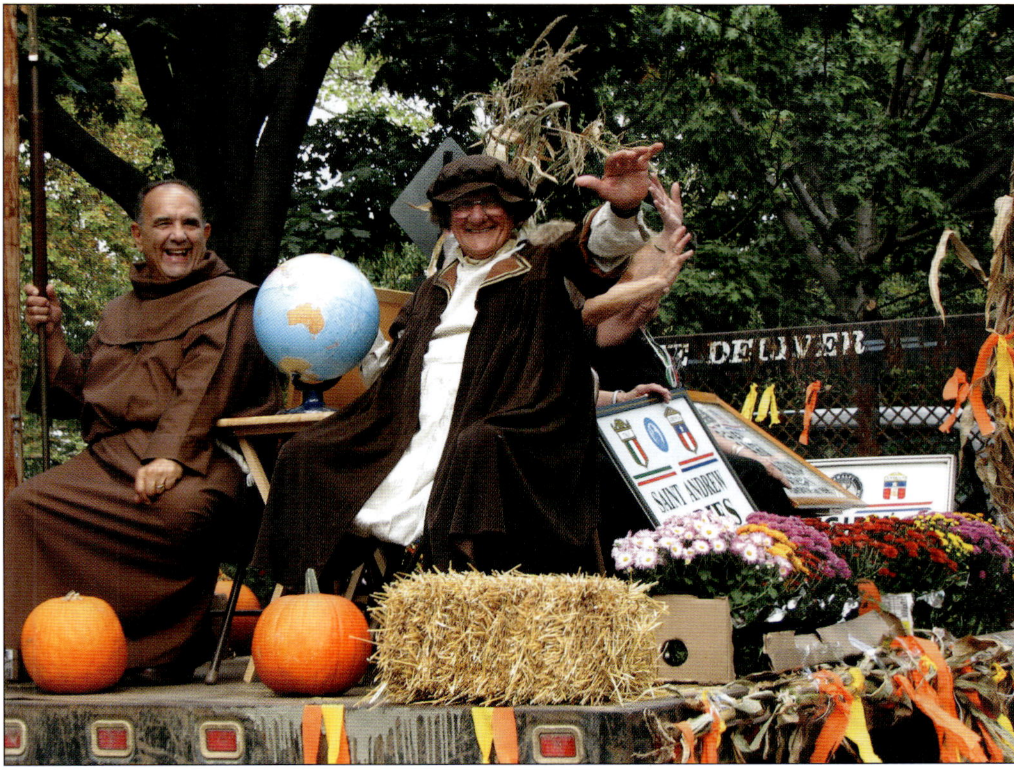

Societá di Sant'Andrea Apostolo. Members of the Societá di Sant'Andrea Apostolo dressed as Columbus and a religious figure in the 2007 Columbus Day Parade in New Haven. While the globe has been used in many monuments, including in the original design of the Columbus Monument by Alfons Pelzer, the pumpkins are a subtler touch suggesting the New World. Pumpkins are thought to have originated in North America and are said to have been eaten at the first Thanksgiving. (Photograph by Arthur Giulietti.)

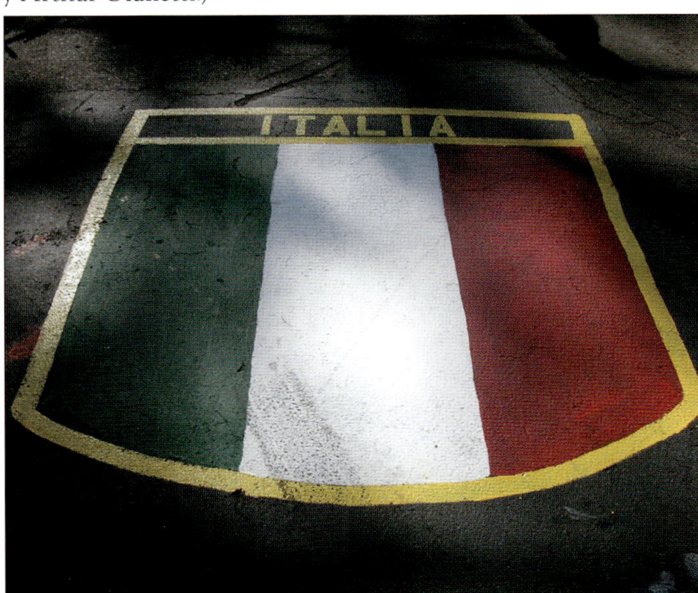

Painting the Streets. Il Tricolore (the flag of Italy) was painted on the street in West Haven for the 2006 Columbus Day Parade. The three colors are said to represent the country in the following ways: green represents the green hills of Italy, white represents the snowcapped mountains, and red represents blood spilled in the wars for independence. These colors are used in many ways in Italy and the Italian diaspora, including on *pizza Margherita*. (Photograph by Arthur Giulietti.)

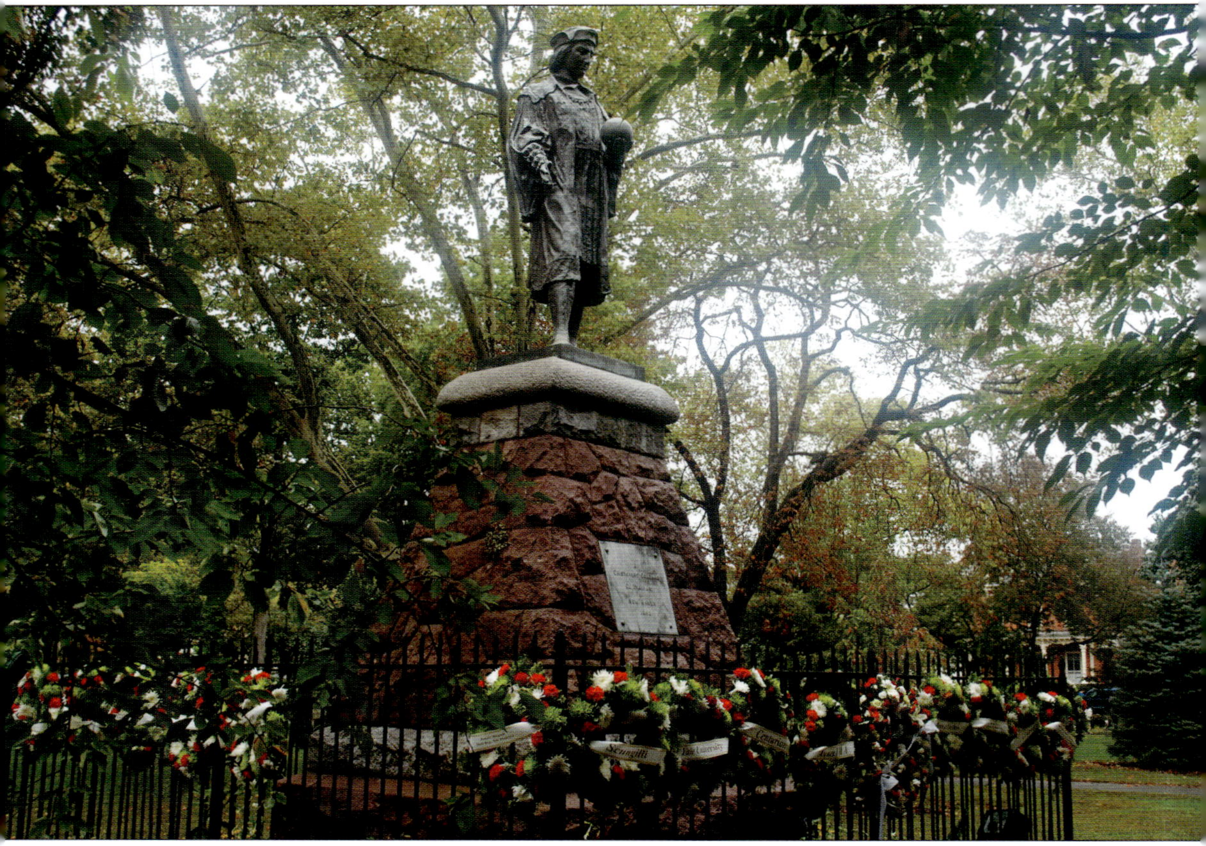

Columbus Monument in Wooster Square. In 1983, Bart Giammatti, the president of Yale University and a scholar of English Renaissance literature, spoke at the Columbus Day Dinner at the Park Plaza Hotel in New Haven. Giammatti said of the inspiration of the Italian navigator, "Because of Columbus, we are all here together. We each have our contribution to make. Our responsibility as Italian Americans is, I believe, special. When we fulfill it for all, we will have continued even more to enrich and ennoble the freest country the world has ever seen." Giammatti's sentiment resonates today, 125 years after the Italian community of New Haven came together to install the Columbus Monument in Wooster Square. His words remind everyone—just as Rep. Rosa DeLauro does in the foreword—that the city and state's Italian populations, like so many before, and so many after, are all part of the American experiment, a country unlike any other in the history of the world. Angelo Bartlett Giammatti died at age 51 and is buried in Grove Street Cemetery in New Haven. (Photograph by Arthur Giulietti.)

Bibliography

Appelbaum, Stanley. *The Chicago World's Fair of 1893*. New York: Dover Publications, 1980.

Barberio, G. Chiodi. *Il Progresso degl'Italiani nel Connecticut*. New Haven: Maturo's Printing & Publishing, 1933.

Biondi, Richard D. *Piccola Italia di Wooster Square, A Pictorial History*. Vol. 1. Privately printed, 2016.

Brown, Elizabeth Mills. *New Haven, A Guide to Architecture and Urban Design*. New Haven: Yale University Press, 1976.

Cannelli, Antonio. *La Colonia Italiana di New Haven, Connecticut*. Stabilimento Tipografico, 1921.

Cupelli, Alberto. *The Italian of Old New Haven, 1847–1900*. Privately printed, 1972.

Ethnic Heritage Center. *Walk New Haven: Wooster Square*. Privately printed, 2016.

Fappiano, Gene. "The Columbus Controversy and Beyond" (Winter 2015), "Columbus and the Slavery Controversy: Toward a Better Understanding of the Historical and Theoretical Contexts" (Summer 2016), and "A Note on the Columbus Series" (Fall 2016), *La Storia*, Italian-American Historical Society of Connecticut.

Inside New Haven's Neighborhoods: A Guide to the City of New Haven. New Haven: City of New Haven, 1982. Published in cooperation with the New Haven Colony Historical Society.

Johnston, Michael. "Italian New Haven: Building an Ethnic Identity," *Journal of the New Haven Colony Historical Society*, vol. 26, no. 3 (Summer 1979) 23–34.

Mick, Alice and Lula White. "Italians and Blacks in New Haven: The Establishment of Two Ethnic Communities." Yale-New Haven Teachers Institute, 1978.

Pisani, Larry. "Revisiting Columbus Bashing," *La Storia*, Italian-American Historical Society of Connecticut, vol. 19, no. 3 (Summer 2012) 1, 3.

Riccio, Anthony. *The Italian American Experience in New Haven*. New York: State University of New York Press, 2006.

Townsend, Doris B. *Evolution of New Haven Public Schools, from 1638 to the Present, an Overview*. Privately printed, 2006.

———. *The Streets of New Haven, The Origin of Their Names*. New Haven: New Haven Colony Historical Society, 1984.

Wilford, John Noble. "Columbus and the Labyrinth of History," *Wilson Quarterly* (Autumn 1991) 66–86.

About the Columbus Day Committee of Greater New Haven, Inc.

The purpose of the Columbus Day Committee of Greater New Haven, Inc., is to promote the spirit and celebrate the history of Christopher Columbus in the Greater New Haven Italian American community and the community at large. Membership is open to all persons who subscribe to the purpose of the committee and shall be members by virtue of their own personal involvement and interest in promoting the activities of the committee. Pictured below are, from left to right, (back row) Arthur Giulietti, Robert H. Bonanno, William Zampa, Peter Desio, Louis Criscuolo, Robert Parente, Patrick J. Donnelly, Frank Consorte, Richard Ramadei, Emilio Triano, and Paul Criscuolo; (front row) Terri Vailette, Barbara Criscuolo, Mary Pursell, Laura Florio Luzzi, Magdalen Sparaco, Joanne Mallinson, and Andrew Giannelli. (Columbus Day Committee of Greater New Haven.)

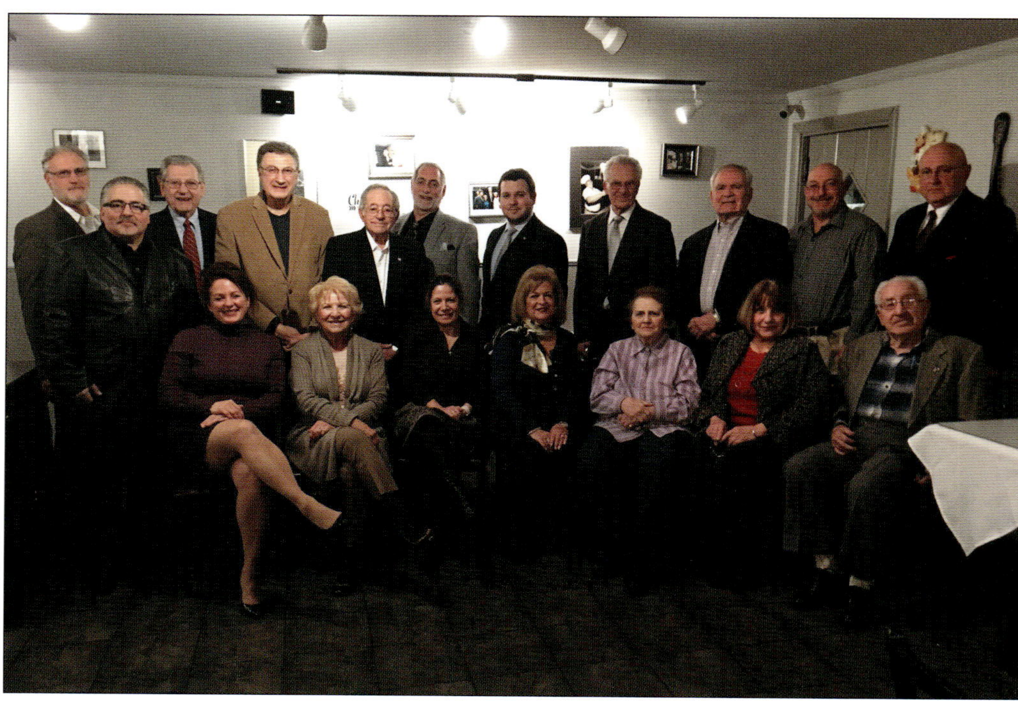

About the Author and Foreword Contributor

Author Laura A. Macaluso, PhD. Macaluso has degrees in art history and the humanities from Southern Connecticut State University, Syracuse University in Italy, and Salve Regina University. She is the author of *Art of the Amistad and the Portrait of Cinqué* (AASLH/Rowman & Littlefield, 2016) and *New Haven in World War I* (History Press, 2017), endorsed by the World War One Centennial Commission. (Photograph by Michelline Hall, author's collection.)

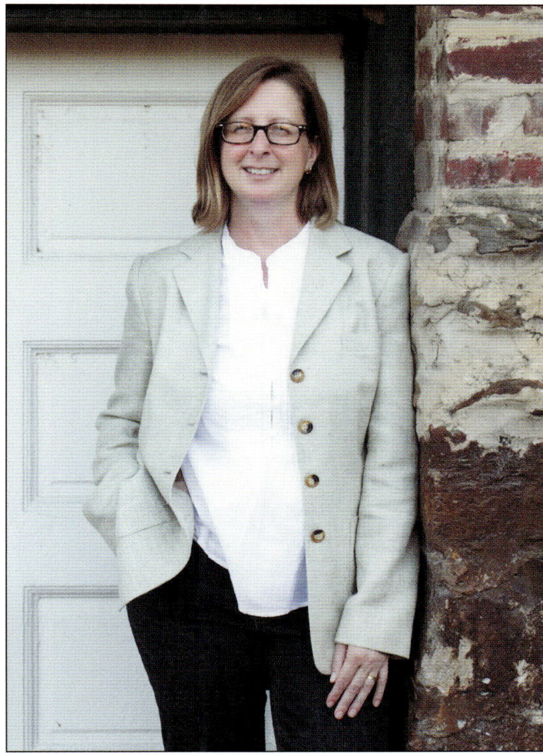

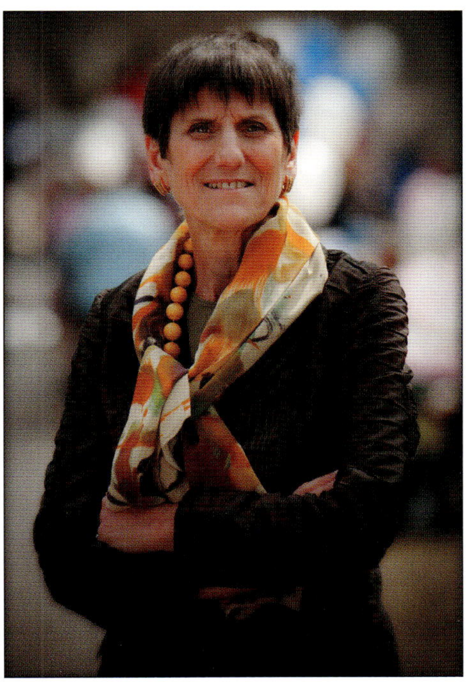

Rep. Rosa DeLauro. DeLauro has been the US representative for Connecticut's Third District since 1991. Her mother, Luisa DeLauro, a longtime Wooster Square resident, is known as a community activist and remains the city of New Haven's longest-serving alderperson. (Rosa DeLauro.)

Chronology

1882 Knights of Columbus is formed in the basement of St. Mary's Church, New Haven

1884 La Fratellanza Italiana, the first Italian benevolent society in New Haven, is formed, quickly followed by many more

1889 The Church of St. Michael is formed; first Italian parish in Connecticut

1892 Columbus Day Parade, held October 11, 1892, in New Haven by the Knights of Columbus; 3,500 Knights march in parade

1892 Columbus Monument unveiled in Wooster Square, paid for by the United Italian Societies. Italians of New Haven and Connecticut march in parade to Wooster Square for both the laying of the cornerstone (October 12) and the unveiling of the monument (October 21)

1893 World's Columbian Exposition held in Chicago

1899 The Church of St. Michael is consecrated on Wooster Square

1908 State of Connecticut's first Columbus Day celebration, with parade held in Bridgeport, Connecticut

1909 Columbus Day Parade held in New Haven

1910 Columbus Day Parade held in Waterbury

1911 Columbus Day Parade becomes an annual tradition in New Haven, the only city in the state to do so

1918 Forty Italian societies gathered in front of the Columbus Monument, escorting Brig. Gen. Emilio Guglielmotti of Italy in a street parade to Woolsey Hall for World War I Liberty loan drive

1930s Columbus Day Parade ceases in New Haven; iron fence is erected around Columbus Monument

1937 Columbus Day is recognized as a federal holiday during the FDR administration

1953 Columbus Day Parade is revived by the City of New Haven, guided by Mayor Richard C. Lee, who appoints members to the Columbus Day Citizens Committee

1955 Copper statue of Columbus is replaced with a similar bronze version, costing city \$5,000; floodlights installed for the first time

1960 Largest Columbus Day Parade in New Haven history; approximately 12,000 marching and 45,000 spectators

1980s The Mayor's Columbus Day Citizens Committee is spun out of city hall and becomes its own nonprofit organization called the Columbus Day Committee of Greater New Haven

1986 Alfonso E. Panico petitions the city to rename Wooster Square as Columbus Park (or Green); the green space is sometimes referred to as Wooster-Columbus Square or Wooster Park on the Columbus Green

1992 "Columbus 500" city and statewide celebrations; a new marker is placed at the base of the Columbus Monument

2000 Last year Columbus Day Parade in New Haven is held

2000 Knights of Columbus install *Columbus, the Evangelizer* in the refurbished plaza of the newly opened Knights of Columbus Museum

2003 New Haven's Columbus Day Parade restarts with a parade in North Haven; the parade begins a tradition of traveling to four other cities in New Haven County: East Haven, Hamden, North Haven, and West Haven

2004 The Columbus Monument is conserved with funds from the Knights of Columbus and the City of New Haven

2008 José Buscaglia's *Rodrigo de Triana* bronze and steel sculpture is inserted over the entrance to Columbus Family Academy in addition to Barry Svigals & Partners' *Winds of Discovery* bas-relief around the exterior of the school building

2013 Town of Branford joins the rotation for the annual Greater New Haven Columbus Day Parade

2017 The presence of Columbus in Wooster Square turns 125 years old